THE
COLLEGE
CARTEL

THE COLLEGE CARTEL

SAHAJ SHARDA

ABOUT THE AUTHOR

Sahaj Sharda is currently a student at Columbia Law School. His main academic focus is antitrust law. Sahaj believes that antitrust laws can be more vigorously enforced to fight the abuse of monopoly power in higher education.

"The foundation of every state is the education of its youth." – **DIOGENES**

TABLE OF CONTENTS

INTRODUCTION

———

I watched a young girl recklessly light herself on fire in the media. It was a fire that blazed brighter with every lie she told. When the flames finally subsided, she was burned beyond recovery. Her reputation was ruined. Her future was marred. The great tragedy was that she suffered all this for a few fleeting moments of validation.

That girl's name was Sara Kim. It was the spring of 2015, and hope was in the air. As college admissions results trickled in, my entire high school fantasized about the future. Where would the seniors go next? What would they accomplish? The whole world was up for grabs. Yet, for a few frenzied weeks, a student named Sara Kim was the main topic of conversation at my high school.

Sara claimed to have been admitted into both Harvard and Stanford. At first, everyone was excited for her. Then, Sara's story got weirder. One day, during my lunch break, someone whispered, "I heard Mark Zuckerberg personally called Sara to convince her to go to Harvard instead of Stanford." Someone else responded, "Why would Mark care? Didn't he drop out of Harvard?" Skepticism started to grow. We didn't know then, but there was a good reason to be skeptical. Sara was fully lying.

Sara was certainly a gifted student. At most high schools, Sara would probably have graduated at the top of her class. However, Thomas Jefferson High School for Science and Technology, also known as "TJ", isn't like most high schools. Consistently ranked as the best public high school in the country by U.S. News & World Report, TJ is a hyper-competitive magnet school. Students from five Virginia counties, nearly 3,000 students, apply to get in each year. These applicants compete for only 480 spots. In this hyper-qualified pool of students, Sara was merely another smart person among many others. So when rumors started swirling that Sara had gotten into both Harvard and Stanford, a notable achievement even for the very best students at TJ, her peers were confused.

The speculation about Sara was wide within TJ because it was even wider outside it. One day, there were South Korean news crews broadcasting from outside the main doors of my American high school campus. In their fervor, South Korean reporters interviewed random TJ students to ask if anyone knew the "genius girl." Sara, who has South Korean heritage, had somehow attracted interest from South Korean press outlets. Suddenly, Sara's admissions success was an international human-interest story.

In this greenhouse of media coverage, Sara and her family made claims that Mark Zuckerberg called Sara to convince her to choose Harvard. There were even claims that both schools had come to a special agreement whereby Sara could go to each school for two years each. Harvard and Stanford had never done this before.

To get into either Harvard or Stanford was unlikely enough. To get into both was deeply impressive, but it was still theoretically possible. However, Sara's peers called bullshit when they read that Mark Zuckerberg had called Sara. Sara's peers weren't the only ones. Slowly, the story started to unravel. Once the skepticism started, it didn't stop. Her peers began to question if she got into either school at all.

As scrutiny over her claims increased, Sara tried a Hail Mary. She impersonated a Harvard math professor named Joseph Daniel Harris and sent an email to the entire senior class at TJ. The email, allegedly from Professor Harris, said the following: "We've heard various rumors related to Sara, and I am here to put it to an end…In addition, we've heard numerous comments related to her research and achievements, but we know much more than all of you guys know, so it needs to stop."[1]

Of course, it wasn't clear how a Harvard math professor would have heard high school gossip from a few states away. It also wasn't clear why he would care. Yet, even if he had heard and even if he did care, it wasn't clear why he would write an email to a whole high school senior class at TJ. Sara's ploy backfired. It only increased skepticism. Now it was only a matter of time before she was exposed.

Eventually, Harvard and Stanford officials came forward in the press and denied that Sara had been offered admission to either school. Her admissions letters were exposed as forgeries. The Zuckerberg call was debunked. Facing the harsh light of media coverage, Sara's father went on record to apologize for the fiasco. Thus, a human interest story turned into a Greek tragedy.

The scandal was newsworthy domestically. It was reported by The Washington Post and CNN. Yet, the scandal was even bigger in South Korea. South Korean press coverage of the scandal was more critical. Many years later, when a South Korean friend found out that I had gone to TJ, he promptly asked if I had known Sara. Apparently, over the course of this scandal, Sara had become well-known in South Korea as a negative example. Sara was someone you didn't want to be.

Sara's hoax was clumsy. It was obviously poorly thought out from start to finish. Instead, Sara's actions gave the distinct feeling of someone who felt deeply insecure and told a lie that constantly had to get bigger or blow up. I remember seeing Sara in the halls at TJ. I was only a year below her. I remember feeling sorry for Sara. I was probably in the minority.

I don't approve of what Sara did, but I understand it. I remember when I first arrived at TJ, in the ninth grade. For my first few months, I often cried when I came home from school. I had been "the smart kid" my whole life. Now, at a high school filled with gifted students, I was just another kid. I didn't know who I was anymore. It took me years to fully adjust to my new surroundings. As I grew older, I realized that almost all my peers at TJ felt similarly. It's why when we started to apply to colleges, our entire grade became so desperate for admission to top-ranked schools. Students needed to prove how smart they were once and for all. Only admission to Columbia could quiet one's crisis of confidence. We were trying to solve internal issues with external results.

I'm sure that Sara had a similar struggle. I doubt that she ever overcame it. The shock of realizing that you're not as special as you thought can be emotionally violent. It destroys your self-esteem. It feels like something was taken from you. You want it back. So, you feel a need to impress everyone all the time. You need to show them how smart you are. When you strip it down, isn't that what Sara was trying to do in her deeply flawed way?

Of course, it's easy to dismiss an eighteen-year-old girl as a morally lost liar. Yet, is that the whole story? Is that even the most crucial part of the story? Or is the real story bigger than one young girl who felt so pressured to achieve that she lied in a desperate attempt to nourish her self-esteem?

Our first impulse is to frame things personally, but it's not just Sara Kim that has poorly handled rejection from America's elite colleges. In 2007, a girl named Azia Kim made her way onto Stanford's campus. Azia lived in the dorms for eight full months before Stanford administrators figured out that she had never been admitted as a student.[2] Azia Kim frequently talked to her peers about school papers and upcoming exams. Azia regularly ate at the dining halls. Azia was so good at pretending to be a student that many actual students were completely shocked when they found out that she was a fraud. Imagine going through all that trouble for eight months, with every intention of going on for four years. When did Stanford become so desirable that even pretending to attend was better than not attending at all? When did we agree to let elite colleges allocate self-esteem in this obviously toxic way?

Sara was wrong, and she'll have to live with the consequences of her actions every time someone searches her name on Google. So will Azia. But what about our system? Is our system not wrong? Is keeping enrollment artificially low, as the elite colleges have done for decades, not wrong? Are acceptance rates below four percent not wrong? Is fraudulently soliciting applications from low-scoring students who will never be admitted not wrong? Sara and Azia are facing the consequences of their actions, but when will the elite colleges be equally confronted with consequences?

With elite seats so limited and with so much importance placed on them, is it really so surprising when talented young people struggle to accept a decision that feels like being labeled second class? Isn't Sara's scandal what our system is designed to produce? I didn't know it then, but Sara's media firestorm was just a prologue. In the years since, admissions scandals have become shockingly common.

The next scandal I witnessed directly occurred in the spring of 2019. I was now a junior at Georgetown University. I viscerally remember when the media grenade exploded on our campus. There was a feeling that there was more to the story because, in parallel, similar media grenades kept exploding on campuses across America. It all began when an FBI investigation, code-named Operation Varsity Blues, was made public.

The center of the controversy was an "admissions consultant" named William Singer. William Singer wasn't a normal consultant. He was an agent of corruption. William Singer repeatedly bribed coaches at elite colleges and falsified test scores on standardized tests to help wealthy clients' kids achieve admission to top colleges. William Singer's key insight was that athletic recruiting at elite colleges attracted little scrutiny. Thus, William Singer deviously assessed that bribery was most likely to work in the athletic recruiting process.

For many years William Singer had organized a conspiracy of titans of industry, famous celebrities, and other wealthy people who all illegally converted assets into access. This scandal was made public when William Singer was dragged into the light by law enforcement. Under pressure from the FBI, William Singer promptly flipped and snitched on his patrons. Thus, with William Singer came dozens of prominent families who collectively spent millions of dollars to rig admissions to elite colleges for their children.

Manuel Henriquez was one of the titans of industry who employed William Singer. Manuel was the founder and CEO of a publicly traded venture finance firm called Hercules Capital.

When the scandal broke, Hercules Capital had a market cap of over a billion dollars. Manuel and his wife were wealthy and powerful. Yet, in 2015, Manuel and his wife made the regrettable decision to pay William Singer over $400,000 to rig the college admissions process for their daughter.

At first, the rigging worked. Manuel's daughter Isabelle Henriquez got a higher score on the SAT when one of Singer's associates posed as a test proctor but actually just fed her the answers. Armed with a higher test score, Isabelle Henriquez then posed as a top tennis recruit. She falsely claimed that she played club tennis for 20 hours a week in high school. She also falsely claimed that she was ranked in the Top 50 in the Junior Girls' Tennis category by the United States Tennis Association.

In fact, there is no evidence that Isabelle Henriquez ever played in a United States Tennis Association tournament in high school. Frankly, there's no evidence that Isabelle Henriquez played a tournament of any kind.

How do you get a non-tennis player admitted through the tennis quota? You bribe the tennis coach. This is precisely what William Singer did. In total, Georgetown's tennis coach, Gordon Ernst, accepted around $2.7 million in bribes between 2012 and 2018.[3] This is how William Singer swung the door open for clients like Isabelle Henriquez. Isabelle wasn't the only one who got in through this back door. At least eleven other students got into Georgetown through fraudulent athletic recruiting.

To keep up appearances during the application process, William Singer had Isabelle Henriquez send Georgetown's tennis coach, Gordon Ernst, an email that read as follows: "I have been really successful this summer playing tennis around the country. I am looking forward to having a chance to be part of the Georgetown tennis team and make a positive contribution to your team's success."[4] Isabelle Henriquez was obviously not a tennis player. Gordon Ernst knew it. Yet, when William Singer came with a new "recruit" like Isabelle, Gordon Ernst closed his eyes and went along.

Because Georgetown's admissions department trusted Gordon Ernst, Isabelle used his name over and over in her Georgetown application. As Isabelle's Georgetown application essay falsely stated: "Being a part of Georgetown women's tennis team has always been a dream of mine. For years I have spent three to four hours a day grinding out on and off-court workouts with the hopes of becoming successful enough to play college tennis, especially at Georgetown. What is most amazing is how quickly I connected with Coach Ernst. He spent time with me while on campus and at several tournaments I played in."[5]

There was very little truthful representation in Isabelle's Georgetown application. Isabelle's essays, her test scores, and her recruitment were all lies. Nonetheless, in the fall of 2016, Isabelle started at Georgetown University. Coincidentally, so did I.

The scandal finally became public in the Spring of 2019. When it came out, it was pandemonium. Major reports kept being published. The circle of exposure kept getting wider and wider. The story struck a chord with the broader public because it reinforced an existing impression that the rich use their power to rig the system in their favor.

I didn't personally know Isabelle at Georgetown, but Georgetown is a small school. We had mutual friends. I distinctly remember the feeling on campus when the scandal broke. There was weird anxiety hanging around the place. Yet, something was different this time. Whatever denunciations were being hurled at Isabelle and the other students caught up in the scandal, they were coming mostly from the media and outside critics. Within

Georgetown's campus, her peers were mostly just embarrassed by her.

As I reflect on it now, I can understand why the campus reaction was soft. Many students at Georgetown had paid for admission in one way or another. Some students had gone to expensive private high schools, which naturally gave them a leg up. Some students had hired professional essay writers for their college essays. Others had participated in expensive extracurricular activities that set them apart. Some students' families had made multi-million dollar "donations" through Georgetown's development office. These donor families had paid for access more directly than Manuel Henriquez, and yet Georgetown put their names on buildings and on plaques. At Georgetown, where so many came from much and so few came from little, Isabelle's main crime was being distasteful. Her family hadn't followed social protocol. The bribe was supposed to be paid to the development office, not the tennis coach. The bribe was also supposed to be much bigger.

Obviously, Manuel Henriquez should have known that he couldn't trust William Singer. Any man who will cheat the system for a price can also be persuaded to cheat you for a price. When the FBI closed in, Singer snitched. Singer cooperated with law enforcement to help gather evidence against his powerful clients. For example, in October 2018, William Singer called Isabelle's mother, Elizabeth Henriquez, and recorded the call at the direction of law enforcement agents. The transcript of the call is as follows:

William Singer: "Okay. Excuse me. So my-- so my foundation is getting audited now."
Elizabeth Henriquez: "Oh."

William Singer: "Uh--"

Elizabeth Henriquez: "Well, that sucks."

William Singer: "Right. And they're going back like they always do."

Elizabeth Henriquez: "Yeah."

William Singer: "Pretty normal. So they're taking a look at all my payments. So they asked me about the large sums of money that came in from you guys."

Elizabeth Henriquez: "Okay."

William Singer: "And so, essentially--"

Elizabeth Henriquez: "For all the good deeds that you do."

William Singer: "Absolutely. So, of course, I didn't say anything-- you know, I'm not gonna tell the IRS that, you know, [CW-2] took the test for [your eldest daughter] or that Gordie--"

Elizabeth Henriquez: "Right. Yeah."

William Singer: "--or that Gordie-- you know, we paid-"

Elizabeth Henriquez: "Like-- Yeah."

William Singer: "--Gordie to help her get into Georgetown, right?"

Elizabeth Henriquez: "Right."

William Singer: "So I just want to make sure that you and I are on the same page--"

Elizabeth Henriquez: "Okay."

William Singer: "--in case they were to call."

Elizabeth Henriquez: "So what's your story?"

William Singer: "So my story is, essentially, that you gave your money to our foundation to help underserved kids."

Elizabeth Henriquez: "You-- Of course."

William Singer: "And--"

Elizabeth Henriquez: "Those kids have to go to school."
William Singer: "Absolutely."[6]

The legal verdict wasn't forgiving to the Henriquez family. As the dust settled, it was only a matter of time before someone from the family went to jail. Eventually, both Manuel Henriquez and his wife, Elizabeth Henriquez, were sentenced to jail time. With tears in his eyes, Manuel Henriquez admitted to the judge that he was "humiliated, a broken man, a criminal and, as you rightfully said, a common thief."[7]

Analyzing the Henriquez scandal, I can't help but ask a simple question. Who has the power in our system? In which direction does the power flow? The common narrative is that elite colleges serve the wealthy. In this narrative, wealthy families hold all the power. But is that true? Was that true for a titan of industry like Manuel Henriquez?

One could protest that Manuel is a bad example, so let's speak more generally. For the generic uber-wealthy law-abiding family, what exactly does a family get in exchange for a million-dollar donation? They get a somewhat fancy certificate. Is the juice worth the squeeze? Who's really being taken advantage of here?

I think the common narrative should be flipped. The elite colleges don't serve the wealthy. In fact, it's the opposite. The wealthy serve the elite colleges. They serve the elite colleges by paying full-price tuition. They serve the elite colleges by paying huge donations on top of that. They serve the elite colleges by becoming trustees. They serve the elite colleges by going into government and then propagating policies that shield elite colleges from tax liability. Wealthy men like Manuel are willing to go to jail to procure seats at elite colleges. The elite colleges themselves are all-powerful, not the wealthy people who fund and serve them.

I decided to write this book a few years after the Varsity Blues scandal. The year was 2021, and I encountered my most impactful elite college scandal yet. The scandal began as the global pandemic eventually made its way onto elite campuses. Contextually, the outbreak of COVID-19 completely changed the social contract on college campuses across the country. Whereas elite colleges prided themselves on in-person learning, they now moved en-masse to online learning. Students felt cheated. They were forced to pay the same price for what they felt was an inferior service. This led to protests, lawsuits, and even agitation on a variety of college campuses. However, the effort that came the closest to generating real change was a tuition strike on Columbia's campus.

I first got interested out of mere curiosity. After I graduated from Georgetown, I started thinking about going to law school. As I researched Columbia Law, I found articles about an unrelated but dynamic story. An undergraduate tuition strike was taking place on Columbia's campus. The Guardian reported that 1,100 Columbia undergraduates wouldn't pay their tuition until Columbia decreased tuition by 10 percent and increased financial aid by 10 percent.[8] This student effort struck a chord with me. I had to learn more.

I went online and found the group responsible for organizing the tuition strike. It was the Columbia chapter of the Young Democratic Socialists of America. I then connected with one of their leaders, a dynamic student named Emmaline Bennet. I called her, and we spoke for over an hour. Emmaline explained why students were striking. These Columbia student strikers had a genuine cause. The strikers felt their educational experience had been degraded by the move to online learning, which Columbia had instituted in response to the pandemic. These students felt that they shouldn't be paying the same amount of money for a lesser amount of services. They had tried asking for refunds. They had tried softer methods. They had been ignored. So, they decided to strike.

Tactically, I was shocked by the strikers' success. Only seven students had persuaded nearly 1,100 undergraduates to strike. These seven students had worked day and night to put out op-eds, call and text peers, and speak at other clubs and across campus. They had been rewarded with a strong response. Their tweets started going viral. Reporters wrote about their strike in major newspapers, including The New York Times.[9] They had momentum. If they kept going at this pace, they would reach a critical mass of students. Columbia would be powerless in the face of such strong financial leverage. The students would win!

Unfortunately, the momentum didn't continue. The growth stalled. The strikers hit a ceiling of support. Still, even without growing larger, one would expect a strike of 1,100 students out of a total undergraduate population of nearly 6000 students would exert some pressure on Columbia. But it didn't. Columbia refused to acknowledge the strike. Instead, Columbia offered vague promises of increases to financial aid in the future, increases that were always likely to happen regardless.

Why didn't the strike work? Why didn't it get large enough? Why did the strikers hit a ceiling of support? Ultimately, wouldn't each student gain from 10 percent lower tuition? Plus, if everyone joined the strike, it was destined to succeed. After all, Columbia couldn't really punish its entire undergraduate population. Acting collectively, the undergraduate population could have a tremendous amount of leverage. So, what gives? After all this momentum, why did the strike fail?

My own conclusion is that the demographics of the student body doomed the strike. Columbia has a total undergraduate enrollment of roughly 6,000 students. Of these students, only an estimated 5 percent of students came from families who comprise the bottom 20 percent of income earners. Meanwhile, an overwhelming estimate of 62 percent of students came from families who comprise the top 20 percent of income earners.[10] In the end, a lot of rich students were just apathetic. The strike needed to sign more people up to succeed, but if you're not on financial aid, maybe you don't care if it goes up by 10 percent. At a certain point, the strike just ran out of students who cared about how much tuition cost. Faced with the opportunity to force Columbia into tuition reform, rich kids just shrugged.

The Columbia tuition strike had a big impact on me because it was really three scandals in one. The first scandal was that the elite colleges were so powerful that they could degrade the quality of their product at will and get away with it. By moving schools online and not offering tuition discounts, elite colleges proved that proposition. The second scandal was that in the face of over a thousand students striking, an elite college like Columbia was completely non-reactive. With the safety net of multi-billion-dollar endowments, elite colleges hold an overwhelming amount of power over their student bodies. Most businesses must listen to their customers. Elite colleges don't have to. The third scandal was that our elite schools are filled overwhelmingly and disproportionately with rich brats. I refuse to believe that our nation's best and brightest all come from the same zip codes. Instead, the better explanation of Columbia's demographics is that we have a system designed to accept a few rich kids and reject almost everyone else.

Watching the Columbia tuition strike stall and end abruptly was deeply demoralizing. Yet, that feeling of demoralization finally moved me to action. The elite colleges had become too powerful. They had become too corrupted. I was going to show the world this truth one page at a time. Thus, this book began.

Who has more power than the elite colleges? It's not smart students because smart students have subordinated their own self-image to the mercy of acceptance from Harvard, Stanford, and others. For the sake of prestige, elite colleges openly reject students who can obviously handle the academic rigor. Elite schools should have tripled their enrolments over the last few decades, but they didn't. This has made students so desperate to get in that they feel pressured to exploit their own trauma for the sake of compelling essays. Later, when capable students get rejected, the feeling of alienation can be so violent that they'll even lie. This is what Sara did when she made up elaborate stories. It's what Azia did when she walked onto Stanford's campus to play pretend. Smart students are clearly at the mercy of ruthlessly rejective elite colleges.

Who has more power than the elite colleges? It's not wealthy families. They're so desperate for admission for their children that they must donate millions or else risk jail time to guarantee spots for their kids. Titans of industry end up in tears and in court, or else they write checks worth magnitudes more than any certificate could ever be worth. They're getting way less in value than however much they pay in money.

Who has more power than the elite colleges? It's not even the students already enrolled at the elite colleges. Elite schools can degrade their product quality whenever they want, knowing that students can't do much to stop them. When students strike, elite schools have the luxury of responding with silence.

Who has more power than the elite colleges? The answer is clear. No one does. Comprehensively, the media has done a poor job of framing the problem with the elite colleges. The college question keeps shifting in the public mind. Some days it's admissions. On other days it's affordability. Some say it's diversity. Others say it's debt. But the common thread that runs across all the issues and all the scandals is the absolute power that elite colleges have. Worse than that, no one has systematically examined how elite colleges accrue this power. This book fills that discursive black hole. This book also explains what we need to do to fix our system.

I know how elite colleges became so powerful, and in this book, I explain it to you. The main thesis of this book is that elite colleges have formed an implicit cartel that routinely engages in anti-competitive behavior to consolidate power. Some of their anti-competitive behavior occurs in broad daylight. You can see it when elite colleges make you sign early decision contracts. You can see it when they increase tuition every year in unison. Where there ought to be competition, you find only collusion. This collusion is the source of the tremendous power that elite colleges wield. To consolidate that power, elite colleges collude to create artificial scarcity in seats, fix prices, cannibalize aid, and distort the market. We study all these tactics in this book.

This college cartel can rig the market because elite colleges have built a moat to isolate the elite colleges from competitors. Even worse, elite colleges coordinate to fully stagnate the number of seats available at those very few elite schools that exist within the moat. The rarity of admissions at these elite schools is what is driving crazy behavior like Sara's lies or the corruption of Varsity Blues. Its why wealthy families will pay such large bribes to the development offices at elite schools. Further, the scarcity of seats makes possible all sorts of other anti-competitive behavior. This is how elite colleges stuff billion-dollar endowments with billions more in cash.

President Kennedy had a famous refrain that, "Our problems are man-made; therefore, they can be solved by man." I believe an analogous logic can be applied to the elite colleges. We gave them power; therefore, we can take it away. If we refuse to allow elite colleges to collude unfairly, a competitive market will naturally produce a tenfold increase in elite seats. In doing so, we will dispel collusion and restore competition. In doing so, we will restore some of the most powerful engines for social mobility back to their rightful purpose.

The elite colleges are undeniably corrupt, but that's not all they are. I've seen the elite schools up close. I graduated from Georgetown, and presently I study law at Columbia. Elite colleges can be amazing places. They can take students and launch them into an entirely better trajectory. They can change lives, produce new knowledge, and improve the world. I don't believe that students shouldn't go to elite schools at all. I believe that dramatically more students should have the opportunity to go to elite schools. We should expand the seats at elite colleges by a factor of ten. This book is animated by a simple belief. Education is supposed to be the panacea, not the problem.

There is a serious urgency to this book. Because of scandals like Varsity Blues, the public is open to the reform of elite colleges. This is why serious lawsuits have been recently filed against elite colleges for price-fixing, admissions decisions, and quality degradation. Yet, addressing the symptoms of the real problem isn't enough. We have a narrow window of opportunity to expand the debate and talk about the industrial organization of elite colleges. If we can bust the anti-competitive industrial structure, every student in the next generation of learners will actually have the option to get a world-class elite education. Students might choose not to go, but challenges like not getting in anywhere or not getting enough financial aid will never foreclose the future for a student again.

I'm probably not the best author for this book. I openly acknowledge that there are authors far better credentialed than myself. Yet, this type of argument can only come from a relatively unknown person. Many of the best academics are vested in upholding the elite colleges. These academics teach at elite schools, research at elite schools, or graduate from elite schools. To be taken seriously, they need a good relationship with elite schools. Thus, serious academics don't really have the incentive to criticize elite institutions too harshly. Apart from academics, few people seem to seriously understand how elite colleges work. There is a de-facto assumption that since education is a good thing, everything educational institutions do is probably well-intentioned. This bias is why there are few books on how elite colleges nakedly behave anti-competitively. I didn't write this book because I wanted to. I wrote this book because no one else has the temerity to. Only an idiot like me would do it. Importantly, this is a topic we desperately need to address. Maybe I'm not the best author for this book, but I'm the one you got.

I'm also an unlikely author, especially for this book. I grew up in a middle-class suburb in Virginia. The ambitions of the people I grew up around were to get into the elite schools, not to criticize them. I was always taught to work within the system. In fact, there might be people from my past who deeply dislike this book. These people might misinterpret my intentions. To clarify, I didn't write this book because I was motivated by some anti-intellectual ideology. Quite the opposite, I think intellectuals play an important role in society. Intellectuals think about how to solve big problems. Elite colleges might not like me saying it, but right now they are one of those big problems.

I affirmatively wrote this book because I believe in our elite colleges. The story of our elite colleges is the story of America. These are colleges founded by men like Benjamin Franklin and Thomas Jefferson. The founders of these schools built elite schools to build a stronger America. Yet, with each day that passes, our elite colleges stray further from that legacy. I wrote this book because I believe in an America where ambition is rewarded, where substance matters more than status, and where credentials and caste are less important than character and competence. This is an America where elite colleges aren't exclusive but expansive. This is an America where change is possible, and that change begins one page at a time.

CHAPTER 1

―――――――

THE HEAD START

Why do students want to go to elite colleges? Why do a few elite schools get so many applications, and why do so many other non-elite schools get so few applications? These are the questions we explore in this chapter.

In the fall of 2015, I began the process of applying to colleges. To start, I scheduled an appointment with my high school counselor. Almost a week later, I finally went in to see my counselor. During my lunch break, I sat in the cramped faculty room at my high school. Once the meeting commenced, I asked my counselor, "Does applying early increase my likelihood of admission?" He responded, "Yes, if you apply through a binding early decision program." My immediate thought was: where do I sign?

By my senior year of high school, I had taken a deep interest in the University of Pennsylvania. It was more than a deep interest; frankly, I was desperate to get in. In my nervousness over the college scramble, I recklessly signed a binding early decision contract with Penn. Importantly, so did many of my friends. Everyone had a strategy on where to apply early to maximize the likelihood of a good outcome. One of my friends applied early decision to UChicago. Another one gave me some company by applying early to Penn. In hindsight, I cringe, thinking about my decision-making at the time. I didn't think anything through. Instead, I was in a trance. It was a trance that took me years to snap out of.

One day that fall, I rushed home from school. Having made myself a peanut butter sandwich, I opened the Penn application form on my laptop computer for the very first time. As I munched on my sandwich, I started to research exactly what essays I would have to write for my application. Eventually, I started drafting outlines. Yet, the essay that should have been the easiest one to complete was the one that stumped me the most. That essay prompt was: Why Penn?

For weeks I struggled to draft and redraft an essay on this topic. I obviously had reasons for why I wanted to go, but none of them would sound particularly good in an essay. The truth was that my reasons were very shallow. I liked that Penn was a prestigious Ivy League school. I liked the fact that it was in a city. Plus, based on my numbers, I felt I had some chance of getting in. Obviously, I couldn't write any of that in an essay. They'd reject me on the spot.

Instead, over the next few days and weeks, I continued to research Penn's history in my free time. I never visited the campus, so the bulk of my research consisted of Google searches and Google street view. In the end, I bullshitted something about Benjamin Franklin with a "personal anecdote" about the feeling I got from being on campus during a visit, even though I had never been. Once I clicked submit, I waited nervously for a response.

My wait dragged on for weeks and then months. Finally, later that winter, I got an email from the Penn admissions office. The email arrived during a free period at my high school. I was sitting in a Geosystems classroom chatting with some friends. By chance, I was right next to my friend who had also applied early to Penn. After I saw an email notification on my phone, I rushed to open the email. My friend opened a similar email on his phone. Briskly, I scanned through the words before I found the ones that mattered. I had been rejected.

It took a few seconds for me to fully absorb the words. Then, almost immediately, my eyes went to my friend's phone and his to mine. He had been rejected too. We took turns punching each other on the arm in a friendly frustration. Eventually, the frustration diffused into full-fledged humor. We started laughing. This college admissions thing wasn't going to be easy.

Reflecting on it now, I still can't articulate a particularly good reason for why I wanted to go to Penn other than the fact that it would have looked good on a resume. I'll openly admit I could have written a better essay. Yet, truthfully, anything else I would have written would have also been dishonest noise. I wanted admission to Penn because it was a prestigious school, and I wanted to borrow some of that prestige for myself. There wasn't a good way to spin that.

Yet, I also don't think I was particularly unique. Even for the students who were admitted, I'm pretty sure prestige is why a lot of them wanted to go too. In fact, many students will openly admit that prestige was dispositive to their decision. For those that don't, the reasons they list often boil down to prestige too.

For example, some students claim that they want to go to certain schools because they have very strong programs in a certain area. Yet, if you often ask these students what makes a school's program so strong. They often draw a blank. Is it the professors? If so, which ones? Is it the method of instruction?

If so, how does it differ from other schools? Is it the textbooks? No, it can't be the textbooks; they're usually identical. When pressed in this manner, students often default to the response that the program is strong because it has a strong reputation. They default to describing prestige by a different name.

Moving beyond anecdotal argument, numerous studies prove that students are deeply motivated by prestige. For example, in 2013, a team of economists constructed a ranking of colleges based on each college's head-to-head record against other colleges. Essentially, every time a student in the study's sample got multiple offers of admission, these economists observed which college eventually "won" that student. Controlling for differences in price, these economists finally aggregated such head-to-head contests for thousands of students to construct a ranking based on which college students had actually chosen when they had a choice.

The results of their ranking were definitive. According to their study, if a student was accepted to both Harvard and Wellesley, then there was a 93 percent chance of that student choosing Harvard.[11] I'll admit Harvard is a slightly more prestigious college but is the difference in academics so drastic between the two schools to explain such a choice gap? Their study was full of such drastic implications. For example, if a student was accepted to both Yale and Notre Dame, there was a 92 percent chance that the student would choose Yale. Again, is the difference in academics at the two schools so drastic? No, it isn't. Instead, the preference for prestige is exceptionally strong among students. As demonstrated in their study, when ranked in this head-to-head manner, the eight Ivy League schools were all in the top 15. As were Stanford and MIT. Meanwhile, the University of Virginia was the only public school to make it into the top twenty schools.[12]

This student obsession with prestige also shows up in studies about the influence of US News' college rankings. For example, when Cornell rocketed from a rank of 14th in the US News ranking in the fall of 1997 to a rank of 6th in the fall of 1998, applications to Cornell rose by over 10 percentage points. Students went wild for the higher ranking.[13] Generally, a Harvard Business School study from 2013 found that "a one-rank improvement leads to a 1-percentage-point increase in the number of applications to that college."[14]

The question is why. Why are we all so obsessed with how prestigious Penn is, or Harvard is, or Yale is? Why does Harvard have a 93 percent chance of beating Wellesley? Turning inward, why was I so obsessed with getting into a fancy school? Having grown up in the internet age, with more knowledge available for free than ever before, couldn't I have gotten a great education at a lot of different schools?

In 1834, Abraham Lincoln was a young man who had fallen in hard times. After a series of failed business ventures, Lincoln was buried in debt. Worse, Lincoln had no obvious path to digging his way out of debt. Lincoln feared for his future. This was when a stroke of fortune changed his entire trajectory.

Lincoln caught a massive break when he was lent some law books by another attorney. Finally seeing a way out of his struggles, Lincoln worked retail during the day, and he studied the law at night. Finding solace in legal thinking, Lincoln eventually mastered legal argument. In 1836, he was admitted to the Illinois bar. This is how a man initially headed towards a life of debt and despair course corrected all the way into the Presidency of the United States.

If Lincoln could teach himself the law with a few used books, what could he have accomplished on his own today? Imagine arming Lincoln with Google, Wikipedia, or Youtube. This begs a bigger question. In the internet era of accessible information, why aren't more students emulating Lincoln? Why aren't more young people self-taught? Why do so many able students inevitably go to college?

Contextually, MIT OpenCourseWare makes more than 1,400 courses available for free. These course modules are composed of real recorded lectures, syllabi, and assignments. You can simulate an MIT undergraduate education with nothing more than an internet connection. Frankly, during the pandemic, you basically got the same education whether you were actually enrolled at MIT or merely using the MIT OpenCourseWare website. Nevertheless, students continued to opt into paying tuition at MIT instead of using the courseware website for free. We can learn something from this paradoxical behavior. Obviously, students don't go to college merely for education or merely to build skills. Yet, since students are overwhelmingly going to college, there must be another factor at play. We can isolate this factor through a simple thought experiment.

Imagine you were turned into an invisible ghost and thus able to attend lectures, access assignments, and take exams at MIT. Since no one could see you, no one would know of your attendance. Now imagine that you followed around and therefore completed exactly the same coursework as another MIT student for four years. Imagine you got the exact same answers for every single question in every single course, but the other student actually got grades on his record, and you did not. Lastly, imagine that on the day of graduation, you turned back into a human, having received the exact same education as the student you shadowed. The only difference between you and this person would be that you wouldn't have a degree certificate. That other student with the MIT degree on his resume would get a job interview wherever he wanted, but what about you? Would McKinsey give you an interview if you didn't have a degree? Would BCG?

Most students don't go to college merely to acquire skills; instead, most students also go for a credible certificate that acknowledges that they have those skills. They go for a signal of their skills. But why is this important? Maybe another Illinois political anecdote can help us understand the importance of signals of competence.

In 1948, on a cold Chicago night, Abner Mikva walked towards his local ward headquarters. Despite being a young and nervous law student, Abner Mikva gathered up his courage and opened the door. Walking into the ward headquarters, Abner Mikva announced, "I'd like to volunteer to work for Stevenson and Douglas." Hearing Abner's offer, a Chicago ward committeeman turned to face the door. This committeeman took his cigar out of his mouth, but he didn't get up from his seat. He looked Abner up and down. He asked, "Who sent you?" Abner responded, "Nobody sent me." The committeeman started puffing on his cigar again. A few puffs later, he concluded, "We don't want nobody that nobody sent."

Abner Mikva would go on to become an Illinois state representative, Congressman, federal appellate judge, and political mentor to a young Barack Obama. But, in the parochial world of 1940s Chicago politics, Abner Mikva couldn't even become a volunteer. In hindsight, the committeeman obviously made a mistake in rejecting Abner Mikva. But the more important question is why did the committeeman reject Abner?

Essentially, Abner Mikva's problem in that pivotal moment was that he couldn't be trusted. The ward committeeman didn't say, "We're not hiring." He didn't say, "Leave your resume." He said, "Who sent you?" If the right person had sent him, maybe Abner would have been more plausible to the ward committeeman. If Abner could be trusted, maybe he would have been hired.

This type of trust gap isn't a problem specific to new deal-era political machines; it's an incredibly general and timeless problem. Definitionally, young people are too young to have a record. Thus, employers of all kinds, not just cigar-puffing ward bosses, have trouble evaluating young people for entry-level job openings. Employers need to know that the person they're hiring is competent and culturally fitting. Without a prior record, young people pose a challenge to employers.

In economic jargon, this trust gap problem is described as information asymmetry. There is almost always an asymmetry in information between the young person seeking employment and the person providing it. Young people know more about their competence than the employer does. Frankly, young people can easily lie on resumes or in interviews. Even if they're honest, maybe they're foolishly convinced that they're more talented than they are. How is an employer supposed to know if an applicant is actually capable or not?

George Akerlof won a Nobel Prize in economics for his famous paper, The Market for Lemons, which exactly explained the dynamic of this information asymmetry problem.[15] In his paper, Akerlof studied the slightly different context of the used car market. Specifically, Akerlof explained that any seller in the used car market necessarily knows more about the condition of the used car that he is selling than the buyer knows about that same car. Thus, a seller could lie and pass off a low-quality car as a really great car to an unsuspecting buyer. If many sellers did this, swindled buyers would spread the fear of being swindled to future customers in the car market. This deterioration of trust in used car sellers would cause the whole used car market to collapse.

In practice, products, regulations, and heuristics emerge to prevent a market collapse. In the used car market, CarMax offers certifications that serve as an independent signal of quality. In Abner Mikva's time, political referrals served as an independent signal that the potential volunteer wasn't an untrustworthy spy.

Much like the used car market, information asymmetry is a significant problem in the first job market. Hiring an incapable person imposes significant costs on employers as employers must go through the trouble of firing such unqualified people and then looking for new hires who might also turn out to be unqualified. This is not as much of an issue in non-entry level labor markets because once an employee has developed a track record, you can do things like ask former employers about job performance, view work product, and more directly verify competence. Not so when a young person is applying for that first job in a specific industry.

Throughout American history, labor markets have produced a variety of solutions for the information asymmetry problem in the first job market. If we were to go back to colonial-era America, the information asymmetry problem was solved by a demonstration of skills. In those days, young people interested in a particular trade would become apprentices to an acknowledged master of that trade. For example, Ben Franklin was a printer's apprentice. After years of service and learning, young people would finally get a chance to showcase all they had learned by producing a masterpiece. For example, a tailor's apprentice would have to produce a well-tailored suit in the newest fashion. Or a printer's apprentice would have to produce a pamphlet. This masterpiece was an honest proof of skills. Essentially, the better the masterpiece, the more you could trust the new tradesman to be competent at his trade. The new tradesman could then use his masterpiece to get hired somewhere else, or he could start his own shop.

In today's knowledge economy, the college degree has emerged as the modern equivalent of the masterpiece. The college degree serves as an independent signal of quality. For example, I recently found an internship role on Google's careers website. Importantly, Google required applicants for that "Product Design Engineering Internship" to be pursuing a bachelor's degree at least.

I'm quite sure that a smart person without a bachelor's degree could do that job. Yet from Google's point of view, it would be quite laborious to figure out who could do the role, and more importantly, it would be even harder to compare the candidates against each other to determine who the best-qualified candidates would be for the role. So much like the Chicago ward bosses from Abner Mikva's story, Google uses a metric with which to start filtering. Unlike the Chicago ward bosses, Google's metric isn't a referral but rather the standard of the college degree.

Generally, in the knowledge economy, employers are looking for at least two things from potential laborers. Employers are looking for competence and a reliable way of telling who is competent and who isn't. Framed differently, knowledge economy employers are looking for both skills and a signal of those skills. Accordingly, students looking to get that first job have to be genuinely competent and able to demonstrate it.

Historically, college degrees used to be relatively rare in America. Other methods of signaling, such as masterpieces or referrals, were more relevant. Yet, this began to change in the late 19th and early 20th centuries. There was a boom of land grant colleges as the nation expanded west. Robber barons of the gilded age further endowed great universities like the University of Chicago, Vanderbilt, and Stanford. As America industrialized, the knowledge economy increasingly employed more people. Scientists, engineers, and technicians were needed to design and develop the technologies of the future.

Yet, the biggest expansions in college enrollment came from policy initiatives designed to specifically send young people to college. The most famous of these policy initiatives is the G.I. Bill. Passed in 1944, the G.I. Bill paid for veterans of World War II to attend college. In total, 2.3 million veterans used the benefits of the G.I. Bill to attend college. Later, Lyndon Johnson passed the Higher Education Act of 1965. This act made student loans readily accessible. Suddenly, easy credit meant expanded enrollment at colleges across America. This expansion of enrollment has continued, and today nearly 66 percent of high school graduates go on to college. The government-led expansion of enrollment has had a flywheel effect. The more students with college degrees, the more employers like Google have required a college degree as a minimum. The more employers require a college degree, the more students go to college.

This massive expansion of college students has created a new signaling dynamic. In the past, so few people went to college that merely attending any college at all was enough to set one apart from others. The fact that Alexander Hamilton attended King's College at a time when virtually no one attended college was enough to signal that he was incredibly gifted. Today attending college isn't special. Nearly two million bachelor's degrees are allocated each year. This poses employers with a new problem. How can an employer compare a student from Michigan to a student from UMiami? How are they meant to figure out which candidate is better between two candidates who each have different and competing signals of competence?

In an economy flushed with college degrees, the diverse nature of college degrees makes direct comparison incredibly difficult. After all, there is such a variety of schools, and the permutations of the college experience available are virtually endless. For example, a math major at MIT likely has a very different experience from a fashion major at Parsons or a music major at Juilliard. Yet, all three have college degree credentials. The college system is incredibly fragmented. Public schools, private schools, and for-profit schools are all constituents of the system. Some schools are big. Other schools are small. How is that any kind of standard of comparison?

The number and diversity of degrees has given rise to a new method of implicit comparison. Essentially, a hierarchy of prestige allows for an implicit comparison between two schools and, therefore, between two candidates. As a thought experiment, ask yourself, who would you find more impressive as a candidate: a Harvard graduate with a 3.5 or a Hilbert College graduate with a 3.9? I'd posit that most people would pick the Harvard graduate. What does this tell us? It tells us that there is some sort of prestige hierarchy that serves as a standard. Where does this hierarchy come from?

Thus, prestige hierarchy comes from metrics of prestige such as the U.S. News & World Report rankings. Rankings centralize and standardize the fragmented and diffuse college market. If you accept rankings at face value, they give you a neatly arranged list of which schools graduate better-qualified students. Accordingly, these rankings allow for the standardization of a system that otherwise is very fractured.

If you have a loose hierarchy of prestige to work from, you can easily compare the Harvard candidate versus the Haverford candidate. Even if that evaluation might be wrong, it is easy to do. Whether rankings are incorporated strictly or more loosely, relative prestige is a way for employers to evaluate signals of competence against each other. In today's economy, prestige is king in getting that first job.

Employers need this sort of standardization if they are to use the college standard to compare students. Empirically, this is exactly what they do. A study commissioned by Indeed concludes, "There is a clear bias towards graduates of top colleges when it comes to hiring. However, it is difficult to predict how that will impact an individual's career. Top school degrees have the highest impact at the entry and executive levels, often the most competitive times in a career."[16]

Attempting to quantify the impact of degree prestige, that same study conducted by Indeed clarifies, "When asked about the role of education in hiring, 29% prefer to only hire candidates from top institutions, while almost half (48%) of respondents believe the institution a candidate graduated from plays a somewhat important role in hiring. Only 4% don't care about the name on an employee's degree as long as educational requirements for the role are met." Framed differently, this study concluded that 96 percent of those surveyed believe that the school brand plays at least some role in hiring decisions.

The direct implication here is that a student's signal of competence in the job market is directly related to the prestige of the institution he or she attends. It might be true that the prestige of the institution doesn't form the entirety of the signal of competence. For example, there are other things that may be relevant such as GPA or relevant internships, but it is undeniable that the prestige of an institution directly impacts a student's signal of competence. The more prestigious a school, the stronger the signal of competence.

Prestigious signals beat non-prestigious signals in the first job market. This simple truth about the value of prestige is why I applied early to Penn with little thought put into it or why my friends applied to other prestigious colleges like UChicago or Yale. Just as my high school classmates intuitively understood that prestige would probably help us compete down the line, so do hundreds of thousands of other students each year.

Elite colleges want to attract the brightest students. To do so, elite colleges have to maintain prestigiousness since a strong signal is what students need for their entrance into the first job market. Yet, prestige is hard to manufacture. Ultimately brand perception and prestige are not actually in the control of any college. Prestige depends on the perception of others. So, the competitive dynamic of colleges today is a constant zero-sum battle over relative prestige. Non-elite colleges try to climb the rankings. Elite colleges try to maintain rank. Thus, US News' influential ranking is able to become a conductor to the elite colleges' orchestra. Whatever the rankings incentivize, elite colleges do. In later chapters, we explore this dynamic in-depth. We also analyze why it is so harmful.

CHAPTER 2

THE ELITE AFTERGLOW

The first chapter in this book implies that the prestige of elite degrees gives graduates a head start in their careers. However, the first chapter also tells an incomplete story. Even if prestigious degrees give graduates a head start, does that head start endure over the entirety of a career? How much does prestige actually matter in the long term?

We might naturally assume that elite degrees offer career-spanning advantages. As one study found in 2013, not only had 45 percent of America's billionaires graduated from elite schools but also 41 percent of US Senators and nearly 41 percent of US Federal Judges had too.[17] Even just looking at average outcomes, as the Harvard Business Review quantified in 2020, within six years of graduation, the average salary for graduates of the top ten most elite colleges was 108 percent higher than that of graduates of the CUNY school system.[18] With all this evidence, do we really need to ask if elite degrees make a difference?

We do, actually, because correlation doesn't always mean causation. Yes, very successful people often graduated from elite colleges, but did those schools actually help these students succeed, or were those particular kids already likely to succeed when they got in? Are we mistakenly finding causation where only correlation exists?

In January of 2007, a reporter from The New York Observer sat down with Joe Biden for an interview. As the questioning began, Joe Biden answered the reporter's questions openly and candidly. Biden periodically flashed a grin, in his characteristic style, and the conversation quickly jumped from issue to issue. Finally, the reporter asked Senator Biden to evaluate Senator Barack Obama's chances in the upcoming Presidential campaign. Excitedly, Joe Biden responded, "I mean, you got the first mainstream African-American who is articulate and bright and clean and a nice-looking guy."[19] As these comments trickled into reports in newspapers and on cable news, I imagine that Joe Biden's communications team sat cringing with their heads in their hands.

The day these comments were made public, Senator Obama was mobbed by a reporter in the Senate. As Senator Obama walked briskly, the reporter asked him what he made of Senator Biden's comments. Senator Obama quickly responded, "Making news, being Joe."[20] Senator Obama clearly didn't want to engage with the reporter, but the reporter pressed him again. Senator Obama again tried to avoid the topic. He kept walking, but the reporter wouldn't give up. Finally, Senator Obama responded, "Joe didn't mean to offend." But the reporter then asked Senator Obama if he thought Senator Biden had a shot at the nomination. On this question, Senator Obama passed entirely. Still walking, eventually Senator Obama was able to escape the reporter by ducking into an exit.

Understandably, there was interest in interpreting what Senator Biden was trying to say. What did Senator Biden mean by bright and clean? What did he mean by articulate? What did he mean by first? Joe Biden, even in 2007, was famous for what is called "gaffes," and many in the media certainly offered that interpretation to explain his comments. For example, shortly after Senator Biden's statement, political pundit Jonathan Darman wrote in a column, "If the gaffe does destroy Biden's chances, few in either party will be particularly surprised. The senator's biggest enemy has always been his own mouth."[21]

But is gaffe the correct interpretation of that particular quote? Or is there something more fundamental that Senator Biden was trying to communicate? Was he really taken out of context, or was that just a convenient excuse once his comments weren't well received? Frankly, I dispute the gaffe interpretation of Senator Biden's comments because, in quarters less gaffe-prone, there seemed to be different words used to communicate a similar idea.

For example, during Senator Obama's run, the media unceasingly reported that Barack Obama had graduated from Harvard Law school. This media obsession stood in stark contrast to the fact that Senator Obama rarely mentioned it himself. Importantly, the media didn't focus on elite degrees to the same extent for other candidates who graduated from elite colleges. Sure, an elite education might be mentioned, but it was never a central part of the story the media told about other candidates. So, why did the mainstream media care so much about Senator Obama's elite pedigree in particular? Wasn't the media trying to frame Senator Obama in a certain way? Fundamentally, was the media's framing so different from Senator Biden's controversial one?

Consider a simple thought experiment. If the name on President Obama's law degree had been changed from Harvard to Howard, would his credibility as a candidate for the Presidency have decreased in the eyes of the mainstream media? If yes, then wasn't the media subtly using Senator Obama's Ivy League pedigree to imply what Joe Biden explicitly said when he called Senator Obama articulate, clean, or mainstream? Wasn't the Ivy League degree used by the media to communicate something about what kind of a black person Senator Obama was?

It is undeniable that there is implicit and explicit bias in various aspects of American society. Senator Obama's presidential run is just one example of this kind of unfair bias. If we zoom out some more, we notice that race is often unfairly used as a signal in other job markets too. Empirically, a study was conducted in 2021 by researchers at Berkeley and UChicago that proves this point. In the study, researchers sent 83,000 fake applications with random characteristics to 108 of the largest US employers.[22] The results were saddening. The study concluded that changing the name on a resume from a distinctively white name to a distinctively black name decreased the likelihood of employer contact by 2.1 percent.[23] Plainly, by America's biggest employers, the name John was preferred to Jamal.

While this is obviously wrong, it is also a reality. It is a sociological fact that humans often assume things about other people solely based on one's race. Some people are given the benefit of the doubt because of their race. Others are doubted more because of their race. Although it shouldn't be, one's race is often used as a signal in job markets. Employers often make judgments on what type of employee someone will be based on their race.

Thankfully, one's race isn't the only signal in job markets. Education is an important signal in job markets too. For example, as we explored in the last chapter, a prestigious degree serves as a powerful signal in the first job market. Sometimes these two signals work in opposite directions. For example, a black job candidate might be wrongly and unfairly regarded as less desirable because of his race, but that same candidate might also attract a more positive assessment because of a prestigious degree from Yale. The impact of the prestigious degree might even totally overpower the initial racial bias. For example, one interpretation of the obsessive media coverage of President Obama's Harvard Law education is that his prestigious degree helped him overcome some racial bias in the Presidential job market in 2008. Importantly, this anecdote about President Obama's elite degree can be generalized quite broadly.

In 2002, economists Stacy Dale and Alan Krueger published a landmark economic study. Their study grew out of a broader question.[24] Contextually, it is a fact that elite colleges graduate billionaires, presidents, lawyers, and laureates. But these economists still wondered if the schools were responsible for the success of their distinguished alumni. Or were these students already likely to be successful to begin with?

To answer this question, Stacy Dale and Alan Krueger designed a study where they compared the career earnings of students who went to elite colleges with the earnings of students who were also accepted by those elite colleges but chose to go to less elite colleges. Their results were very shocking.

What Stacy Dale and Alan Krueger found is that attending an elite college especially increased career earnings for Black students, Hispanic students, and students whose parents hadn't earned a college degree.[25] Later studies have extended these results to conclude that elite degrees also benefit female students. In fact, one recent study concludes that graduating from a college with a 100-point higher average SAT score increases a woman's career earnings by 14 percent![26]

However, Stacy Dale and Alan Krueger and other more recent studies have also shockingly and counter-intuitively found that for other types of students, there were zero earnings benefit from attending an elite college instead of a non-elite one. For example, for a wealthy white male, as long as he got into Harvard, it didn't decrease his earnings if he went to Haverford instead. As Dale and Krueger explain in their study: "students who attend more elite colleges may have greater earnings capacity regardless of where they attend school."[27]

At this point, you might object! How could that be? Didn't we just spend the first chapter discussing how elite degrees help in the first job market? Yes, we did. However, a career is longer than just one's first job, and these studies conclude that over time the effect of the first job boost evaporates. In effect, as careers begin to extend through time, people develop new signals. Referrals from former bosses. Work product from past jobs. New industry networks. News coverage from previous work. Eventually, those signals begin to make more of a difference in who gets what opportunities. In the end, amongst people who are not discriminated against and who already have access to connections, cream generally rises to the top. Shane Hunt puts it bluntly: "The C student from Princeton earns more than the A student from Podunk not mainly because he has the prestige of a Princeton degree, but merely because he is abler. The golden touch is possessed not by the Ivy League College but by its students."[28]

To prove this point, let's indulge in another thought experiment. I'm a massive Manchester United fan, but like almost all other fans, I reached the sad conclusion long ago that I would never play for Manchester United. Unfortunately, I'm just not that good at soccer. Even if I was magically drafted onto Manchester United's starting team today, it would only take a few minutes for me to expose myself as terrible. A few games in, the coach would dump me. I'd be right back where I started.

Just as I would be unable to play for Manchester United even if I got a chance, there are many people who would be unable to sustain or advance in other jobs or industries even if they were to get their foot in the door. In the longer term, signaling can only do so much. At a certain point, you have to actually perform. It is no surprise then that when you zoom out beyond the first job advantage that a more prestigious degree confers, the advantages of a prestigious degree begin to fade away.

You might still be skeptical about the assertion that elite education provides little economic value. What about the alumni network? What about the fact that at elite schools, you can learn from the very best professors? How could these studies possibly be true? How could an elite education make no impact at all?

On January 11th, 2000, George Bush made his way onto a stage in Florence, South Carolina. Brimming with confidence, he smiled and waved at an adoring crowd. Standing tall in a windbreaker, the American flag was pinned up behind him. George Bush was vigorously campaigning for the Republican presidential nomination. At the time, his nomination wasn't a sure bet. Instead, Governor Bush was up against a stiff challenge from Senator John McCain. So, Governor Bush decided to largely stake his candidacy on the issue of education. In fact, education reform was a major theme in his speech that day in Florence, South Carolina. As he smiled and waved, you could feel that George Bush was winning over the crowd. As his speech went on, Governor Bush then framed the education question in a way only he could. He paused his speech for emphasis before he asked his audience, "Rarely is the question asked: are our children learning?"

President Bush became known for his Bush-isms over the course of his political career. Once to a reporter, he said, "One of the great things about books is sometimes there are some fantastic pictures." Another time he empathized, "I know how hard it is for you to put food on your family." In 2004, President George Bush once observed, "Too many good docs are getting out of the business. Too many OB/GYNs aren't able to practice their love with women all across the country."

In all of this context, it might be lost on many that George Bush went to the most elite schools his entire life. He went to Phillips Academy, an elite prep school, before he matriculated to Yale for his bachelor's degree and Harvard for his MBA. There are few people in America with a more elite educational pedigree. Yet, when most people think of George Bush, they don't immediately think of an elite educational background.

There's a reason for this. George Bush's father and grandfather were successful American politicians. His dad was a Congressman, Ambassador, CIA Director, Vice-President, and later President! Because of his father's extensive political network, George Bush was already a phone call away from any person he ever wanted to speak with. If George Bush had gone to Young Harris instead of Yale, he likely would still have had many of the same opportunities. His own life likely would have followed a similar trajectory whether or not he went to Yale or Harvard. After all, how much did he really uniquely benefit from the networking at Harvard?

Contrasting President Bush's presidential campaign with President Obama's, a clear distinction is immediately evident. President Bush's elite pedigree didn't have to compensate for racial bias against him. It is likely for this reason that the media very rarely reported on President Bush's academic credentials. For President Obama, his Harvard diploma was harped on endlessly by the media. Contrasting George Bush with Barack

Obama illustrates a broader truth. As Derek Thompson asserts, "Research suggests that elite colleges don't really help rich white guys. But they can have a big effect if you're not rich, not white, or not a guy."[29]

Elite colleges help students whose parents aren't college-educated gain access to professional networks that their parents might have been entirely disconnected from. Plus, elite colleges help counter-signal for students whose racial or gender characteristics are wrongly undervalued by society. Networks for the disconnected and signals for the misjudged are the two places where elite colleges provide value.

On the other hand, if your dad can pick up the phone and call his buddy to help you get a coveted internship or job, you don't really need the prestigious degree. This fact poses a paradox. If so many other students, especially rich, white, and male students, don't really benefit from an elite education, then why are they so interested in attending?

John Kennedy was 17 years old when he first applied to Harvard in 1935. In those days, the Harvard application was written by hand. Even so, there was an essay that each applicant had to complete. The prompt was: "Why do you wish to come to Harvard?"

According to documents recently released by the JFK Presidential Library, John Kennedy wrote the following: "The reasons that I have for wishing to go to Harvard are several. I feel that Harvard can give me a better background and a better liberal education than any other university. I have always wanted to go there, as I have felt that it is not just another college but a university with something definite to offer. Then too, I would like to go to the same college as my father. To be a 'Harvard man' is an enviable distinction and one that I sincerely hope I shall attain."[30]

Kennedy's college essay is instructive. Why are people who won't extract financial benefits from it so interested in attending expensive, prestigious schools? One fairly straightforward answer is vanity. Degrees confer status. While things have changed from 1935 to the present day, this idea of a Harvard diploma being "an enviable distinction" hasn't really changed at all.

So, why is it so important to be a "Harvard man"? As Carnevale, Schmidt, and Strohl theorize in their book, The Merit Myth: How Our Colleges Favor the Rich and Divide America, "An expensive college education represents what economists call a 'positional good.' Like a pricey designer handbag or a luxury car, its value stems partly from its price, artificially inflated by the inability of most people to afford it. The additional money spent on it signals wealth and status as much as any additional measurable quality. People are welcome, of course, to engage in conspicuous consumption, such as the purchase of Gucci purses or Lamborghini roadsters, with their own money."[31]

Importantly, this framing of an elite college degree as a positional good reframes an elite degree from an investment decision to a consumption purchase. When seen through the consumption lens, the lack of a rate of return on investment starts to make more sense. One relevant question within this new framing is, of all the things to spend one's fortune on, why is the college degree the one that captures so many resources? Aren't there better luxury items to signal status?

I don't know the answer to why college takes such preeminence among positional goods. Yet, if I were to speculate, I think that elite degrees serve a deep psychological need for the very wealthy. In a mostly global capitalist system, such as ours, where the disparity between "winners" and "losers" is quite stark, an intrusive question might naturally trouble wealthy people: "Why me?"

This question might not be so troubling for self-made successes, but for those who inherit wealth, the question might take on a nagging quality. Of course, acknowledging one's luck is probably the right response, but it can leave one morally unsatisfied. Against this emotional backdrop, an elite degree can serve as an indication of merit. If you inherit wealth but also attend Harvard, you might be lucky, but you might not see yourself as undeserving. After all, you've been educated amongst the best and brightest. So what if it was easier for you to get in? You still had to graduate like everyone else, didn't you?

"Why me?" turns into "Who else?" when you have an indication of merit on your side. Each time someone asks where you went to college, and you respond with an elite name, the sub-communication becomes more important than the communication itself. Of course, with each whisper of "Princeton" or "Penn" what you're really saying is, "I'm qualified. I deserve it."

Understanding prestigious degrees as positional goods helps to explain why people are so willing to spend so much money both to get admission and also complete attendance. One study from 2021 by economists Peter Blair and Kent Smetters finds that, in dollar terms, an average person admitted to a top 2 percent college, like Cornell, would be willing to shell out $114,942 in order to get into a more prestigious college like Harvard, Princeton, Stanford, or Yale.[32] To many people, this might sound crazy. Why would someone be willing to pay more than $100,000 for admission to a slightly more exclusive school?

I agree with those who characterize this frenzied and desperate behavior as crazy. Yet, I also acknowledge it is real. In fact, $100,000 dollars might even sound reasonable compared to the amount some people spend every single admission cycle. Routinely, applicants from wealthier families donate in the millions to get into Harvard, Princeton, Stanford, and Yale. When interpreting the $114,942 figure that Blair and Smetters calculate, we have to remember that this dollar value corresponds to a switch between colleges which are both somewhat elite.[33] The amount students would be willing to pay gets larger the further they get from the very top. In fact, as Blair and Smetters explain, many applicants would be willing to pay a similar amount to make a jump from a college in the top 10 percent to a college in the top 2 percent. Just as there's a frenzy for students from Cornell to get into Harvard, there is a frenzy for students from UNC to get into Cornell.

The main takeaway of this chapter is that there is an economic benefit to going to an elite college for certain people. For others, like modern-day Kennedys, it is merely an exercise in social vanity. The high value on vanity consumption that many people place contrasts with the high value for society that the right admitted students generate. This tension has massive implications for how elite colleges ought to structure their admissions policies. If seats are truly limited, who do we want to get them? Do we want to fill the halls of Harvard with rich posers? Or do we want to fill those halls with unappreciated merit? Only by expanding enrollment can we do both.

CHAPTER 3

THE COLLEGE OF CARDINALS

My graduation ceremony was originally meant to be held in May 2020. However, things didn't play out that way. Unfortunately, the COVID-19 pandemic completely scrambled the normal flow of events. As plague and pestilence spread through the globe, my Georgetown graduation ceremony was postponed. I didn't know it then, but it would be nearly two years before my graduation ceremony was rescheduled.

In the intervening two years, I spent a lot of my time research-ing and writing this book. This was a deeply instructive period in my life. With the world frozen in place by the pandemic, I had more time alone to think through ideas. This intellectual isolation allowed me to see beyond the sheen and sparkle of prestigious schools. Beyond the pretense, I didn't like what I found. Essentially, the more I learned about how elite colleges actually work, the more I found objectionable. I wasn't the only one coming to this epiphany.

On January 10, 2022, I remember waking up to texts from many of my friends. The texts were all worded differently, but in their essence, they were alike. Each one linked to the same article in that morning's Wall Street Journal. There was breaking news. A class-action lawsuit had been filed against Georgetown and other elite colleges for fixing prices on financial aid offers.[34] With the canon fire of the lawsuit, the reform movement against the college cartel had begun.

For over a year before that headline made it into the Wall Street Journal, I had been telling anyone who would listen that the elite colleges were organized in a cartel. So, when my friends started texting me on that day in January, it was a gratifying moment. With this lawsuit, my ideas were making it into the mainstream.

I discuss the substance of this price-fixing conspiracy in more detail in a later chapter, but the lawsuit was also important to me symbolically. After all, the lawyers who filed the case forced me into intellectual clarity. If they were doing something to confront the college cartel, why wasn't I? In the weeks and months after their lawsuit was first filed, I decided that this book on its own wasn't enough. After all, there was a high chance no one would read this book, although I'm quite glad that you are. Plus, this book wouldn't be done anytime soon. So, feeling the urgency of the moment, I decided to shine a light on the price-fixing issue by organizing protests on various campuses. This included my own.

The day before my graduation ceremony, my dad asked, "Why are you doing this?" My sister objected, "Why are you so weird?" I tried to explain my rationale to them, but they didn't seem to understand me. So, I decided to ignore their objections. I was going to protest at my own graduation ceremony. I felt that I had a responsibility to do it.

On the day of my graduation ceremony, the campus swarmed with alumni in their hats and gowns. It was a sunny day, and we all got to campus early in the morning. That morning, as I sat down in a classroom with some peers, I realized that it had been over two years since I had seen so many of these classmates. I was happy to see them. I didn't want to ruin anyone's graduation ceremony. So, I decided to keep my protest targeted, short, and sweet.

As the ceremony commenced, I sat in a folded chair on our campus lawn with my sweaty palms. Although I was dressed in the customary cap and gown, I also had a small duffel bag stashed under my seat. In that bag was a top hat, a monocle, and a stick-on mustache. My plan was simple. On my way on stage, I planned on switching out my cap for my top hat, monocle, and stick-on mustache. I was going to confront the President of Georgetown University dressed up as the monopoly man. The names were starting to be called. In just a few moments, my name would be next.

Then my name was called. I walked towards the stage, scrambling to assemble my costume. With my costume on, I heard a few giggles. I first walked on stage, and then I walked across. I was handed my diploma. The first handshake began. I then walked towards President John DeGioia. I shook his hand too. Then, I kept shaking his hand. I said, "Mr. DeGioia, you need to pull out of the 568 price-fixing cartel. If you announce that you're pulling out publicly, the whole conspiracy will fold like a tent. You have a real opportunity for leadership. Do it." Mr. DeGioia just stared away from me. He whispered, "Congratulations."

Although I'm disappointed that President Jack DeGioia didn't affirmatively pull out of the price-fixing conspiracy, I think the more productive question is why? Why didn't he? Further, why didn't the other college Presidents affirmatively pull out of the price-fixing conspiracy? Maybe college presidents are motivated by some base greed. But that can't possibly be the whole explanation. After all, elite colleges are non-profits. If George-town makes more money, it doesn't directly go into President Jack's pockets in the form of dividends or a higher share price. The explanation is not as simple as pure greed. There's a more complicated story at play. What is it?

To understand that story, we need to understand how some-one like President Jack DeGioia ends up as President of a major elite college in the first place. What gets him the job? What helps him keep it? How does he get a raise? This chapter answers those questions. In doing so, this chapter explains some of the incen-tives that push elite college Presidents to behave in ways that are so obviously contrary to the public interest.

This chapter connects to the broader narrative of this book by explaining how decision-makers at elite colleges are pushed to behave in anticompetitive ways by their internal incentive struc-tures. As we explore later, changing those internal incentives can help break the structural logic which results in anticompetitive conduct.

I want to start our analysis with an anecdote from medie-val history. In 1241, Rome had been blockaded by Fredrick II's armies. To move militarily against Rome was a brazen move, but then again, Fredrick II was a brazen man. Brazen might even be an understatement. In fact, Pope Gregory IX condemned him openly as an antichrist. Yet, there was a method to Fredrick II's madness. This ambitious Holy Roman Emperor wanted some-thing. Frederick II had moved in his armies for a very specific purpose. Audaciously, Fredrick II wanted a hand in choosing the next Pope.

To a political animal like Fredrick II, the intrigue was irre-sistible. The elder Pope Gregory IX had just passed away. A new Pope was yet to be selected. In this interim, influence could

A Picture from My Protest at My Georgetown Graduation

be exerted on the Cardinals who would choose the next Pope. Frederick II sensed an opportunity. So, he decided to kidnap some cardinals and block others from entering Rome. With his military, he controlled entry into the city. He was, therefore, able to rig the electorate.

In the face of this pressure, the elector Cardinals couldn't agree on whom to select. There was great polarization in the electorate. Some Cardinals wanted a hardline Pope who would continue the papal fight against the oppressive Fredrick II. Other Cardinals wanted a detente. Finally, the Roman civilians had enough of the impasse. These civilians wanted a Pope! So, the civilians locked the Cardinals in a monastery and refused to let them out. They wouldn't let the Cardinals out until these Cardinals did their job and a Pope was selected.

It was under these oppressive conditions that the Cardinals finally chose Pope Celestine IV, one of their oldest and weakest members. In fact, Pope Celestine IV was so old and weak that on his seventeenth day as Pope, he passed away. The whole process would have to be repeated!

The story of Pope Celestine IV's election serves to highlight a broader truth. The interests of the electorate heavily determine the selection of the elected. In the case of Pope Celestine IV, the Cardinals really didn't want to decide. So even when forced to select, the Cardinals cynically chose someone likely to die soon. This decision allowed the elector Cardinals to continue to procrastinate on a real choice for the longer term.

This medieval papal history might seem entirely unrelated to our story about elite colleges, and in some ways, it is. Yet, I believe that we can understand the role of elite college presidents through an analogy with the Catholic Pope. For just as each Pope reflects the papal conclave that elected him, so too is each college president a reflection of the board of trustees which selected him. To understand this relationship in more depth, let's begin with the organizational basics.

All elite colleges are organized slightly differently, but there are common themes in the governance structure. All elite colleges have a board of governance. At most private schools, this is called the board of trustees. At many public schools, this is called a board of regents or a board of visitors instead. These governance boards have various responsibilities. For example, at Stanford, "The Board of Trustees is the custodian of the endowment and all properties of the University. The Board administers the invested funds, sets the annual budget, and determines policies for operation and control of the University."[35] In other words, the board decides the direction of its university. These board members are the people who, through subcommittees and general meetings, chart a vision for the future of their respective elite college. They then appoint and remove executives to fulfill that vision. Internal change starts and ends with them.

While governance boards often outline a direction for their respective universities, they don't execute that vision. Instead, a governance board appoints the president of the university. It is the president who is ultimately responsible for running the university. The board merely provides oversight. If the president is mismanaging the university, it is up to the board of directors to fire and replace him or her.

In this respect, we can understand a governance board by analogy with the College of Cardinals. Just as the Pope reflects the interests of the Cardinals, so too is the president of an elite college a reflection of the interests of the trustees. In fact, this analogy might even understate the influence of the board of trustees. After all, the College of Cardinals can't fire a Pope.

The board of trustees can fire a president. As a result, both in the selection and in the execution of the president's job, the board of trustees is the president's ultimate constituency. Metaphorically, the board of trustees holds a hatchet over the president's head, and they can swing that hatchet at any moment.

In 2012 there was exactly such a hatchet swing at the University of Virginia. On June 7, 2012, Helen Dragas, a member of the board of visitors at the University of Virginia, asked Terry Sullivan, the President of the university, if they could meet.[36] President Terry Sullivan was confused. Why did a board member want to meet her now? It was the summer, and there was no meeting that had been scheduled either. Nevertheless, the next day, President Terry Sullivan texted board member Helen Dragas that she'd be back at her office around 5 pm. They could meet then.

President Terry Sullivan had no idea what she was in for. In fact, few others had any idea either. The Governor of Virginia had been briefed. Fifteen other board members had been briefed. A handful of mega-donors had been briefed. Apart from these chosen few, no one saw the dagger coming.

As the clock struck five, the meeting began. Only it wasn't much of a meeting. It was an ambush. Helen Dragas brutally explained to Terry Sullivan that she had no choice but to resign as President. Helen Dragas mentioned that she had the votes of 15 members on a governance board of 16 total members.[37] If Terry didn't resign, she would be fired by the board. Terry took a day to talk it over with her husband. She came to a sad conclusion. There was no other option. The next day Terry announced her exit.

But why did Helen Dragas and fifteen other board members start this coup? As Helen explained to a faculty member at the University, "Virginia was falling behind competitors like Harvard and Stanford."[38] To the board, this was unacceptable. Importantly, it wasn't just board member Helen Dragas who supported the coup. Instead, UVa's biggest donors were largely behind it.[39] In fact, billionaire mega-donor Paul Tudor Jones wrote an op-ed immediately after President Sullivan's resignation. He praised the decisive action. For mega-donors like him, the coup was, as he wrote, "a clarion call from the Board of Visitors that business as usual is not acceptable anymore. Why be good when there is outstanding to be had?"[40]

As far as what trustees and mega-donors considered to be "outstanding," Billionaire Paul Tudor Jones spelled it out even further in his op-ed. He wrote, "Individually, each of us has a larger role to play than we used to if Virginia is to continue to occupy its historical place as one of the elite universities in the United States. Here are a few alarming facts about the university: UVa's U.S. News and World Report ranking has fallen steadily since 1988 — from No. 15 to No. 25, with a ding from No. 24 taking place as early as last year."[41] To paraphrase the general sentiment. If the University of Virginia didn't improve its ranking, it would lose touch with the elite private colleges it used to compete with. This was unacceptable to the donors. It was unacceptable to the board. But President Sullivan hadn't inspired these power brokers that she had a solution to the problem of the ongoing ranking backslide. President Sullivan hadn't done enough to close the resource gap between UVa and the top dogs like Harvard and Stanford. Therefore, President Sullivan had to be forced out.

In the days immediately after the firing, President Sullivan's allies fought back. Naturally, there was a massive whiplash on campus to the board of visitors firing the President in such a rushed and nefarious way. Faculty didn't like it because they worried that the board might try to fire some of them next. Plus, students perceived the firing as a coup orchestrated by wealthy donors. In fact, protestors spray painted the letters "G-R-E-E-D" in big font across the campus rotunda.[42] Eventually, the national media picked up the story, and pressure built on the board of visitors to bring Sullivan back.

As the days dragged on, the media attention on UVa started to look bad for Virginia's Governor, Bob McDonnell. So, on June 22, Governor McDonnell wrote a stern letter to the University's board of visitors. He demanded that he receive a final decision from the board within a few days. Governor McDonnell just wanted an end to the drama. As he threatened in his letter, "If you fail to do so, I will ask for the resignation of the entire board on Wednesday."[43]

Board member Helen Dragas wanted to tough it out. She tried to lobby other board members to stay the course and find a new President. Helen explained that the criticism would subside. Yet, some of the other board members began to lose their nerves. They didn't like being profiled in the media. They were portrayed as a greedy, nefarious, and ruthless bunch. It was getting bad. Plus, the Governor had put them on an incredibly tight deadline, and they had to decide immediately. Slowly, the sentiment on the board flipped. Could President Sullivan come back?

When Helen Dragas lost the backing of much of the board, she was forced to flip also. Finally, Helen Dragas asked to meet with former President Terry Sullivan again. As they sat down across from each other, Helen Dragas said, "It's time to bring the U-Va. family back together."[44] Helen Dragas continued, "I believe real progress is more possible than ever now. It is unfortunate that we had to have a near-death experience to get here."[45]

Finally, former-President Sullivan agreed to come back a mere eighteen days after she was first fired. She would stay on as President for another six years before she retired from the University of Virginia in 2018.

Although the board's coup was poorly planned and executed, it did deliver some results. President Sullivan, who came back eighteen days later, wasn't the same President Sullivan who left. The new President Sullivan started paying more attention to fundraising. Within a year, President Sullivan led the University to the completion of its $3-billion capital campaign.[46] Importantly, over the span of her presidency, the philanthropic cash flow increased from $203.8 million in FY10 to $283.4 million in FY17.[47] As more money came in, the University's ranking stabilized, even if it didn't improve drastically. The assault on Sullivan also sent a signal to future Presidents. When Sullivan's successor James Ryan was asked about rankings, he responded, "I'm competitive enough that if we are going to be ranked, I'd like to be ranked highly."[48] Mr. Ryan had seen what happens to presidents who ignore concerns about rankings. He knew better than to say or act differently.

Truthfully, this type of palace intrigue is relatively rare at elite colleges. But that's because the threat of firing is often enough to incentivize college Presidents to dance to the trustees' tune. Usually, that tune is unbelievably repetitive. There is an intense focus on rankings and resources, but there is little else that trustees aggressively push for. While governance boards are quite powerful, most lack imagination. Very few boards have an innovative or affirmative vision for what elite colleges can be. Very few have radically new directions in mind for what they should do. Instead, many default to the mere mimicry of high rankings and large endowments.

One reason for this lack of vision is that most trustee positions are part-time commitments. These trustees often have high-intensity day jobs that occupy most of their attention and time. Plus, the large number of trustees often diffuses responsibility among them. As a report by McKinsey quantifies, "Many boards skew large, making them unwieldy—among top 20 universities, board size can range from 19 to 72 trustees, with 40 being the average."[49] In the absence of time commitment and true responsibility, the stale rankings obsession reigns.

Beyond the structural organization of boards, the demographics of boards create a certain set of incentives to focus on rankings also. After all, there is a very specific type of person who often ends up on boards of elite colleges. That type of person is often very rich. In fact, centi-millionaires and billionaires are not uncommon on boards. Generally, the board of trustees at elite colleges is usually composed of some mixture of partners at big law firms, partners at private equity funds, partners at real estate funds, prominent hedge funders, former political figures, partners at major consulting firms, and executives at major Fortune 500 companies. You wouldn't know most of the names included on a board of trustees. But, on some boards, there will be a few names that might ring a bell. For example, UChicago's board includes David Rubenstein and Satya Nadella.[50]

Why do boards look like this? This is because one of the main qualifications to be on a board of trustees is to be a major donor to the university. To donate such large sums to these elite colleges, board candidates must be wealthy. Further, the boards at elite private colleges often choose their own replacements. As a result, there is a reproduction that occurs as current trustees support new members who share a background and outlook with them. Composed of members who represent sameness, a certain timidity often manifests itself amidst boards of trustees at elite colleges.

It can be inferred that these trustees are not people deeply upset with the status quo. Further, they are not strangers to exclusive elite institutions. Most of them graduated from the same elite colleges they now oversee. In their lives, they're surrounded by such institutions. In fact, they might not see anything wrong with highly rejective elite institutions. Institutions defined by extreme selectivity, prestige, and exclusion might even feel normal to them.

Although governance boards are in the best position to press for internal change, the members who compose these boards often lack the desire to push change aggressively. Yet, if board members don't have a real vision for how to change these institutions, why do they want to join these governance boards to begin with? If you're a prominent business or political figure, why would you want to be on the board of trustees at a major university? Aren't you busy enough as it is? It's a part-time job, it doesn't pay well, and you often must donate huge sums of money to get the role. The incentives of trustees aren't always obvious. What gives?

The most cynical explanation of trustee motivation is that being on a board at an elite university helps some trustees raise money for their hedge funds, private equity funds, and venture capital funds, allowing these trustees to get rich via management fees. As Charlie Eaton explains, "Even among billionaire alumni of top 30 private colleges, private equity and hedge fund managers are almost twice as likely as billionaires to serve on these boards. This is because elite university boards are especially valuable to financiers as conduits for endowment capital and private information from other elites that they use to raise capital and invest in assets that they think are undervalued by public financial markets."[51]

The fact that hedge fund elites use massive university endowments to get rich is deeply scandalous, yet it is often true. In one anecdote that Charlie Eaton relays, "hedge fund billionaire Tom Steyer learned from a friend at the 1988 Yale homecoming football game that Yale's endowment manager, David Swensen, was considering investing in hedge funds. Steyer reached out and, after some persuasion, raised $300 million, a third of his initial capital, from Yale's endowment."[52] If Tom Steyer charged Yale's endowment the industry standard two percent initial fee and twenty percent of all investment gains, one can easily imagine just how massively lucrative such a redirection of Yale's endowment would have been for Tom Steyer.

But it's not just Tom Steyer. Charlie Eaton suggests that the ability to harvest endowment wealth in the form of management fees is one reason why private equity and hedge fund representation on elite university boards "increased from 3 percent in 1989 to 9 percent in 2003 and to 18 percent since 2013."[53] In fact, as Charlie Eaton explained in The Washington Post, "Harvard, Brown, Columbia, Cornell, Penn, Princeton and Yale all disclosed in 2013 that they also had investments involving at least one board trustee."[54] Quantifiably, in 2013, The New York Times reported that "[Dartmouth] said that 13.5 percent of the assets were in funds led by trustees or members of the college's investment committee."[55] One anonymous letter to the New Hampshire Attorney General's office in 2012 critiqued that "For years, Dartmouth has been run by and has paid sky-high fees to a group of investment manager trustees, all Dartmouth graduates, who have then recycled some portion of the fees...as generous donations." As one might imagine, such conflicts of interest are obviously troubling.

The most troubling implication of this theory of trustee motivation is that trustees who benefit from large university endowments, which can potentially be redirected into their own funds, will naturally support policies that allow university endowments to grow larger. As we explore in future chapters, this corrupt financial interest might be why financially motivated trustees support elite college cartel tactics like seat scarcity, price-fixing, and subsidy cannibalism which extract money from students but fill endowment coffers.

In fairness, a corrupting financial motivation can't explain every trustee's decision to join an elite university's board. After all, many trustees have no direct connection with finance. So, a different explanation of trustee interests is that trustees want to serve on governing boards not for direct financial benefit but for status and prestige for themselves. This type of non-financial benefit can be hard to quantify, but it is nonetheless real. Like titles of royalty, Nobel prizes, or knighthoods, markers of status and prestige can be powerful motivators. This theory certainly rings true in the elite college context. As William Bowen explained in Harvard Business Review, "Fortunately, many busy executives join nonprofit boards because of deep personal commitments to the organizations' values and purposes. But others, I suspect, participate for reasons of status and with the expectation that they will be able to enjoy a kind of vacation from the bottom line."[56] Of course, trustees with this type of motivation have very little incentive to scrutinize the general direction of the elite colleges they oversee. This is because criticism only serves to darken the glow of the institution's prestige, a glow they seek to bask in. Maybe they're all just prestige junkies.

There is certainly evidence for the prestige junkie theory. Remember how the board of visitors tried to fire the President of the University of Virginia in 2012? Well, billionaire mega-donor Paul Tudor Jones explained why he supported that decision in his op-ed. As he explained, "When I was applying to colleges in 1972, I was debating among Harvard, Virginia, and West Point. All three were destination schools, as opposed to safety schools. Each had its own unique set of advantages. I chose to apply early to Virginia because it had the cross-section of attributes that most appealed to me. (It also helped that my father told me I could go to college anywhere in the country as long as it was in Albemarle County!) Today, conversations around UVa seem confined to "top state schools" or "top public universities" rather than best outright, far less than what most of us aspire to when thinking about our beloved institution. We can do better."[57] In other words, it was more important to him that people thought of the University of Virginia as prestigious, a "destination school" than that the University did a really good job at teaching students. Although Paul Tudor Jones wasn't a trustee himself, he was quite close with many who were. His thinking largely aligned with theirs, and prestige likely mattered to all of them.

A less cynical explanation of trustee motivation might be that trustees genuinely care about their alma mater. However, this motivation might also shield monopolistic elite college practices from scrutiny, as trustees might be reluctant to dissent from university policies because of their deep loyalty to the institution they are charged with overseeing. Indeed, nostalgia might cloud their oversight. As William Bowen explained in Harvard Business Review, "Other motivations for joining boards represent a more general set of problems for certain classes of nonprofits. For example, the commendable desire of many college and university graduates to "give something back" can lead them to inject excessive doses of nostalgia into boardroom deliberations—what colleagues at Princeton used to call the furry-tiger syndrome."[58]

For trustees driven by internal motivations of status and loyalty, the primary priority is protecting and improving the brand of the elite institutions they oversee. This primary emphasis on a college's reputation might be why trustees even define a president's role around protecting the institution's brand. Importantly, this emphasis on brand transposes into an emphasis on maintaining rank. As a survey of southern college Presidents conducted by John Head quantifies, <u>80 percent</u> of Tier 1 college Presidents responded that an institution's ranking was "<u>important to trustees</u>."[59]

If any trustees choose to chart a course that diverges from what the rankings incentivize, then they invite scrutiny from alumni, faculty, and students onto their own oversight and their commitment to the institution they oversee. Instead of furthering their own prestige and status, these trustees would then become liable for enhanced scrutiny and criticism, which is the opposite of what they would want.

A different and more generous explanation of trustee motivation is that trustees might be genuine in their commitment to philanthropy. Yet, these same trustees might see their role not expansively, as committed not to the welfare of society at large, but rather quite narrowly, as committed to the welfare only of the institution they oversee. From this narrow point of view, their elite institutions are doing better than ever before. Each year more and more students apply. Each year more and more money come in. Why radically change anything?

Even if trustees are well-intentioned saints completely free of bias, the non-profit structure of all elite colleges might itself lead to flawed decision-making. This is because, in the absence of a profit or loss bottom line, non-profit organizations are sent into a bit of a mission drift. Ultimately, their key goals and how to measure them are imposed by cultural norms. As Richard Vedder explains, "Profits are the bottom line of competitive market business enterprises, and they are signaling devices that inform and direct decisions. The lack of a bottom line in higher education means it is hard to tell if schools are meeting goals and what the goals are. Did Stanford have a good year in 2006? Who knows? Firms like U.S. News & World Report try to create a non-market bottom line, often based on dubious measures (e.g., inputs used instead of outputs). Instead of cutting costs to increase profits, colleges often enhance costs to buy things (good students, more faculty) that improve magazine rankings, not knowing if it truly improves teaching and research. Unlike in the private sector, buildings lie empty months of the year because there are no real incentives to use them more efficiently."[60]

Whether trustees are selfishly motivated or structurally handicapped, the result is the same. What's important to trustees becomes important to the presidents whom they appoint. Endowment maximization and prestige maximization become all important. Climbing the US News rankings, which helps to accomplish both goals, slowly morphs into the overarching mission of the institution, and university presidents who don't value rankings get replaced by presidents who do.

We already discussed the attempted coup at the University of Virginia. However, this pattern also holds true at non-elite colleges. One such example is from Syracuse University, a relatively non-prestigious college. In 2004, Syracuse University's governance board selected Nancy Cantor to be its new chancellor. During her reign, Nancy Cantor did something truly radical. She decided to define Syracuse University's mission expansively. Instead of focusing on increasing rejectivity as some other similarly ranked universities had done, she decided to accept more students. She accepted more low-income students and more minority students. She accepted students with lower SAT scores that other similarly ranked schools routinely rejected. Shockingly, she felt that giving disadvantaged students a chance at Syracuse was a worthwhile mission.

As a result, Syracuse began to slide down the rankings. During her tenure, Syracuse went from fifty-second to sixty-second in the US News ranking.[61] Some couldn't stomach this. There was a widespread clamor from alumni and faculty. They wanted better rankings! Under pressure, Kent Syverud took over as chancellor in 2014. Kent wasn't Nancy. He made that very clear. In fact, Kent explicitly pledged to pay more attention to the rankings. Syracuse has started moving upwards in the US News ranking again. By 2022, the university had clawed its way back to number fifty-nine in the US News ranking.[62]

If the pressure at mid-tier colleges to climb the rankings is so high, imagine if Yale slid ten spots in the rankings. Would the board ever allow such a thing? Imagine the horror. Knowing the board's likely reaction, would any Yale President ever offer reforms that might benefit students but hurt the university's ranking? The answer is probably not. Instead, elite college presidents focus intensely on maintaining and improving rank. How they allocate their budgets, how they set prices, and how they decide admissions policies flow from this important metric. Conforming to the ranking becomes very important.

Fundamentally, these organizational incentives to climb in US News' ranking influence the direction of governance. The way US News' ranking works is that there are a variety of metrics that the website weights in its formula to create a single number through which it can compare one school to another. Responding to these incentives, elite colleges orient their internal policies to maximize the metrics that the ranking cares about. In 2015, Jeongeun Kim found that whenever US News changed its criteria between the years 1987 and 2009, elite colleges changed their spending priorities to conform with the new rankings criteria.[63]

What's more is that the influence of the US News ranking isn't simply limited to expenditure but also extends to admissions. As that same 2015 study found, when the US News ranking changed its criteria to further reward student selectivity, elite colleges became even more selective. Anecdotally, elite college presidents will often try everything before increasing class size. In 2012, when President Sullivan of the University of Virginia was facing pressure from her board of visitors, she needed to find money from somewhere. Yet, even amidst all this pressure, President Sullivan categorically rejected expanding the student body. "The alumni and student body believe there is huge value in the relatively small size," Sullivan said.[64]

Of course, what President Sullivan really meant is that alumni and students want the prestige that comes with a high ranking. If President Sullivan expanded enrollment, UVa would lose rank. Alumni donations would fall. New student applications would fall. The board of visitors would be pissed. Therefore, higher enrollment was off the table.

Sometimes slightly more edgy college presidents push back against the US News ranking and its arbitrary criteria. For example, in 1996, Stanford President Gerhard Casper was upset after a lower-than-expected ranking for Stanford. Burning with internal indignation, Casper sent a letter to James Fallows, the then editor of the US News. In his letter, Casper inveighed, "Were U.S. News, under your leadership, to walk away from these misleading rankings, it would be a powerful display of common sense. I fear, however, that these rankings and their byproducts have become too attention-catching for that to happen. Could there not, though, at least be a move toward greater honesty with, and service to, your readers by moving away from the false precision? Could you not do away with rank ordering and overall scores, thus admitting that the method is not nearly that precise and that the difference between #1 and #2 - indeed, between #1 and #10 - may be statistically insignificant?"[65]

But even edgy college presidents like Casper only highlight how powerful US News' ranking is. After all, even as Mr. Casper made his iconoclastic attack on the false precision of US News' ranking, he had in the back of his mind that alumni and donors care about US News' ranking. As Mr. Casper complained to The New York Times in 1996, "While Stanford dropped from No. 4 to No. 6 among national universities, the drop "definitely didn't cost me any sleep,"[66] Mr. Casper said. "But people will ask for a reaction. Alumni read these things."[67] And although he didn't say it, I'm sure Mr. Casper had his board of trustees in mind also. The pressure on elite college presidents to ace the rankings is intense.

While the US News rankings obviously impact admissions policy and spending priorities, it also influences the total amount of money a university is incentivized to spend. After all, the more money you can spend on areas like faculty expenditure, the better you will be ranked.[68] As a result, elite colleges have become obsessed with raising money from donors and through other sources, like higher tuition costs. It is a never-ending race for resources. This might explain part of the reason why Georgetown's John DeGoia pushed so hard to organize a price-fixing conspiracy or why the sticker price of tuition at elite colleges has gone up dramatically over the last decades.

I don't only blame Georgetown's John DeGioia for the broader price-fixing conspiracy. I understand that there is a lot of pressure pushing Mr. DeGioia in the wrong direction. It's not just him either. At most elite colleges, these pressures exist. In fact, when elite colleges look to interview candidates to take over as president, they make increasing resources and ranking obvious criteria. As a report published by Deloitte relates, "The president of a private university told us he recently received a call from a search committee looking to hire a president who would turn the university into a national brand. 'I know the last president was fired,' the president said."[69] That same report quotes the same President as disclosing that, "selectivity and tuition discount rates were suboptimal for what they wanted to do." Elite college presidents are pushed to improve their rank by increasing rejectivity and by increasing expenditures.

To increase expenditures, Presidents also must raise revenue. This desperation for revenue explains why fundraising has become such a big part of presidential jobs. For example, facing the displeasure of her board, UVa's President, Terry Sullivan, spent a lot of her tenure begging donors for more money. As The New York Times reported in 2012, "UVA's fund-raising staff maintained a list of 50 "targets" capable of giving at least $10 million. Sullivan met 45 of them in person."[70] The art of eliciting donations is a delicate dance. Mega-donors often have their own eccentric ideas. In fact, President Terry Sullivan was once approached by a mega-donor with the idea of endowing a new yoga center. Playing with the wording a bit, she later announced a $15 million donation for a "contemplative sciences center."[71] Donations like that help the University of Virginia compete in the US News ranking, but does anyone really believe that a "contemplative sciences center," a yoga studio, makes the education at the University of Virginia much more robust?

It's not just the elite colleges playing catch-up that place such an emphasis on fundraising. The top dogs are even more serious about resources. In 2001, when Larry Summers left his powerful post at the Treasury Department to become Harvard's President, he famously spent weeks preceding his Harvard appointment on airplanes.[72] He was flying all over the country to meet with Harvard's mega-donors. He felt it was important to cultivate their support early. Coincidentally, Harvard raised a staggering $658 million in 2001.[73] Maybe Larry Summers wasn't wrong to focus on donors.

Unfortunately, fundraising and prestige are intimately connected. Alumni want to see that their donations are being used to improve the university. Rankings serve as their barometer for seeing improvement. Just as few would donate to a political campaign with no chance of winning, few want to donate to a university slipping in the rankings. Importantly, this type of Alumni reaction is internalized into administrative decision-making at the universities. As we explored earlier, even as Stanford led a critical reaction to the influence of US News' ranking in the mid-1990s, the reaction of alumni to Stanford falling in that same ranking was on the mind of then Stanford President Gerhard Casper.

There is a feedback loop that has developed at elite colleges. These colleges need resources for better rank, and then they need a better rank for more resources. The circular relationship between rank and resources indicates what the administrative priority at elite colleges really is. Since elite colleges are organized in a non-profit manner, they don't covet resources solely for profit's sake. Instead, they covet resources because of the prestige they can buy with them. Prestige is the ultimate priority at elite colleges.

With trustee motivations around maximizing prestige, endowments, and brand power, administrative motivation to make that a reality, and very little critical reevaluation of the educational mission at elite colleges from internal parties, the result is a deep mission drift at most of our nation's elite colleges. This mission drift stems from a lack of clarity in purpose. As Carnevale, Schmidt, and Strohl describe, in their book, The Merit Myth, "No matter how lofty their stated missions, colleges' desire to climb and their fear of going into a tailspin keep them focused on doing whatever is necessary to take in more money."[74]

In 2021, a Yale administrator named Jamie Petrone put 94 boxes of consumer electronics in the back of her Range Rover and drove it to a FedEx facility in the state of Connecticut.[75] What she didn't know at that time was that she was under federal surveillance. In less than a year, her whole life would change. She was about to be arrested.

At the time of her arrest in 2021, Jamie Petrone suspiciously owned two Mercedes Benz cars, two Cadillacs, one Range Rover, three properties in Connecticut, and one property in Georgia. This was incredibly odd. After all, her formal title was "lead administrator and director of finance and administration for the Department of Emergency Medicine at Yale University." How did a university administrator acquire all this wealth?

As the Justice Department uncovered, Jamie Petrone wasn't any normal administrator. Instead, she was an incredible grifter. For over a decade, Jamie Petrone had been stealing money from Yale without anyone finding out. One of her schemes was to order iPads and Microsoft Surface Pros for "medical studies" and then resell those devices to different companies in exchange for personal payments to her own company named, Maziv Entertainment LLC. When she was driving those 94 boxes to a FedEx facility, this was exactly what she was doing. As the Justice Department quantified, "In total, Petrone caused a loss of approximately $40,504,200 to Yale."[76] She stole $40 million dollars, and no one noticed for years.

This anecdote illustrates a shocking truth. Spending is so out of control at elite universities that small figures like $40 million don't even register. As The Economist once quipped, "Derek Bok, a former president of Harvard, once observed that 'universities share one characteristic with compulsive gamblers and exiled royalty: there is never enough money to satisfy their desires.' This is a bit hard on compulsive gamblers and exiled royals."[77]

Of course, most spending isn't just outright fraud. Instead, most spending is rankings oriented. Whatever the US News wants to see more of, elite colleges spend more on. While elite colleges are classified as "non-profit," they produce huge profits. The only distinction is their profits are accounted for and described as costs. As Arthur Austin explains, "tax laws allow private colleges to designate themselves not-for-profit enterprises, which in turn allows them to include in their costs some amounts that are really profits."[78] In any other market, we would recognize this.

One interpretation of the massive endowments at elite colleges is to see them as an accumulation of profits over time. Maybe that explains why elite colleges are so obsessed with growing them. As Leon Botstein, the president of Bard College, once observed, "We've reduced our definition of worth into fame and wealth, and it carries over into the way institutions think about themselves. An overwhelmingly huge part of what Harvard is about is managing its money."[79]

Harvard is not the only college with a multi-billion-dollar endowment. As The Washington Post reported in 2015, "More than 800 colleges and universities across North America hold endowment assets of $516 billion. But the top 10 schools in terms of assets have about $180 billion of that total, more than one-third of all the holdings. Harvard University alone has a $35 billion endowment."[80] Beyond Harvard, there are at least fourteen colleges with endowments over $10 billion. There are many dozens more with endowments over $1 billion. If the goal is charity, why do these non-profits have such sizable treasure chests?

The real answer for why elite colleges have such big endowments is simply because they can. Elite colleges have no interest in reducing tuition beyond a certain point. The greater their revenues, the greater their prestige and power. Why would any elite college unilaterally deleverage itself? Elite colleges squeeze as much money as they can because they have the power to do it. Endowments are just the most obvious proof of what the genuine priority at elite colleges really is: purse, prestige, and power.

Some combination of trustees, faculty, students, alumni, and college presidents will push back on the characterization of elite colleges as motivated by resources and prestige. Instead, they might mention their commitment to diversity, research, innovation, and learning. They might posit that more resources merely support those primary priorities. But if elite colleges are interested in diversity and inclusion, why are they so non-diverse and non-inclusive? As we examine in the following chapters, the rhetoric of elite colleges on diversity doesn't match their record. This discrepancy between phrase and fact can only be explained by an obsession with prestige and resources, not diversity and inclusion.

This organizational lust for prestige and resources is what drives the anticompetitive behavior we examine in later chapters.

Prestige lust is what explains seat scarcity. It's what explains the cozy relationship between elite colleges and US News. It's what explains the price-fixing and early decision contracts. In fact, prestige lust even explains subsidy cannibalism. These are all areas we explore in later chapters.

CHAPTER 4

THE DIVERSITY PARADOX

In the early-2000s, federal authorities were about to score a big win. With each day that passed, the DOJ was getting closer to a conviction against dodgy New Jersey real estate tycoon Charles Kushner. When the Justice Department managed to flip Charles Kushner's sister to testify against him, the odds of the case shifted drastically in the government's favor. Charles Kushner panicked.

For years, Charles Kushner had cooked his tax returns by failing to report a variety of things he should have. By 2004, the government had caught on. Now, the DOJ was building a tax-evasion case against him. With his own sister against him, Charles Kushner was on the ropes, but Mr. Kushner wasn't ready to go to jail without a fight.

In his desperation, Charles Kushner decided to hatch a truly unbelievable scheme to nullify his sister and prevent his own conviction. When asked about Mr. Kushner's scheme years later, Chris Christie responded, "I mean, it's one of the most loathsome, disgusting crimes that I prosecuted when I was U.S. attorney. And I was U.S. attorney in New Jersey."[81]

Basically, Charles Kushner needed leverage against his sister. So, Charles decided to hire a sex-worker to seduce his sister's husband. Preemptively, Charles set up a hidden camera in a hotel room to catch the whole affair on tape. He then sent his sister the tape of her husband having sex with the sex-worker. Charles Kushner thought he could intimidate his sister into not testifying by holding the sex tape over her head. He was trying to blackmail her.

Unfortunately, Charles' plan backfired. Not only was Charles Kushner prosecuted for tax evasion, but also, he was punished for witness tampering. In 2005, Charles Kushner was sentenced to two years in prison. Charles Kushner's sex-tape blackmail isn't relevant to this book, but some actions he took in the late 1990s are. I decided to include this anecdote about Charles Kushner because it helps us frame an important question. If Charles Kushner was confident enough to subvert the justice system with such lurid acts of corruption, what other systems had he previously subverted without any consequence?

A few years before his conviction, Charles Kushner schemed the college admissions system just as he attempted to scheme the justice system. But Charles' college admissions scheme was nowhere as creative as his sex-tape blackmail. Instead, he just cut some checks. In our country, rigging admissions at elite colleges isn't illegal, it's easy.

In the late 1990s, Jared Kushner, Charles' son, attended The Frisch School. At this private Jewish high school in New Jersey, Jared Kushner was enmeshed in an academically competitive environment. Yet, Jared never really distinguished himself while in school. Instead, Jared Kushner was mired in mediocrity. Jared's high school grades were unimpressive.[82] His SAT score was unimpressive. Nor did he have impressive extracurricular qualifications. So, when Jared Kushner matriculated at Harvard in 1999, his former classmates, teachers, and counselors were all surprised. In fact, one administrator at his high school openly objected, "There was no way anybody in the administrative office of the school thought he would on the merits get into Harvard."[83]

Jared's unimpressive record inspires questions. If Jared Kushner was so undistinguished, then how did he get into Harvard? After all, even in the 1990s, Harvard was difficult to get into. In Jared's application cycle, only one in nine applicants was accepted. Investigative reporter Daniel Golden's theory is that Jared's father used donations to swing Harvard's door open. Knowing Charles' other exploits, this tale isn't so hard to believe.

By the late 1990s, Charles Kushner, Jared's father, was a well-known New Jersey real estate tycoon. He owned tens of thousands of apartments, many plots of undeveloped land, and plenty of offices and retail space. Perhaps this financial success is what landed Charles on Harvard's list of top donation targets. In fact, Charles was often courted and dined by Harvard administrators and faculty. Essentially, Charles got the red-carpet treatment, and Harvard finally got his donation. As investigative journalist Daniel Golden reported in ProPublica, "I learned that in 1998, when Jared was attending The Frisch School and starting to look at colleges, his father had pledged $2.5 million to Harvard, to be paid in annual installments of $250,000. Charles Kushner also visited Neil Rudenstine, then Harvard president, and discussed funding a scholarship program for low- and middle-income students."

Of course, it's impossible to say that Charles' large donations are the only reason that Jared Kushner got in. Maybe Jared had an amazing essay. But administrators at his former high school don't seem to think it was his essay that did the trick. As one administrator complained, "His GPA did not warrant it. His SAT scores did not warrant it. We thought for sure there was no way this was going to happen. Then, lo and behold, Jared was accepted. It was a little bit disappointing because there were, at the time, other kids we thought should really get in on the merits, and they did not."

The curious case of Jared Kushner is a very extreme example of a very general truth. Donors' kids get a leg up in college admissions. Importantly, the market rate for this type of bribery has been trending upwards over the last few decades. While Charles Kushner got away with a $2.5 million donation, today, the going rate to secure admission for your academically mediocre scion is often upwards of $10 million.[84]

This type of bribery in admissions is obviously unfair, but the administrators at elite colleges disagree. For administrators, bribery is reframed as "development." After all, million-dollar donations can erect new buildings, create new programs, and generally increase the prestige and power of elite universities. As a result, the mediocre children of such super-powerful people are called "development cases."

Elite colleges play very close attention to possible donations in the admissions process. For example, the following is an email between Harvard administrators discussing how to adjust a student's chance of admission based on his or her donor relatives:

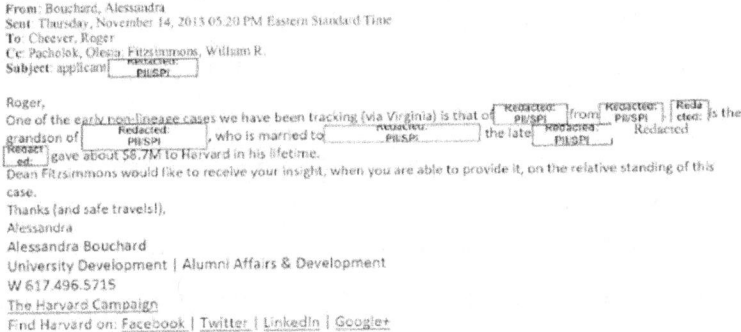

From: Bouchard, Alessandra
Sent: Thursday, November 14, 2013 05:20 PM Eastern Standard Time
To: Cheever, Roger
Cc: Pacholok, Olesia; Fitzsimmons, William R.
Subject: applicant [Redacted: PII/SPI]

Roger,
One of the early non-lineage cases we have been tracking (via Virginia) is that of [Redacted: PII/SPI] from [Redacted: PII/SPI] [Redacted] is the grandson of [Redacted: PII/SPI], who is married to [Redacted: PII/SPI] the late [Redacted: PII/SPI] Redacted [Redact ed] gave about $8.7M to Harvard in his lifetime.
Dean Fitzsimmons would like to receive your insight, when you are able to provide it, on the relative standing of this case.
Thanks (and safe travels!),
Alessandra

Alessandra Bouchard
University Development | Alumni Affairs & Development
W 617.496.5715
The Harvard Campaign
Find Harvard on: Facebook | Twitter | LinkedIn | Google+

*Email Record from Students for Fair Admissions, Inc.
v. President and Fellows of Harvard College*[85]

Development cases with a high expected donation value are routinely given a massive boost in admissions. As the Washington Post reported in 2019, "Children whose parents have given big money in the past or are likely to pony up upon admission are ushered to the lead of the line. At nearly all top universities, the fund-raising office furnishes admissions with a list of these 'development cases,' who are often accepted even if they rank near the bottom of their high school classes or have SAT scores 300-400 points below some rejected applicants. University presidents generally have a right-hand man, from Joel Fleishman at Duke to the late David Zucconi at Brown, whose role, whatever his title, is to gratify key donors and alumni, including facilitating the admission of their children."[86]

Of course, while bribery carries a tone of legal implication, there is nothing directly illegal about this donation-for-seats scheme. Instead, donations to elite colleges are tax-write-offs for wealthy people. As a result, hyper-wealthy but academically unqualified students take up seats at the expense of socioeconomically disadvantaged students. At Dartmouth, up to 50 applicants a year are considered through this "development" status, and most of them are admitted.[87] In extremely stark contrast, Dartmouth's overall acceptance rate in 2022 was 6.2 percent.[88] As one lawsuit alleges, nearly 5 percent of Dartmouth's class consists of "development" cases.[89] Put plainly, nearly one in twenty students at Dartmouth got there through bribery.

Of course, this truth of systemic advantage for the ruling class is hard to square with the narrative we hear from elite colleges. Generally, elite colleges claim that diversity on campus is a big priority. As Princeton claims on its website, "Princeton aspires to be a truly diverse community in which individuals of every gender, race, ethnicity, religion, sexual orientation and socioeconomic status can flourish equally."[90] I'm not sure how Princeton can make that claim with any credibility. Empirically, as The New York Times reported in 2017, "At 38 colleges in America, including five in the Ivy League – Dartmouth, Princeton, Yale, Penn, and Brown – more students came from the top 1 percent of the income scale than from the entire bottom 60 percent."[91]

Beyond Princeton, at elite colleges generally, the diversity numbers are terrible. As the Washington Post reported in 2015, "Low-income students who qualify for Pell Grants, most of whom come from families making less than $60,000 annually, make up 15 percent or less of the student body at Stanford, Princeton, and Yale."[92] Almost all the elite colleges claim to be need-blind in their admissions policies. They're not.

This general discrepancy raises a simple question. If diversity is so important to elite colleges, and they certainly claim it is, then why are elite colleges so bad at producing diversity on campus? Welcome to the diversity paradox. This chapter is relevant to the broader narrative of the book because by solving the diversity paradox, we further conclude that what elite colleges really care about most is prestige and access to resources. This exploration of motivation helps explain otherwise baffling anticompetitive behavior throughout the rest of the book.

In this chapter, I don't address the artificial scarcity of seats, even if the artificial scarcity of seats is one of the primary structural reasons for the lack of diversity at elite colleges. Instead, in this chapter, I take the scarcity of seats as a given. Even so, why is the proportional distribution of those few seats so skewed? The answer is that socioeconomic diversity is a subordinate goal, if it is a goal at all.

Beyond boosts for donors' offspring, at elite colleges, many other admissions policies also provide significant structural advantages to wealthier applicants. Some of these policies include legacy admissions, athletic recruiting, early decision, the use of standardized tests, and even the use of college essays. In this chapter, we briefly explore how all these policies are biased to benefit the wealthy. Let's start with legacy admissions.

In 1922, Harvard's president felt a crisis looming on the horizon. President Lowell grasped for a preemptive solution, but it wasn't clear which way to turn. After all, it was a sensitive problem that he was trying to solve. What was the problem? According to President Lowell, the problem was that there were too many Jews at Harvard. By 1922, Jews comprised more than twenty percent of Harvard's enrolled students.

As President Lowell once wrote, "The anti-Semitic feeling among the students is increasing, and it grows in proportion to the increase in the number of Jews. If their number became 40% of the student body, the race feeling would become intense."[93] So, the anti-Semitic Lowell decided to figure out how to stop the Jews from getting in. First, he proposed a quota on Jewish enrollment, but then his board of trustees told him that it didn't support such explicit discrimination. "The Jewish Question" remained unsolved.

One day, President Lowell had a eureka moment. He finally found a more discreet solution. Instead of an explicit quota, Harvard began factoring in geography and legacy status into the admissions process. Considering legacy meant that students whose parents or other relatives had attended Harvard would be favored in the admissions process. Because Jews used to comprise less of the Harvard enrollment, by considering legacy, Lowell was able to lock-in more of the previous demographics. Over time, the Jewish question began to phase out of view.

The history of the development of legacy admissions illustrates a plain point. Legacy admissions have always been morally compromised. While legacy preferences now serve a different purpose, they are still unfair.

Because of legacy admissions policies, children and relatives of alumni get admissions boost at elite colleges. Importantly, the legacy admissions boost can be quite significant. As the Harvard Crimson quantifies, "Between 2014 and 2019, the acceptance rate for legacies, 33 percent, dwarfed Harvard's overall acceptance rate of only 6 percent."[94] Of course, these are not students who need further boosts. As the Harvard Crimson describes, "For starters, the children of Harvard alumni are disproportionately wealthy; nearly a third of legacy freshmen hail from half-a-million dollar households."

The simple logic of the legacy policy directly contradicts the quest for diversity that elite colleges espouse. It is obvious that those with elite degrees likely earn more money. Accordingly, students whose parents did not attend an elite college, or any college, are likely to be poorer. So, why would you penalize first-generation college students in the application process?

The answer that Harvard gives in response is a nakedly financial one. As the Harvard Crimson reported in 2021, "The argument that the University has put forth comes down to money: alumni donate more if they know their children are given extra consideration, irrespective of their abilities. That cash, in turn, allows Harvard to further its educational mission." Empirically, some fifteen percent of the undergraduate class at the most elite colleges are legacy students. Actions speak louder than words. When asked to choose between diversity and resources. Harvard and its peers pick resources.

Another advantage for the wealthy in admissions comes from elite college athletic recruitment. Before she posed as a highly accomplished rower, Olivia Jade Giannuli had never competitively rowed in high school. Nor was she a competitive rower in middle school. She had never even rowed recreationally. But all of that changed when notorious admissions "consultant" William Singer approached actress Lori Laughlin and her husband, fashion designer Mossimo Giannulli, with a scheme to help their daughter, Olivia Jade, get into USC as a recruited rower.

I'm sure it was embarrassing for Olivia. After all, her parents forced her to take photos pretending to be a rower so that they could email those fake photos to William Singer. She had to get dressed up in athleisure for the photo. She had to fake good form. She had to find a rowing machine. I kind of feel for her. In her place, I would have felt so embarrassed.

After all, the real tragedy of the Olivia Jade situation is that it didn't even seem like she wanted to go to USC. On a VLOG she posted on her Youtube channel, Olivia told her fans, "I don't know how much of school I'm gonna attend."[95] Instead, Olivia Jade was more excited about the extracurricular parts of USC. As she said in that same VLOG, "But I do want the experience of like game days, partying...I don't really care about school, as you guys all know."

Nevertheless, Olivia went along with the scheme. Once her rowing photos were taken, her dad emailed them to William Singer:

From: Mossimo Giannulli ▮▮▮▮▮▮▮▮▮▮▮▮
Date: July 28, 2017 at 10:47:22 AM PDT
To: Rick Singer ▮▮▮▮▮▮▮
Cc: Lori Giannulli ▮▮▮▮▮▮▮▮▮▮

Images of Email Records Published by The Sun.[96]

The real puzzle of the Olivia Jade situation was that her parents didn't have to do all this. Instead, all they had to do was not be cheap. Charles Kushner had shown them exactly what they needed to do: just pony up and pay the market rate for a "development" case. A Giannulli donation would have been written off as a tax benefit, and therefore it probably wouldn't have even been that expensive for a family as wealthy as theirs.

Yet, that's not what happened. Instead, Olivia Jade's parents were just cheap. When Olivia Jade's father asked William Singer if he should say anything to USC's athletic director, William Singer replied: "Best to keep [the USC Athletic Director] out of it. When I met with him a year ago about [your daughter], he felt you were good for a million plus."[97] To this idea that Mossimo would pay the "fair" market rate to rig the admissions process, Mossimo responded, "HAH!!"

Of course, like with the other Varsity Blues parents. Mossimo's cheapness came to bite him in the ass. When the FBI flipped William Singer, Mossimo was toast. The following is a taped conversation between admissions "consultant" Wiliam Singer and Olivia Jade Giannulli's father, the fashion designer Mossimo Giannulli:

William Singer: "I'm calling 'cause I just want to make sure you're-- give you a heads-up that-- so my foundation is being audited..."

Mossimo Giannulli: "Okay."

William Singer: "--which, as you know, is normal."

Mossimo Giannulli: "Yeah."

William Singer: "And so they're looking at all the payments. So they-- they asked me about your 2 payments of 200,000."

Mossimo Giannulli: "Uh..."

William Singer: "And, of course, I'm not gonna say anything about your payments going to Donna Heinel at USC to get the girls into USC, through crew. So..."

Mossimo Giannulli: "Sure."

William Singer: "--that's for sure."

Mossimo Giannulli: "Right."

William Singer: "But what's funny-- It's funny. Because Donna called me couple weeks ago and says, "Hey, uh," you know, "going forward, can you use the same format you used for [the GIANNULLIS' older daughter] and [their younger daughter], and the regattas that you put in there, for any girls, going forward, that don't row crew?" So it's funny how-- I thought I was just makin' stuff up."

Mossimo Giannulli: "Uh, right. Uh..."

William Singer: "But-- but they loved it, love..."

Mossimo Giannulli: "Uh, right. Perfect."

William Singer: "So I just want to make sure out stories are the same, because..."

Mossimo Giannulli: "Yeah."

William Singer: "--and th-- and that your $400K was paid to our foundation to help underserved kids."

Mossimo Giannulli: "Uh, perfect."[98]

Once this conversation was on record, the DOJ had an easy time prosecuting the case against Mossimo. A few months after being sent away, Mossimo later complained to a reporter that he wasn't enjoying jail. While the Olivia Jade story is entertaining, I want to zoom out from the story of one person and one family. What insights does Olivia Jade's story give us about athletic recruiting generally? We know that Olivia Jade wasn't a real athlete, but what if she was? Is athletic recruiting fair, to begin with? I think not.

When we think of college sports, we think of basketball or football, but at elite schools, many recruits practice far more niche sports, like rowing, lacrosse, tennis, or squash. As The Atlantic reported in 2018, "When it comes to college athletics, football and basketball command the most public attention, but in the background is a phalanx of lower-profile sports favored by white kids, which often cost a small fortune for a student participating at a top level. Ivy League sports like sailing, golf, water polo, fencing, and lacrosse aren't typically staples of urban high schools with big nonwhite populations; they have entrenched reputations as suburban, country-club sports."[99]

These recruited athletes are empirically from wealthier backgrounds. As The Atlantic reported in 2018, "It's no surprise, then, that per The Harvard Crimson's annual freshman survey, 46.3 percent of recruited athletes in the class of 2022 hail from families with household incomes of $250,000 or higher, compared with one-third of the class as a whole." Importantly, at elite schools, like Harvard, these niche athletes take up a huge number of slots. Empirically, one in five students at Harvard is an athlete.[100]

It is incredibly difficult to understand why elite colleges persist in recruiting athletes for niche sports. It cannot be explained without the lens of prestige. Squash, tennis, sailing, and rowing are all prestigious, expensive sports. Winning in these narrow-domain sports garners prestige for the elite colleges amongst their elite donors, alumni, and trustees. Plus, reserving a quota of seats for specifically wealthy athletes opens a way to further benefit those students whose families are most likely to donate. The motivation for this policy is obviously neither racial nor socioeconomic diversity. It certainly isn't academic quality, either. I personally know someone who plays squash at an elite college, and he is a complete idiot.

But it's not just the development, legacy, or even athletic recruiting policy that favors wealthy kids. Instead, even the way elite colleges measure "merit" can be interpreted to be anti-diversity. Truthfully, standardized tests like the SAT and ACT, long held up as objective measurements of merit, are biased by family wealth.[101]

I did well on the SAT. For the longest time, I thought that meant something about how smart I was. I had peers who did even better than I did. Some of these peers were even obnoxious enough to bring up their scores in random conversations or ask leading questions so that others would ask what their scores were. It was super annoying then, but I understand where they were coming from. Vanity is a hell of a drug. I was vain about my score too.

It's only recently that I've reflected on how I got that score in the first place. I grew up around people who started prepping for the SAT with prep books, courses, and tutors starting very early in their high school careers. That's just what everyone did. Like many of my peers, I immediately started a prep course after my sophomore year had ended. In 2014, over the course of the summer, my parents spent over five thousand dollars on prep courses alone. My parents were supportive enough to drive me back and forth between tutoring sessions. I remember I woke up super late on the weekend once. I was planning on taking the SAT within the month. That day, my dad sat me down and gave me "the hairdryer." He yelled and yelled and yelled. "Why are you so lazy," he asked. "Do you want to fail in life?" he posed. I didn't appreciate it at the time, but I did get to work. I recognize now that if I did well on the SAT, it was by standing on my parents' shoulders. That fact is inescapable.

As the Brookings Institute explains, "Standardized tests that are used for the purposes of college admissions don't predict college success very well. Scores on the widely used SAT and ACT tests only adequately predict grades earned in a student's first year in college. And those scores are worse predictors for black and brown students. For what it's worth, scores from the SAT and ACT tests are good proxies for wealth. The more money a student's parents make, the more likely he or she will have a higher score. It follows, then, that the less money your parents make, the more likely it is that you'll be denied at a selective institution."[102]

A lot of normal people have trouble internalizing the evidence of wealth bias in standardized testing. Many claim that anyone can choose to self-study for these tests, and even if prep books might cost hundreds of dollars, skeptics might posit that the cost barriers are not impossibly high for motivated students. What these skeptics miss is that lower-income or first-generation college students often don't know about the importance of these standardized tests until way later in the application cycle. Middle and upper-class students grow up knowing that to get into elite schools, they need high scores. They have parents who give them the "hairdryer." They start studying for the SAT or ACT in their sophomore or junior years. This is simply not the cultural norm at lower-income high schools. By the time lower-income students start thinking about applying to college and start studying for standardized tests, it is often far later in the application cycle than wealthier students who have already been preparing for years. Further, it is difficult to accept the argument that better teachers and better tutors have no impact on test score performance. Obviously, resources spent on mastering a test matter. I can personally attest that standardized tests can be mastered with the use of resources. In my case, my performance was largely a function of time, tutors, and practice tests.

Colleges have some rationale for the use of standardized testing in admissions. Obviously, it's difficult to compare a student from a high school in rural Virginia to a student from a high school in urban Los Angeles. The grading systems at the two high schools might be quite different. Without some standardized measure, how can college administrators conduct a reasonable comparison of intellectual ability?

Even if this is the rationale that elite colleges propose, it isn't super compelling in the light of the evidence. Obviously, standardized testing doesn't give you much of a comparison of intellectual ability either. It's notoriously bad as a predictor of college performance.

Instead, a better method of comparison might be a non-standardized one. For example, when I was a senior in high school, I applied for admission to Oxford, a prestigious university in the United Kingdom. Oxford had a very different system. To get into Oxford, I had to participate in three different academic interviews. During the interviews, I was quizzed by the Oxford faculty on concepts like monetary policy. Further, I was asked to make arguments about political trends and philosophical paradoxes, and I was also given a game theory problem set and asked to solve it. I didn't get into Oxford. So, you can imagine how I did in the interviews.

It was difficult to prepare for this type of interview because I had no way of knowing what the faculty was going to test me on. Importantly, it allowed them to compare my performance to other students in a qualitative way. I'm not sure if this method of comparison is less biased to reward raw wealth, but it proves that there are other methods of comparison. Importantly, it is likely that no matter how colleges try to evaluate students against each other, wealthier students will likely have some edge just because of their willingness and ability to spend more time and money to prepare. So, while the goal of a completely unbiased system might be impossible, it is important to find less biased systems than the present ones. Non-standardized methods might be better suited to reducing bias than standardized methods because standardization allows wealthier students to learn to game the standard. Non-standardization at least makes it harder to prepare.

There is a further argument for non-standardization. When colleges all adopt the same standards of comparison, colleges come to the same conclusions about which students are the most "gifted." Yet, if you've seen the movie Moneyball, you might concede that standardized metrics, like the SAT and others, might be missing something, just as the conventional wisdom of scouts had been missing talented baseball players in the movie. There might be "gifted" students who are undervalued when evaluated by the prevailing metrics. Of course, in a world where colleges were competing on the genuine quality of their incoming class, it would be in any college's self-interest to drop the convergent standardized metrics and adopt their own Moneyball-like evaluations, finding value and merit where others might miss it. The fact that colleges don't do this brings us to another inference. Colleges aren't really competing on the quality of the incoming class. Instead, they are competing on the <u>perception of the quality</u> of the incoming class. In a world where perception matters more, standardization is king.

Elite colleges know all about the drawbacks of relying on standardized tests. Some even make a show out of being test optional. Yet, most continue to rely heavily on standardized tests to evaluate students. There are all sorts of admissions calculators online which evaluate your chances of getting admitted to a given school based solely on two metrics, GPA and SAT. These calculators are often quite accurate. So, despite knowing all the drawbacks and the empirically anti-diversity outcomes, why do elite colleges persist in favoring high standardized test scores?

Elite colleges do so because their primary priority isn't diverse outcomes; instead, it is prestige. Not only do reports of high test scores create prestige on their own, but also commercial rankings incentivize high test scores. For example, the US News rankings currently place a heavy 5 percent weight on standardized test scores.[103] Further, there is a stealthy way in which standardized test scores are used. Because standardized test scores correlate strongly with wealth, high scores allow colleges to proxy select wealthier students who will be able to pay higher tuition prices. Standardized test scores are perfect for this stealthy wealth discrimination because, to the outside world, elite colleges can claim that they are being technically "need-blind" in their admissions policies. The extra revenue generated by enrolling wealthier students allows elite colleges to increase spending on metrics that the rankings value. Obviously, more resources are heavily weighted in the US News rankings. Importantly, if you want to compete for the top slots in the commercial rankings, you must maximize almost all the metrics US News optimizes for.

The cumulative effect of all these incentives is a heavy reliance on standardized test scores at elite colleges. According to the Department of Education College Scorecard, in 2021, the median ACT score at Harvard was 34, the 25th percentile was 33, and the 75th percentile was 35. With the ACT being out of 36 points total.[104]

I'll be one hundred percent honest. I wrote much of my little sister's college essay. Although I was only meant to help her edit it, I just couldn't help changing it. In the end, it would be difficult to spot a single sentence that she entirely wrote herself.

Importantly, I must have done something right because my sister got into NYU with middling stats. I know I'm not the only older brother to help a sibling with an essay. Nor is my case anywhere near the most egregious.

In fact, relatively few kids submit their own work when it comes to college essays. As a recent study from Stanford qualifies, "Results show that essays have a stronger correlation to reported household income than SAT scores."[105] The reason this is the case is that wealthy applicants can game the essay writing process. As reported in Wired, some well-known essay editing services can charge in the hundreds of dollars per essay.[106] As the Los Angeles Times recently reported, one well-known journalist charges $150 an hour to write college essays.[107] Anecdotally, I've heard of rich families paying in the thousands per essay.

In the college admissions process, essays are meant to differentiate different applicants. Essays are meant to qualify softer skills like writing, communication, and self-reflection. They're supposed to be written by the students who submit them, but they often aren't. If elite colleges were interested in diversity, likewise, they would have reworked the essay component of their applications. Maybe essays would be timed and written under supervision like the SAT is.

Lastly, the increasing use of binding early decision admissions by elite colleges is also anti-diversity. Binding admissions systematically favors wealthy applicants. Early decision programs increase an applicant's likelihood of admission, but they bind that student to attend college if admitted through the early decision program. Intuitively it might be hard to see why an early decision is biased towards the wealthy. One might posit, can't anyone apply early? How does early decision benefit wealthy students only?

While it is true that anyone can apply through early binding programs, to understand why early decision systematically favors wealthy applicants, we must think about what happens after admissions, and not just admissions itself. Remember that students must negotiate financial aid after they are admitted into a college. Accordingly, if a working-class student applies through an early decision program, he is deleveraging his own negotiating position. This is because this student can now no longer threaten to go to another school if the financial aid package he or she receives is insufficient. Fear of deleveraging one's negotiating position leads poorer students to often forgo applying through binding programs. These disadvantaged students end up applying for a regular decision where their chances of admission are lower.

If you press administrators at elite colleges for the truth about early decision policies, they'll admit it. For example, Georgetown's former dean of admissions, Charles Deacon, said the following to The Atlantic: "A cynical view is that early decision is a programmatic way of rationing your financial aid. First, the ED pool is more affluent, so you spend less money enrolling in your class. And then there is absolutely no need to compete on financial packages. I am dealing with a very attractive candidate right now, admitted to our nonbinding program, who is comparing our aid package with [that of a prestigious university that offered her a full grant]. If she had applied their early decision, they wouldn't have had to do that."[108] As a legal scholar, Adam Henry concludes, "The foregone opportunity to negotiate for financial aid that ED entails leads many financial aid candidates to forestall application until the regular round. As a result, ED pools tend to include disproportionate numbers of students able to pay full sticker prices."[109]

Early decision might have started out as a niche admissions policy, but it has morphed into something entirely different. At the University of Pennsylvania, an Ivy League school, nearly half of the enrolled class is filled through binding admissions. As The Daily Pennsylvanian reported in 2021, "This year, 7,795 students applied through the University's Early Decision Program, a 2% decrease from last year's 7,962 applicants. Penn offered admission to 1,218 students, who will comprise about half of the Class of 2026."[110] Similarly, other elite schools use binding admissions to secure a plurality, if not an outright majority. This is an incredibly systemic bias benefiting wealthy applicants. Again, it can only be explained by a lust for resources and prestige.

Reviewing our case, through bribery, legacy admissions policies, college sports recruitment, reliance on standardized testing, professional essays, and heavy use of early decision, the wealthy are systemically favored in elite college admissions. These policies can't be defended by saying that they improve academic quality either. One study of Harvard admissions found that nearly 75 percent of the students who benefitted from a donor, athlete, faculty relationship, or legacy status would have been rejected if they were not given a boost in the admissions process at Harvard.[111]

Elite colleges say they care about diversity, but they care about prestige and resources. This is the real answer to the diversity paradox. Importantly, this lust for prestige and resources explains the motivation behind the tremendously anticompetitive behavior they engage in, which we explore in later chapters.

CHAPTER 5

THE MOAT

In 1852, the California Gold Rush was on. Every day, new and dramatic fortunes were being minted on the wild western frontier. Ambitious young men rushed west in growing numbers. That year, a hungry 28-year-old named Leland Stanford also made his way to California. He didn't want to miss out on the action. In just a few years, Leland Stanford would remake the state of California in his own image. He didn't know it then, but Leland Stanford was destined to become one of the greatest robber barons of all.[112]

Leland first started out in business with a general store where he sold goods to the waves of miners making their way to the West. One day, one of Leland's customers paid for his groceries with some shares of his gold mining company. Leland held onto those shares, and when the mine struck gold, so did he. Leland quickly amassed a fortune of half a million dollars.[113] Sometimes, when it rains, it pours.

Relatively quickly, Leland Stanford turned his attention to politics. In 1856, Leland helped organize the California

Republican Party. For the next few years, he ran for multiple elected offices. However, in these years, Leland never quite made it. He kept losing his elections. But, in 1861, the wave turned decisively.

Essentially, the Civil War split the California Democrats. This created the opportunity for the Republicans, through their candidate Leland, to power their way to the governorship. Leland Stanford found an opportunity and seized it with both hands. Yet, while he was finally finding success politically, he was laying the seeds for what would become one of the largest fortunes in the world. In 1861, a few months before the gubernatorial election, Leland and his business associates, known as "The Big Four," formed the Central Pacific Railroad. They positioned themselves perfectly for Leland's political exploits.

A Republican in office during the Civil War, Mr. Stanford made great fortune through graft and grit. He and his business associates milked the state and federal government for subsidies and loans to build the Central Pacific Railroad. Leland specifically positioned himself to benefit from the federal government's Pacific Railroad Act of 1862 and moved the California legislature to help his railroad company with subsidies and grants. In total, Leland and his business partners raked in some $62 million, in 1860s dollars, from constructing their transcontinental railroad. A famous satirist once dubbed Leland Stanford as "Stealin Landford."

By 1870, when Leland's son was born, Leland Stanford was one of the wealthiest men in the world. And Leland spent like it. In 1876, he had a house fit for a king built in San Francisco's Nob Hill. Around the same time, he bought a big farm in Palo Alto. He increased his land holdings all over the Bay Area. Leland's life was a life of luxury.

Unfortunately, when Leland took his young son on a tour of Europe in the 1880s, his son contracted typhoid and died. His son's death affected Leland greatly, and Leland resolved that henceforth "the children of California shall be our children." So, in 1885, Leland Stanford endowed The Leland Stanford Junior University with his farmlands in Palo Alto.[114] In 1891, Stanford University opened its doors. Thus, a great university was born.

But Leland Stanford wasn't alone. In fact, he was only one of the very many robber barons who started universities. In that same era, in the midwest, John D Rockefeller endowed the University of Chicago. In the south, Cornelius Vanderbilt endowed Vanderbilt University. In the mid-east, Andrew Carnegie and Andrew Mellon both endowed universities. In Texas, William Marsh Rice endowed Rice University. These were the boom years for elite universities. As the nation closed the frontier, new elite colleges populated the whole country with astonishing speed.

The relationship between the robber barons of years past and elite universities directly contrasts with our experiences today. When was the last time you saw a new elite university spring up? Is Bezos any less rich than Stanford, Vanderbilt, or Mellon? Is Musk too poor to start a school? Probably not, and yet, amongst the most elite universities in America, the "youngest" is CalTech. Indeed, CalTech was founded in 1891.

What happened? Why hasn't some new technology or product wiped out elite colleges? Why isn't anyone new entering the elite college market? If being an elite college is so lucrative, and it certainly is, then why aren't there more elite colleges? Why don't existing non-elite colleges try to compete with the elites? Why doesn't Harvard lose sleep over competition from an ambitious Hofstra? If the elite colleges are so inefficient, and they certainly are, why don't entirely new colleges emerge to challenge the elites? When was the last time you heard about an elite college startup? What is the nature of the force field protecting the elite colleges from new competitors? What is this magical moat made of? These are the central questions of this chapter.

When I graduated from college, Georgetown mailed my diploma to my childhood home. One day, the mailman dropped off a cylindrical tube. I hadn't expected my diploma in the mail, so I naturally wondered what that cylindrical tube contained. Maybe it was a map? Who ordered a map? In my curiosity, I popped off the caps on both sides of the tube and took out the furled paper. I ripped through the plastic covering. When I finally unfurled the paper, I saw my diploma. It was completely unexpected. I looked at it for a minute. Then, I felt a bit let down. I thought this was something I could have made at home.

Of course, the value of an elite education isn't in the piece of paper we call the diploma. Instead, the real value is in the signal that the diploma sends. The value is in the head start it gives one in the job market. And, for some, the value is in the afterglow the credential provides throughout a career. We've explored these themes in earlier chapters, but they are once more relevant. The basic conclusion of this chapter is that to compete with elite colleges your institution must have a strong standardized signal, and creating a strong standardized signal is very difficult and expensive. As a result, new competitors never emerge.

My grandfather was born in 1938. He was raised in an era so far removed from our own that India was still a British colony when he was a boy. Yet, in the many decades since his birth, my paternal grandfather's life changed quite dramatically. This transformation started when he first displayed an aptitude for scholarship. He used to study in his rural town late into the night by using candlelight and lanterns because his town was not yet electrified. In an era when attending college was remarkably rare, my paternal grandfather went on to graduate from both college and from graduate school. He later even earned a Ph.D. In his life, he saw both great personal progress and great societal progress.

For that reason, I was very happy when he got a chance to visit me at Georgetown. Having grown up so enamored with scholarship, it was his great dream that I got the opportunity to educate myself in the most intellectually stimulating environments possible. His rural Indian family could never have afforded to send him to an elite American college, but if they could have, he would have gone in a minute. By seeing me at Georgetown, he had the opportunity to live vicariously.

When he met me on Georgetown's campus, I showed him everywhere. I took him to the libraries, to the classrooms, to the lecture halls, and to the dorms. Weirdly, everywhere I took this elderly man in his early 80s, he seemed to already have a feel for what the function of that area was. He recognized the libraries. He recognized the classrooms. He recognized the methodology of lectures, homework, and exams. He recognized everything at Georgetown, a school that was financially and temporally far removed from any institution he had ever attended. At the time, I didn't make anything of his familiarity.

Reflecting on it now, his familiarity is a deeply troubling truth. My grandfather struggles to use an iPad or email. He would be quite surprised to see a car drive itself or a drone deliver his food. Yet, he seemed right at home on a modern college campus. Why was he so familiar with Georgetown? Put another way, why has higher education changed so little in his eighty years, even as so many other things have become so different? Why was I even going to college? Why hasn't an elite college education been replaced by something better or more modern?

To be fair, some people have tried. More than a century after Leland Stanford endowed Stanford University, one Stanford double graduate finally took Stanford head-on with a new product that was decidedly not Stanford. That man was billionaire venture capitalist Peter Thiel. In 2010, mere days after he and a friend first came up with the idea, Peter announced a new philanthropic scheme, something he thought could challenge the dominance of elite colleges.

It all happened very suddenly. On stage for a panel at TechCrunch's Disrupt conference, Peter Thiel attacked the higher education system for inflating a massive debt bubble. He said Harvard was status-obsessed, and he laid into the culture of academia. Then, Peter Thiel truly shocked the crowd. He proposed something very controversial. Thiel said he would pay twenty kids under twenty $100,000 each to drop out of college.[115] He later dubbed this program the Thiel Fellowship.

To many outside observers, the Thiel Fellowship felt like a groundbreaking idea. Instead of funding scholarships like most billionaires, Peter was funding an anti-scholarship. In op-eds and interviews, the status quo establishment attacked the Thiel Fellowship for its misguided vision of encouraging young people not to study. Larry Summers called the Thiel Fellowship "misdirected."[116] These critics completely missed the point and responded with an utter lack of proportion.

In reality, the Thiel Fellowship was only a slight variant of something that had already existed. After all, Silicon Valley venture capitalists had been giving money to elite college dropouts for decades. For example, in 2004, Peter Thiel wrote a half-a-million dollar check to a Harvard dropout with a social networking start-up.[117] That dropout was Mark Zuckerberg. That startup was Facebook. It was one of the most successful investments of all time.

The idea of dropping out of college first achieved cultural vogue when famous dropouts Steve Jobs and Bill Gates scaled the ladder of wealth. The idea was further boosted when Mark Zuckerberg dropped out of Harvard to build Facebook into one of America's most valuable companies. In subsequent years, many investors started actively seeking out Stanford dropouts and Harvard dropouts. Silicon Valley venture capitalists felt that there was something special about these particular elite college dropouts. Investors thought that elite college dropouts were capable enough to get into top schools and contrarian enough to drop out. These dropouts also demonstrated an appetite for risk-taking. Investors liked all those traits and wanted to invest in capable but contrarian risk-takers. Suddenly, dropping out from a very elite school became its own signal for the venture capital class.

So, when the Thiel Fellowship took shape, it was just a way to formalize a signal that venture capitalists were already looking for. The Mark Zuckerbergs of the world, who were already planning to quit Harvard and Stanford, were now financially encouraged to apply to a specific program. Thiel was able to send a bat signal to all the young kids that Silicon Valley wanted to invest in, and he was able to stamp his name onto the most promising of that batch.

In the years since 2011, the signal of the Thiel Fellowship has only gotten stronger. Thiel Fellows have been known to start successful companies and launch important products. One example is Vitalik Buterin, who dropped out of college in 2014 when he was accepted into the Thiel Fellowship.[118] While a Thiel Fellow, Buterin built Ethereum. Today Ethereum is a flagship cryptocurrency, and Buterin is worth more than a billion dollars.

It is unlikely that Buterin was only successful because of the Thiel Fellowship. In fact, he had written the white paper for

Ethereum in 2013, before he ever became a Thiel Fellow. But causation is beside the point. The point is that the Thiel Fellowship has developed a track record of identifying capable and contrarian people. To the outside world, the Thiel Fellowship is a credible signal of ability and nonconformism. So, when the next Vitalik knocks on doors to raise money for his new startup, he will be likely to have an easier time if he is a Thiel Fellow. Since venture capitalists like to invest in Thiel fellows, the signal has power.

Each year, twenty to thirty kids benefit from that signal. But if the Thiel Fellowship is so successful, why doesn't Peter expand it to more than thirty kids a year? Why not three thousand or thirty thousand? More importantly, why aren't other billionaires copying Peter and launching Fellowships like this of their own? Why aren't fellowships stealing more market share from Harvard and Stanford? Plainly, why isn't the Thiel Fellowship scalable?

The Thiel Fellowship itself isn't very scalable because Silicon Valley is quite unlike the rest of the American economy. Whereas venture investors there are looking for nonconformism, employers elsewhere are looking for conformism. They want employees who will take orders without questioning those orders. For example, investment banks want someone who will work fourteen hours a day doing mind-numbing work without complaining. What investment banks certainly don't want is some young Diogenes. Definitionally, there are only so many people that a Thiel Fellowship could accommodate because the market for nonconformist but capable people is fairly limited in scope. I'm sure the Thiel Fellowship could expand beyond thirty kids, but it couldn't scale that much more.

There is also a more structural reason that new non-college programs have trouble competing with elite colleges at scale. The world can handle one Thiel fellowship. Employers and investors know what it is. But if every billionaire launched a new fellowship, then we'd have a problem. There would be too many new unstandardized signals. All new fellowships would lose their signaling value because of noise pollution. We can better understand this phenomenon by studying some WWII history.

Imagine you are an American pilot in WWII. Flying over the Pacific, you are suddenly fired upon by Japanese airplanes. You radio the headquarters to communicate and ask for support. The noise of guns blazing is in the background. You click the radio button and say, "I need support!" You wait a minute. There's no response. You radio again, "I need support!" The guns in the background get louder. Now, the engine is working overtime and creaking also. The background noise is massively loud. Headquarters radios back, "We can't really hear you." You radio again, yelling, "I need support!" Headquarters yells back, in a baffled voice, "Are you headed for port?!"

This thought experiment might seem overly dramatic to us, but it was deadly serious to the many pilots who faced danger in WWII because they had trouble communicating. When flying, the background noise of the engine, the propellers, and the environment created a massive amount of background noise, making communication very hard to understand. The enormity of the background noise made perception incredibly difficult. Plus, the audio resolution was very low. The signals that pilots were trying to send were getting lost in the noise.

During WWII, some of America's brightest minds worked hard at Harvard's psycho-acoustic laboratory to come up with a solution to these types of communication problems. One great scientist, George Miller, designed an experiment that provided a breakthrough in this field. Miller and two of his students ran an experiment where they asked people to decipher what they heard while Miller modulated the amount of background noise. The results were astonishing.

George Miller learned that people could understand the difference between "boy" and "heel" at very high noise levels as long as they were told in advance they would be hearing one of those two words. However, when the number of possible words was enlarged beyond just "boy" and "heel," Miller's subjects lost the ability to hear. Even if you said "boy" or "heel," as long as the subjects expected that the words could be one of a larger list of possibilities, the subjects weren't able to perceive the word over the background noise.[119]

Eventually, through experimentation, psycho-acoustic researchers applied this insight. If pilots or headquarters could say whatever they wanted, neither party could really understand what was being said. However, if pilots restricted the words they could use, and headquarters focused on matching what they heard with a very limited range of words, then suddenly, the signal could be understood despite the noise. This is why pilots use weird phrases like Whiskey, Tango, Foxtrot, and the rest. By having a standardized vocabulary, the pilot's signal survives despite the noise. Today we have the NATO phonetic alphabet as the standardized radiotelephony spelling alphabet for exactly this reason.

The reason that limiting the possible range of options helps with perception has to do with the field of information theory. When there are only two options, such as "boy" and "heel," you have an either-or situation. You only have to perceive one bit of information. But as the number of options expands, you must perceive more and more bits of information to correctly determine what you heard. The calculations become more and more intense. Once the calculations reach a certain amount of complexity, they become virtually impossible. There are too many variables and not enough data to plug into them.

All of this might seem very theoretical and far removed from our discussion, but it is actually directly related. After all, what is educational signaling if not communication? In many ways, the US News ranking is the NATO phonetic alphabet of the higher education sector. The US News ranking creates a semi-standardized prestige hierarchy. The ranking helps tell us which signals are "better" than others. It standardizes the range of signals that we are looking for. If pilots moved away from the NATO phonetic alphabet, we would have our communication problem reemerge. Similarly, if a new range of non-standardized signals were unleashed into the labor market, the noises would drown out the signals. No one would know who was capable anymore. It would be too difficult to compare!

When someone like Peter Thiel launches the Thiel fellowship, it's like adding just one more letter to the NATO phonetic alphabet. It is well-defined. Easy to understand. It doesn't increase the overall level of noise too much. But if a lot of other entrants introduce non-standardized signals into the market, it becomes virtually impossible to tell water from oil. Eventually, some type of ranking, prestige, hierarchy, or other standardization tool must restore order. But such tools haven't emerged. No current ranking ranks a non-college product alongside colleges. Moreover, definitionally, it doesn't make much sense to do so. This is one reason why non-college alternatives haven't caught on in the elite college market.

Because the knowledge economy labor market is already locked into an elite college signaling standard, any new signal is just increasing the level of noise. Now, if you could get the entire labor market to switch its phonetic alphabet, you could theoretically displace the elite colleges with a new product. The issue is that getting the entire labor market to switch is hard. Standards have natural network effects. This helps to lock in the older order.

We can understand the barrier that these network effects create with a thought experiment. Imagine you invented a language that was way better than English. Imagine that this language was far more precise, easier to learn, more descriptive, and more acoustically pleasing. Who would want to learn your language? Unfortunately, probably no one. It wouldn't be very useful for the first few people to learn this new language because they wouldn't have many people to communicate with. On the other hand, so many people globally already know English. So even if English is less precise, harder to learn, less descriptive, and less acoustically pleasing because it already has so many users, it is far more valuable to learn. Over time, most likely, English would persist, and your new language would die. The standard stays the standard.

Imagine now that instead of a new language, you invented a new teaching technique. Imagine that it is better than anything the elite colleges are doing. Imagine that you started a startup to commercialize that type of teaching. Customers pay you for access to your teaching technique, and your startup offers a certificate in return. Now you go looking for customers. Will the very best students sign up? Unfortunately, I don't think so. The standardization barrier is too strong.

Especially in the knowledge economy, to get someone to recognize your new "certificate" as equal to the pedigree of a Harvard degree is almost impossible. Employers won't recognize your "certificate." Instead, employers will default to assuming that the quality of students who chose your "certificate" program is quite poor. Employers will likely interpret your new "certificate" as noise. After all, employers have a phonetic alphabet already. Until you get employers to recognize it as such, quality students won't apply. But, since you won't get quality students to apply, employers won't recognize your signal. It's a chicken-and-egg dynamic, and this is the prestige standardization barrier at work.

Essentially, the standardization barrier is why many recent education startups, like Coursera, have mostly focused on the vocational demographic. For example, you can get a Coursera certificate to demonstrate knowledge of Google Cloud. While Coursera offers certificates, these are meant to signify some narrow set of skills. Generally, startups like Coursera want their product anchored more in skills than signaling.

As if the deck wasn't stacked enough against them, non-college products also have another challenge. If they want to compete with colleges, they have to fight upstream against a flush of government subsidies. As one estimate from 2016 quantifies, the federal government subsidizes higher education by some $91 billion per year.[120] In aggregate, the fifty states also spend a roughly equivalent amount on higher education.[121] This subsidy barrier is a massive impediment.

Imagine you invented a teaching method that was twice as good for half the cost. Imagine your price on the market was $10,000, whereas the colleges you were competing against cost $20,000. You should win, but will you? Probably not. After all, a kid can get a subsidized student loan to pay for the $20,000 college bill, but it is unlikely that child will get a loan to pay for your program. Furthermore, the child might get a Pell grant to help bring down the cost of college. He certainly won't get any government grant to pay for your program. Because of the subsidy barrier, non-college products fail all the time.

The standardization & subsidy barriers might keep out non-college alternatives, but what about existing college alternatives? Why can't existing less-elite colleges compete with elite colleges for their students? What is stopping UVa from displacing Harvard as the top choice of students? Why can't Virginia Tech catch up with UVa? After all, these colleges don't have a standardization issue. Nor do they have a subsidy issue. These colleges also qualify for student loans and Pell grants. So, what gives? Maybe an anecdote about notorious billionaire venture capitalist John Doerr can help us understand.

In 1974, a young man named John Doerr joined Intel. It was an exciting time to be in the computing business. Because of Moore's Law, things were changing very quickly. By 1974, Xerox Parc had invented the GUI, the mouse, the ethernet, and the personal computer.[122] John Doerr was excited about the future of computing. His excitement showed. John Doerr quickly became a top salesman at Intel.

In 1980, an exciting new opportunity arose for John Doerr. The venture capital firm Kleiner Perkins offered him a job. In those days, venture capital was still an emerging area of investing. In fact, the business establishment was downright skeptical of any business case for venture capital. In fact, when John Doerr mentioned his new job offer to his boss Andrew Grove, Mr. Grove responded, "John, venture capital, that's not a real job. It's like being a real estate agent."[123]

Nevertheless, John Doerr made the leap. In the subsequent years, John Doerr made investments in Netscape, Google, Amazon, Sun Microsystems, and many other massive winners.[124] He was one of the reasons Kleiner Perkins became one of the most famous names in all of venture capital. Personally, John Doerr's net worth also rocketed during this period. Today, he is worth billions of dollars.

In recent years, John Doerr has shifted some of his attention toward philanthropy. In 2010, John signed the Giving Pledge, thereby pledging to give away the majority of his fortune while he lives or in his will.[125] In 2022, John Doerr started to make good on that pledge. In fact, he donated a whopping $1.1 billion to just one organization. Of course, that organization was the ever-needy Stanford University.

Why would John Doerr give so much money to a school that doesn't need it? As we explored in a previous chapter on what motivates trustees, maybe John is interested in the massive amount of prestige he will accumulate with his gift. After all, it is likely that the amount of influence he will now have at Stanford will make him more popular in his billionaire social circle. Or maybe, there is a different calculation at play. Maybe John Doerr wants his money to support the very best scholarship and research, and he feels that Stanford is the very best. Perhaps he truly believes that his money will be put to good use by Stanford.

The incumbency advantage in politics has been well-studied. For context, in the 2020 American general election, 93 percent of incumbents won their reelection bids.[126] One reason the incumbent win rate is so high is that incumbents have a massive fundraising advantage. Incumbents are already well known. Incumbents have a track record of winning. Most importantly, incumbents can often do favors for donors, and they often govern with an eye toward future fundraising. Quantifiably, in 2014, political incumbents had a spending advantage over challengers of 4 to 1.[127] As one study from 2014 concluded, much of those extra funds came from corporate donors in heavily regulated industries.

This fundraising incumbency advantage in politics is quite like the fundraising incumbency advantage for elite colleges. After all, elite colleges are also able to do favors for rich donors. For example, we explored "development cases" in an earlier chapter. Furthermore, donating to an elite college gives the donor a glow of prestige to bask in. The alumni of the most elite colleges are often much wealthier than alumni of other schools. So, when they make donations, they make the rich schools even richer. Even for a more open-minded donor, donating to a less elite college might feel "risky." For all of these reasons, elite college donations are a winner-take-most market. Essentially, the rich schools just keep getting richer.

It's not just private donors that create the divergence in resources. Instead, it's also the federal government. In a big shock, a small number of research universities monopolize virtually all the major government funding for research. As the National Science Foundation admits, "US academic R&D performance was concentrated in a small percentage of higher education institutions."[128] For example, in 2020, Harvard University received $800 million in research funding, with 70 percent coming from the federal government.[129] The other Ivies aren't far behind. Between 2010 and 2015, the eight Ivy League schools got an aggregate of $23.89 billion in federal grants.[130] Non-elite schools don't get anywhere near that amount of money. This creates a massive resource disparity also.

Why does so much federal research money go to the most elite colleges? One answer is that elite colleges have mastered the process of government contracting. They promote faculty that know how to write grants. They network with the major government grant-making agencies. Most importantly, elite colleges play a big role in writing the laws. One report concludes that the Ivy League schools spent $17.8 million on lobbying between 2010 and 2014. While I wouldn't openly call this a fully corrupt process, there is no doubt that when it comes to government contracts, the rich get richer. This advantage doesn't just help with research grants. It also helps with other subsidies and tax exemptions. The same report concludes that between 2010 and 2015, the Ivy League gobbled up a grand total of $41.59 billion in federal support. Other less wealthy, less prestigious colleges can't play the political game quite as well.

In previous chapters, we saw that to attract the best students away from the current incumbents, colleges must climb in the rankings. We also saw that to climb up in the rankings; colleges must gobble more resources. John Doerr's donation helps to frame the fundamental problem for Stanford's competitors. It's not that UVa doesn't want to compete with Stanford for students. As we explored in an earlier chapter, UVa really wants to compete with Stanford for students, but UVa just can't. Plainly, no matter how hard they try, UVa and other less elite colleges just can't close the resources gap with the most elite colleges. Instead, that resource gap keeps getting bigger. The incumbency advantage of private fundraising and government grants is too strong.

This divergence in resources makes it difficult for a non-elite college to attract more "qualified" students to their campuses. Importantly, the benefits of more "qualified" students play out over time. These are students who will have more income to pass back to the college in the form of alumni donations. These advantages begin to snowball. Strong alumni donations lead to strong endowments, which leads to stronger faculty, which leads to a strong student body.

Of course, maybe in a different sector, an investor would come in with a massive infusion of capital into a would-be competitor. Firms in other markets can sell equity to investors and then use that money to compete in a market. But this can't happen in the elite college market. Most current colleges that could reasonably compete with elite colleges are structured either as public or nonprofit schools. A nonprofit corporate structure does not allow for the infusion of massive amounts of private capital because there is no possibility for returns on one's investment.

There is also a structural issue with non-elite colleges becoming more elite. Prestige in our elite college system is inherently zero-sum. If one college is first, all the other colleges are not. As a result, if an existing semi-elite college climbs in the rankings, it means that an existing elite college falls. The net result is unclear. Will the elite college market expand? Or, instead, will the elite college market just gain one competitor to lose another?

My intuition is that the elite college market might expand in the short term, but my fear is that it will correspondingly contract in the longer term, keeping the newly elite college and casting out the formerly elite college. This obviously is a high barrier to entry. In fact, if this intuition is true, the argument can be made that entry is impossible in the longer term. That would be a powerful moat, indeed.

Lastly, why can't a completely new college compete with the existing elite giants? John Doerr gave Stanford $1.1 billion. Why didn't he just start his own school with that money? After all, isn't that what the robber barons of old did? Isn't that what Leland Stanford did?

The reason John Doerr didn't start his own college and the reason that Peter Thiel went with a fellowship instead of a new university is simple. To compete with truly elite colleges, you need somewhere around $10 billion. Without at least that much money, you won't rank highly in your first few years. If you don't rank highly in your first few years, you'll start to attract less "qualified" students. Essentially, your reputation will be mediocre. Once that happens, you'll have all the challenges that a school like UVa has now.

The $10 billion starting number is just a guesstimate, but if you look at the endowments of the top ten ranked colleges in the US News ranking. Only one school's endowment is drastically below $10 billion. That school is Caltech which had a $3 billion endowment in 2020.[131] But of course, Caltech also only enrolled 938 total undergraduate students that year.[132]

As the $10 billion figure might suggest, there are very high capital barriers to entry. Buying and building a campus will cost a lot. So too, will the construction of dorms and other facilities. Meeting payroll for faculty with only one class enrolled for the first year, two classes for the second year, and so on will be difficult. The most difficult of all will be acquiring customers. You will have to pay the very best students massive amounts of money to get them to go to an as-yet unproven university. With no endowment, no alumni base, no students, and no streams of revenue, the cash burn will be incredibly steep, and this is just to get in the game.

All these prohibitive factors combine and create one of the most formidable moats of any industry anywhere. This moat is what allows the colleges within to behave in the nakedly predatory and anticompetitive ways we explore in the following chapters.

CHAPTER 6

ARTIFICIAL SCARCITY

My younger cousin finished applying to college during the 2021-2022 application cycle. So, when I saw him last summer, I naturally asked him about his recent experience. Was there anything that surprised him? Did it all go according to plan? Did he have any stories for me?

My cousin's response exceeded all my expectations. As an anecdote, my cousin told me about a classmate in his grade named Madeline Choi. Madeline's story is a whirlwind tale of unethical conduct. Essentially, Madeline Choi secured admission to a prestigious Ivy League college before a massive scandal tarnished her reputation. As soon as I heard about Madeline's scandal, I thought: this is going into the book.

Madeline's scandal features gaming admission into an elite college, an international media fiasco, and a petition to evict students from an elite college. That petition grossed over six thousand signatures. The story also illustrates a simple truth: when elite seats are artificially scarce, crazy and unethical behavior is encouraged. Often intense parental and societal pressure pushes kids toward unethical conduct. When that conduct is exposed, futures become dimmer. Is that the system we want? Do we really want a system built around scarcity, status, and shame?

The seeds of the Madeline Choi scandal were sown in the Spring of 2021 in Cupertino, California. At the time, Madeline was a junior at Monta Vista High School. Madeline was very well-liked by her peers. After all, she was elected vice president of her high school class. Charming, bright, and charismatic, Madeline seemed to have a bright future ahead of her.

When summer transitioned to fall, the chatter at Monta Vista High School turned to college applications. Every student speculated on where others would end up. Of particular interest was Madeline Choi. Madeline's peers expected Madeline to get into a prestigious college just like her older sister had. Still, the entire senior class knew that rejection was possible for anyone. After all, competition to get into an elite college is perennially tough at Monta Vista High School. In 2021, the average SAT score at the high school was 1416 out of 1600. In Madeline's class, there were 57 national merit semi-finalists out of 501 students.[133] As the application deadlines panned into view, the tournament began.

It's not just Monta Vista High School where the competition is intense. No matter the geography, a high test score or GPA alone doesn't guarantee admission into the very best colleges anymore. If you want to get into a top elite college today, you really need something special on your resume to stand out. This resume competition has created a pressure cooker for high school students to achieve things few high school students are truly capable or ready to do.

For example, when I was in high school, a girl in my grade started a nonprofit with the explicit mission of ending malaria. None of her peers thought she was going to end malaria. Instead, the general interpretation of her nonprofit was that it was a ploy to pad her resume for college applications. Of course, it's not fair to pick on her nonprofit, especially when I must admit that my friends and I also started a nonprofit in high school. Our stated mission was slightly less ambitious. We stated that we wanted to tutor students in elementary and middle school. Of course, we ended up doing a bit of tutoring, but what really motivated our effort was the resume boost.

As I reflect on it now, high school students starting nonprofits to get into college doesn't make any sense. If you know how to start a successful nonprofit already, especially one that can cure one of the toughest tropical diseases, what do you need a college degree for? Thankfully, by the time Madeline Choi applied to college in the fall of 2021, nonprofits had become cliche. But that same competitive pressure to pad one's resume hadn't gone anywhere. Feeling that pressure intensely, Madeline took a wrong turn. She carried out a scheme to game the elite college admissions system. Her upcoming scheme wouldn't become public knowledge for at least a year.

To set herself apart, in the spring of 2021, Madeline published five academic papers in quick succession.[134] She published on a range of topics, from the impact of Covid-19 on autistic people to detecting fake news through machine learning. When Madeline applied to colleges that fall, she had this incredibly impressive academic track record with which she impressed elite colleges. Accordingly, she won admission into the University of Pennsylvania's incoming class. The problem was her papers were plagiarized from other people's research. Her scheme was to copy other people's research methodology and then fudge their numbers with fake ones. It's not even clear if she wrote her papers at all.

She probably didn't realize it at the time, but Madeline's actions would soon set off a chain of events an ocean away. This is because Madeline Choi is related to a prominent South Korean politician. It all happened at once. In April of 2022, Madeline's uncle, Han Dong-hoon, was nominated to be South Korea's Justice Minister, a post akin to the position of the American Attorney General. As soon as the nomination was made, the media scrutiny of Han Dong-hoon's entire family heated up. Some of that scrutiny made it to his extended family too. The political hunt was on, and Madeline was on the menu.

On May 16, an anonymous group named For Justice in College Applications launched a petition on Change.org.[135] The petition asked for the University of Pennsylvania to launch an investigation into Madeline Choi and her sister Annabelle Choi. Specifically, the petition wanted the university to investigate the studies that Madeline and Annabelle claimed they published when first applying to the University of Pennsylvania. For Justice in College Applications concurrently published a document that contained evidence that Madeline and her sister Annabelle's scientific publications were heavily plagiarized.[136] The group's petition started to pick up steam. If you read the document, it's easy to see why.

For example, in 2021, Madeline published a study on the impact of Covid-19 on individuals with autism. Well, it turns out that her paper shared a 75 percent similarity with another paper published earlier in 2020.[137] Reading through both, it was pretty obvious Madeline plagiarized the study. Even more incredibly, to do a study on human subjects, one needs to get prior approval from the FDA. There is no record of the FDA ever approving Madeline's study. Therefore, if she had actually conducted the study, Madeline would have been in breach of the FDA's rules.

What actually happened is that Madeline never did the study at all. Instead, she just copied the earlier study and changed the numbers slightly. A different study conducted by Madeline had an even higher 78.2 percent similarity with someone else's previously published paper. Overall, Madeline and her sister Annabelle basically plagiarized every study they ever published. It was all smoke and mirrors.

The petition to investigate the Choi girls reads like an opposition research dump. It feels politically motivated. Importantly, the entire scandal has been used in a political way. For example, attempting to sling mud onto political nominee Han Dong-hoon, an opposition politician claimed that Han's daughter was also "attempting to build a resume and win awards through ghost-writing and plagiarism so that she could follow the same path as her cousins."[138] Madeline and Annabelle Choi were useful to opposition politicians who wanted to dent Han Dong-hoon's reputation. They seized the opportunity.

Some might argue that opposition politicians even manufactured the opportunity. Indeed, Madeline Choi and her sister maintain that their plagiarism scandal is nothing more than a political witch hunt. When asked by an American newspaper for comment, Annabelle Choi responded, "Innocent until proven guilty. Cyberbullying is overboard and inhumane given the full political context."[139]

Maybe the opposition dump was politically motivated. It certainly seems that way to me. But why was there all this plagiarism to find in the first place? Was admission to UPenn worth the political exposure the Choi girls risked? Why did these bright, ambitious girls feel so much pressure to act in this unethical way? Why is there so much pressure on so many kids beyond the Choi sisters?

Generally, is a system where seats are so scarce morally justified? I certainly don't think so. There's too much pressure, too early, for too few slots. These scandals are telling us something. It's time we listened.

The scarcity of elite seats is particularly repugnant because it isn't natural. This isn't the free market at work. Instead, some unbelievably cynical arrangements have been allowed to corrupt our system. A web of collusion has been spun. The result is the artificial scarcity of elite seats we see today. As economists Peter Blair and Kent Smetters concluded in a 2021 study, if elite colleges had kept the same admissions standard since 1990, enrollments would have increased by 300 percent.[140] That is what a natural market would produce. More abundance of seats. Instead, we're moving in the opposite direction because of a cynical set of arrangements.

In this chapter, we explore exactly what those cynical arrangements are. In other chapters, we explore how to restore a more natural abundance to elite education. If we broke the elite college cartel, then seats would naturally increase drastically. Understanding how that seat cartel operates and produces scarcity helps us understand how to break it up. Let's start with its origins.

The elite college seat cartel began with a series of decisions made by an enigmatic real estate billionaire in the 1980s. That billionaire's name is Mortimer Zuckerman. There was always something a little different about Mortimer Zuckerman. Born in Montreal in 1937, Mortimer Zuckerman was a child of middle-class Jewish immigrants. His father owned a candy and tobacco store, which produced enough income for Mortimer to pursue higher education if he desired.[141] Mortimer Zuckerman made the most of that opportunity. He was a precocious young boy. Mortimer zoomed through his schooling and started accumulating degrees.

Mortimer entered Canada's top college, McGill University, at the tender age of sixteen. He excelled at McGill, and in 1961 Mortimer graduated with first-class honors and an undergraduate law degree. But Mortimer wasn't done yet. That very same year, he raced through an MBA program at UPenn. In 1962, he even completed an LLM at Harvard Law. For most students, any one of these degrees would have been a massive academic accomplishment. For Mortimer, the real challenge was in seeing just how quickly he could finish all three.

Armed with his library of degrees, Mortimer now had a quiet crisis. He found the law exceptionally boring. He once described practicing the law as the opposite of having sex, quipping, "even when it's good, it's lousy." Not having a clear idea of where to apply his prodigious talent, Mortimer Zuckerman took a gamble. In 1962, at the tender age of 25, Mortimer decided to try his hand at real estate development. He was about to find out whether his academic success would translate into meaningful achievements in the real world.

Mortimer first went to work for a man named Jerry Blakely at a firm called Cabot, Cabot & Forbes. While there, Zuckerman was a runaway success. Just a few months after being hired, Mortimer successfully rang the alarm bell that the firm's development project in Laguna Beach, California, was at risk of bankruptcy. With his foresight, he saved the firm a fortune. It soon became clear that Mortimer had a gift for understanding the nuances of real estate deals.

It was no surprise to anyone when Mortimer Zuckerman set out on his own. In 1970, Mortimer Zucker co-founded Boston Properties with his Cabot, Cabot & Forbes colleague Edward Linde. Their first developments were in Boston. But, they soon expanded. San Francisco, Washington DC, New York, and other urban markets became their bread and butter. Today, the market cap of Boston Properties is nearly $11 billion.[142]

Much of the success of Boston Properties is mainly because of Mortimer. As his partner, Edward Linde, once admitted, "Mort had the ability to work with the lenders and give them a sense of confidence that they weren't taking an unnecessary risk. His intellectual power in that area was obvious to the person across the table." But Mortimer wasn't only gifted at one area of business. Instead, Mortimer expressed an interest in a variety of different industries. As Mortimer scaled the ladder of wealth, he began diversifying his personal equity holdings into these other industries.

One asset class he particularly liked was newspapers. In 1995, Mortimer invested $10 million to acquire a majority stake in Fast Company. In 2000, the company sold for $360 million, and Mortimer made over a quarter of a billion dollars on the deal. But Mortimer Zuckerman's most interesting media acquisition, and the one that is most relevant to this book, is his 1984 acquisition of the US News and World Report.

In 1984, US News was one of three major competitors in the weekly news magazine category. The market leader was Time Magazine. Time had a weekly circulation that numbered in the many millions. In second place was Newsweek. Newsweek was right behind Time in circulation. A much further third was US News and World Report. This was the state of affairs when Mortimer Zuckerman made his bid for US News. Whereas other businessmen balked at the asking price, Mortimer confidently offered $168.5 million for the enterprise.[143] Mortimer felt that with the right leadership, US News could knock Time and Newsweek off their perch. Mortimer wasn't interested in third; he wanted first.

In 1983, the year before Mortimer's purchase, US News had accidentally discovered the incredibly popular subject of college rankings. That year, US News published a list with an amateur methodology and little foresight.[144] But the press and public loved it. The college rankings issue was a bestseller. The market was sending US News a message: give us more.

The 1983 US News' ranking methodology was laughable. Essentially, the US News sent around a survey to college presidents and asked them to respond with their opinion of the best five colleges in a certain category, like National Universities or Regional Liberal Arts Colleges. When Stanford was ranked first, its then President responded by saying, "It's a beauty contest, not a serious analysis of quality."[145]

But the popular audience didn't care about such ivory tower criticism. The rankings issue sold like crazy in 1983 and even more in 1985 and 1987 when US News repeated the exercise. Mortimer Zuckerman smelled blood in the water. Mortimer suddenly had a vision for the college rankings. He saw a franchise, something like the Forbes 400 or People's Sexiest Man Alive.

Mortimer reacted quickly and built a serious college rankings team at US News. In 1987, Mortimer hired a man named Mel Elfin and paired him with an underling named Bob Morse. These two men didn't know it then, but they were about to embark on a project that would exercise undeniable influence on the future of elite higher education in America.

Together, Elfin and Morse developed a new rankings methodology. Instead of merely asking college presidents for their list, the new US News ranking now crunched a variety of input data. Starting in 1987, US News sent out surveys to the various college presidents asking for data about areas like institutional spending, student profiles, teacher profiles, and peer reviews of other schools. Taking in those inputs, The ranking became formulaic, almost algorithmic. It gave certain input data weight and used a proprietary formula to calculate a ranking output. Some of that input data is now easily familiar. Selectivity was important. So were yield rates and alumni giving. The criteria of the rankings have been tweaked in the years since 1987, but the broader logic has largely stayed the same. As Nicolas Thompson of Washington Monthly once opined, the US News' ranking favors any school that "is rich, hard to get into, harder to flunk out of, and has an impressive name."

The popularity of this new formulaic annual rankings exploded. By the year 2000, the college rankings edition of US News sold forty percent more than its other issues. Over the years, the ranking became even more popular. In 1999, eight million people visited the US News' website after it launched the annual college ranking. By 2013, when US News published its ranking online, US News earned 18.9 million page views within just one day.[146]

Along the way, Mortimer achieved what he had set out to do. In 1991, US News surpassed Newsweek in total ad pages.[147] In 1992, US News overtook Time in total ad pages. Mortimer knocked both the market leaders off their perch. He won. But, just as the US News took the lead, the entire legacy media market turned.

In the 2000s, when the internet became the dominant place for advertising, newspapers started going out of business. Even US News was losing money in 2006, 2007, and 2008.[148] From a peak print circulation of 2.5 million, US News was down to 1 million by 2008. In the 2000s, many newspapers went bust, facing the same market headwinds. Yet somehow US News survived. Essentially, US News had a secret weapon. To survive, US News decided to go all in on its college ranking.

In the internet age, US News made the college rankings one of the main profit centers of its business. US News realized early that kids applying to college were searching for information on Google. So they began to dominate Google searches on the subject of college. This wasn't so difficult for US News. They had already seen through their print sales that there was a desperate demand for "rigorous" college rankings. As US News transitioned to the web, students gravitated to the site. In 2006, the US News had 1.6 million web visitors in the month of December. By 2013, US News was grossing 20 million visitors a month. The college rankings made for incredibly sticky readers. By the 2010s, the US News was one of the few media companies turning a consistent profit. In fact, in 2013, US News made close to $10 million on nearly $40 million in revenue. That's an incredibly unique margin; but, of course, US News had a very unique product.

During the market disruptions, other news sites eyed the US News' profitable enterprise with a great jealousy. In the intervening years, many other news sites attempted to enter the college rankings market. Niche launched a ranking. Forbes launched a ranking. But none of these efforts even got close to the US News' scale. Instead, the US News totally captured the vast majority of market share in the college rankings market. In other markets, competition usually breeds a bigger split of market share. So, why didn't market competition result in market diffusion? Why does US News still dominate today?

The answer lies in a particularly weird arrangement. US News produces the only ranking which receives access to unique data from college administrators through responses to surveys. Colleges further promote US News by putting out press releases when they do well in the ranking. Most importantly, boards of trustees take US News seriously. All these small signals of insider knowledge and legitimacy add up to a massive advantage for US News. Students feel that US News knows something that other news companies don't. They feel that US News has insider access and knowledge. They feel that employers trust US News. That strong credibility is why US News dominates the college rankings market, even though other alternatives exist. US News is the undisputed winner in a winner-takes-all market.

This explanation of the US News' dominance might seem far-fetched, but it happens to be the interpretation that the company itself believes. The architect of US News' college ranking, Bob Morse, admitted as much to Time in 2009: "I think our rankings make the most sense to the public because our rankings are the most transparent. Our rankings have the methodology that makes the most sense. When the public sees that the schools want to do better in our rankings, they say, well, if the schools want to improve in these rankings, they must be worth looking at. So, in essence, the colleges themselves have been a key factor in giving us credibility."[149]

If you really think about that Bob Morse quote, you become confused. After all, the US News, although profitable, is a company worth a few hundred million dollars. On the other hand, many elite colleges have endowments worth tens of billions of dollars each. If so, why do these unbelievably wealthy organizations lend US News the credibility it needs to dictate to their trustees and administrators? Why do elite colleges crown the US News as their master? In terms of market capitalization, it's akin to the tail wagging the dog.

The relationship is even weirder because, in public, elite colleges moan about US News' ranking criteria. In a previous chapter, we explored how Stanford's then-President, Gerhard Casper, went so far as to send US News a letter asking them to stop publishing the college ranking. Yet, in private, those same elite colleges give US News the very credibility it needs to dictate to them. Most importantly, elite schools do everything in their power to climb the US News' ranking. Sometimes, these all-powerful schools even lie to succeed in the US News ranking.

In 1754, when New York was still a colony, a royal charter from King George II founded King's College. It was the first university in New York and the fifth youngest in the thirteen American colonies. At the time of the American Revolution, King's college counted founding father Alexander Hamilton as one of its alumni. As a new nation emerged out of the Revolutionary War, King's College was renamed Columbia. In the two centuries since, Columbia University has blossomed into one of the best-known educational institutions in the world.

Columbia University obviously has an illustrious and proud history. Today it is one of the richest and most powerful institutions in America, and it routinely turns away some of the smartest and most privileged children from all over the world. In 2021, Columbia University had an endowment worth more than $14 billion. It is this context of Columbia's proud traditions and obscene wealth which makes Columbia's ethical surrender to US News even more shocking.

In 2022, a slightly wonkish Columbia math professor with a middle part and long hair became a modern muckraker. That math professor's name was Michael Thaddeus, and he was a very unlikely candidate to play the role of an ethical broom. After all, in his own research and teaching, Professor Thaddeus' usual focus was on ideas like Riemann surfaces and conformal field theory. Nevertheless, some obscure strands of data caught Professor Thaddeus' eye. When he followed that strand to its origin, he found nothing but moral corruption.

This is why, in 2022, Professor Thaddeus decided to bring sunlight to a dark place. He published a blog post exposing all the ways in which Columbia's US News ranking was juiced. As Professor Thaddeus wrote in his post, "[Columbia's] ascendancy may largely be founded, not on an authentic presentation of the university's strengths, but on a web of illusions."[150] The post raked so much mud it went viral. Columbia University was caught in a media whirlwind.

Once Professor Thaddeus opened the kimono, everyone took a peak. The New York Times then published a long piece explaining the rankings scandal.[151] Other news outlets took Columbia head-on, and they asked them to account for discrepancies in the data Columbia submitted to US News. Of course, Columbia University didn't have a particularly good answer. After all, Professor Thaddeus was telling the truth. The ranking was juiced.

There were a few different techniques Columbia University used to juice its ranking. Historically, one question on US News' survey is about what percentage of a university's faculty have PhDs or terminal degrees in their respective fields. In its response to US News' surveys, Columbia often claimed that 100 percent of its faculty met this requirement. Professor Thaddeus published that he knew of at least 66 professors at Columbia who had neither PhDs nor terminal degrees. Of course, even one such example was enough to disprove the 100 percent claim. A contradiction of sixty-six professors was truly jaw-dropping.

As far as doctored data is concerned, the terminal degree overestimate was small potatoes. Instead, Columbia's big blatant lie was about instructional spending per student. This number was properly juiced, and this doctored data served as the foundation of the highly publicized number two ranking that Columbia scored in US News' 2022 ranking. The scheme was somewhat simple. Essentially, Columbia University also runs a hospital. Being overly "clever," Columbia falsely included spending by its hospital on patient care, something entirely unrelated to instruction, in its submission to US News about instructional spending per student. This sleight of hand boosted Columbia's instructional spending metric by a "substantial portion" of Columbia University hospital's $1.2 billion of spending on patient care.

In response to the media scrutiny, Columbia University first denied that anything improper took place. Then, Columbia claimed to be conducting an internal investigation to gather the facts. Recently, Columbia even announced that it wouldn't participate in this year's US News ranking while it "figures out" what is going on with its data. With no response from Columbia, US News decided to boot it from this upcoming year's ranking.

Doctoring data is not only incredibly strange but also difficult to explain. After all, if the elite colleges feel so much unwanted pressure from US News, why do they continue to participate in their own oppression? US News pressured Columbia University into conduct that borders on fraud. Why didn't Columbia University fight back without resorting to fraud?

It's not like Columbia University's hands are tied. After all, in 2013, President Obama explicitly offered Columbia University and other elite colleges a way out of rankings oppression. Specifically, President Obama proposed launching a new federal college rating system oriented around outcomes, not inputs. A government rankings system could credibly displace US News' ranking. If elite colleges wanted to free themselves from the US News, this was their opportunity to do so. Columbia could have really pushed for it. Elite colleges could have sunk US News' rankings business. Instead, Columbia and others rebuffed the offer.

In fact, the story gets even weirder. Instead of mere neutrality, elite colleges actually organized against the Obama administration's effort. They acted to protect US News with their collective lobbying power. In 2015, The New York Times reported, "Critics, including many of the <u>presidents at elite private colleges, lobbied furiously against the idea of a government rating system.</u>"[152] Why did the same college presidents who routinely complain about US News' ranking protect it when they had a chance to replace it? The New York Times laid out the stated rationale in the same article: "Officials at many schools said <u>the government had no business competing</u> with college rating services like those offered by US News and World Report." Their argument is so contradictory it makes my head spin.

Some might say that this contradiction can be explained. Maybe elite colleges thought that the government ranking would be even more oppressive than US News'. But that still misses the larger point. Elite colleges can do other things to end their oppression. If elite colleges had the will to work together, there are so many ways they could destroy the US News and World Report rankings. They could collectively provide bad data to screw them up, or they could all provide no data at all. They could release their own rankings or support an alternative rankings mechanism, such as the one proposed by the Obama administration. If they wanted to, they would.

Apologists might argue that all these solutions suffer from a collective action problem. But there are many things any elite college could do on its own. Let's talk plainly. Elite colleges have so much money. Why doesn't one just use a small fraction of its endowment to buy US News from Mortimer Zuckerman and slowly change the ranking criteria? Isn't Mortimer Zuckerman a businessman, after all? Is there no price he would agree to?

Columbia University has an endowment of more than $14 billion. US News is worth something in the low hundreds of millions. Surely a deal could be done.

If the elite colleges don't want to buy US News themselves, there are other cleverer tactics. After all, these schools are massive investors in some of the world's largest private equity firms. Can't they "suggest" that one of these private equity firms buy out US News? If Columbia University is willing to bend morally to lie to US News, why isn't Columbia University willing to pressure a friendly private equity fund to buy US News?

Adding to the cynicism, while elite colleges complain about US News, lie to US News, and do everything to climb US News' ranking, they seem to have no problem with US News' owner. Indeed, in 2012, Columbia University accepted a $200 million donation from Mortimer Zuckerman to start a research program studying the human mind.[153] In 2004, Harvard accepted a $10 million donation from Mortimer Zuckerman to start a fellowship at its famous Kennedy School of Government.[154] Princeton and New York University went even further. Both universities had Mortimer serve on their respective board of trustees.[155]

I have an answer for why elite colleges act in all these contradictory ways, but first, let's summarize all the contradictions: Elite colleges feel pressure to climb US News' ranking. They publicly claim indifference or even hostility to US News. Yet, these schools make admissions and expenditure decisions based on US News' criteria. Some elite colleges, like Columbia University, will even fudge their numbers to score higher in the US News ranking. As a whole, the elite colleges take no collective actions to free themselves of US News. Furthermore, the elite colleges take no unilateral actions to free themselves of US News. When the government threatened to step in, the elite colleges rallied to fiercely protect US News. But, these elite colleges also want you to believe they are at the mercy of US News' immense power. How do we explain this contradictory and confusing set of facts?

The thesis of this chapter is that the only way to explain this set of facts is that the elite colleges immensely benefit from <u>dominant and independent</u> US News rankings. They benefit because US News' ranking creates a system-wide artificial scarcity of elite college seats. That artificial scarcity, in turn, gives elite colleges the immense market power they need to generate the insane tuition fees, obscene donations, and other unbelievable revenues which make them so powerful. This is why elite colleges work hard to keep US News both dominant and independent. Throughout the rest of this chapter, we explore the precise dynamic of this cynical bargain. Essentially, US News is the hub in one of the world's most powerful hub-and-spoke cartels. It is a cartel whose time has come.

Empirically, the unnaturally high rejection rates of the elite colleges began around the same time as the start of US News' ranking hegemony. Before US News came to dominate the rankings market, elite colleges used to rapidly grow the number of seats at their schools. From 1920 to 1970, Yale and Stanford increased enrollment by over 250 percent. Since the start of US News' hegemony in the 1980s, the rate of growth in seats at those same schools has stagnated dramatically.[156] This is the impact the hub-and-spoke seat cartel has had.

Essentially, US News' ranking criteria creates a system where elite colleges don't have to explicitly collude with each other to limit seats. Instead, it's in no individual college's best interest to expand enrollment and drop in the rankings. Thus, US News' rankings allow each elite college to focus on maximizing its own prestige while still creating incentives for a system-wide shortage.

One reason why no elite college would ever dream of buying US News is that doing so would permanently destroy the subtle arrangement which benefits all of them. The elite college seat cartel is delicate. It depends on an independent hub that can coordinate between the various colleges without any individual college having to acknowledge participation in a cartel.

The entire setup is cynical, but the real genius of the symbiosis between the elite colleges and US News is that US News' rankings give elite colleges the perfect cover. US News rankings make it easy for elite colleges to benefit from artificial scarcity while still retaining their moral halo and avoiding antitrust scrutiny.

In researching this book, I came across media coverage of a rather remarkable story about a rather remarkable student. That student, Craig McFarland, is an incomparably gifted young person. Craig speaks five languages. Craig scored nearly perfectly on his standardized tests. Craig even graduated from high school with a jaw-dropping 4.98 GPA. Craig's high graduation valedictorian speech was positively inspired. Unsurprisingly, Craig was admitted to all eight Ivy League colleges in the spring of 2020.

Somewhat strangely, Craig's admissions results captured the public's imagination. Craig was interviewed by a number of media outlets, and Craig was even covered by The New York Times.[157] But there was something deeply flawed about the media coverage of Craig McFarland. On the surface, the articles were all about the extraordinary Craig McFarland. Beneath the surface, the articles weren't really about Craig McFarland at all. The media cared about Craig only to the extent that he got into all the Ivy League colleges. To the media, Craig's actual qualities were all footnotes to the verdict elite schools had rendered about his worthiness. Honestly, if just one of those Ivy League schools had said no, then the media wouldn't have covered Craig McFarland.

Sadly, it's not the first time the media has completely missed the plot in this way. Annually, journalists reproduce the same story by replacing Craig's name with the most recent Craig. When only a tiny handful of students manage to get into all eight Ivy League colleges, the media celebrates that chosen few.

I'm sick of reading the same yearly headlines. It's such lazy journalism. The media shouldn't be covering Craig's admissions. They should be covering Craig's accomplish-ments. The fact that it's so rare to get into all eight Ivy League colleges isn't a cause for celebration. It's a cause for critique. Craig shouldn't make news for getting into multiple top-ranked schools because those top-ranked schools should already vigorously compete for each gifted student. In a truly competitive system, all our gifted students would have multiple Ivy League schools to choose from. Therefore, the fact that Craig is newsworthy merely because he had multiple options proves how anti-competitive our elite college system has become.

Amusingly, Craig had so many top options that he struggled to decide. First, Craig said that he was going to choose Yale. However, Craig flipped after painfully agonizing over his decision. Finally, Craig matriculated at Harvard. Craig's story is important to the narrative of this book for one reason. That reason is that Craig, unlike so many others, actually got to choose between a lot of top schools. Most other students aren't nearly so lucky.

What is the incentive for Harvard to improve its campus, courses, and costs if it doesn't have to compete for students who can credibly go to another similarly prestigious school? Harvard must work hard to win the lucky few students like Craig. Yet, with each year that passes, students with choices like Craig become rarer. Because so few students get accepted into multiple similarly prestigious colleges, there is less competition in the elite market. As a result, colleges like Harvard feel little pressure to improve beyond improving prestige.

Scandalously, Stanford's acceptance rate recently dipped below 4 percent. Acceptance rates below 5 percent are the norm at top-ranked colleges. How much closer to zero do we need to get? When is the rate low enough? Suppose aliens landed on earth, and we told them that colleges that refuse to teach students are considered better than colleges that teach as many students as possible. What would the aliens conclude about the intelligence of our species? Seriously, why do we revere those colleges that only accept students who are already likely to be successful?

The rejectivity of the elite schools is even more baffling compared to the ever-increasing demand levels for seats at those schools. Applications to the Ivy League grew from 3.1 million applicants in 2009 to nearly 3.6 million in 2016.[158] Yet the number of seats at most of those Ivy League schools barely budged. In 2005, Yale enrolled 1321 incoming undergraduate students. In 2016, Yale enrolled a marginally higher 1367 incoming undergraduate students. Even more shockingly, high rejection rates are increasingly common, even for non-elite colleges. As authors Carnevale, Schmidt, and Strohl quantify, in their book, The Merit Myth, "There are 1.5 million high school seniors with better than an 80 percent chance of graduating from one of the top 193 colleges, but those colleges annually admit only 250,000 freshmen."[159] There is a demonstrable gap between demand and supply.

Reframing high rejection rates from a business perspective, we must ask a simple question. What kind of business doesn't want more customers? Isn't the first objective of any startup to scale and to scale quickly? If I went to Baskin-Robbins and told them they should sell less ice cream, they would laugh in my face. Yet, if I went to Brown and told them they should accept fewer students, this would be plausible advice. Why is Baskin-Robbins so different from Brown?

The reason this advice is much more plausible for Brown is that Brown operates in a different market structure than Baskin-Robbins. If Baskin-Robbins tried to sell less ice cream, hungry consumers would go to a different ice cream shop. Maybe they would walk to Ben & Jerry's down the street. Or maybe they would drive to the Haagen-Dazs a bit further. Ice cream customers have a lot of options. But if Brown reduced enrollment, where would those unfairly rejected students go instead? They can't go to Harvard. It's even harder to get in there. Likewise, they can't go to Stanford; they probably won't get into Stanford. Maybe, a few of them could get into Duke, but it's not a sure bet for everyone. Most likely, many students would have to settle for a less prestigious college education. So what's the difference between Baskin-Robbins' competitors and Brown's? Baskin-Robbins' competitors want more business. Brown's competitors don't.

In a competitive system, not only would Brown's competitors try to enroll all the talented students that Brown unfairly rejected, but also competitors would try to steal away all the students that Brown actually did accept. In such a competitive market, elite colleges would constantly be trying to get larger, and they would all jockey to increase enrollment substantially. If one of their campuses reached capacity, they would be trying to build a new one somewhere else in the world. Acceptance rates would be far higher. Quality of instruction would be far better. Prices would be much lower. This is obviously not what is happening in the elite college market. This fact pattern, on its own, is actually enough to prove that the elite colleges act like a cartel. Only in a cartel market structure do competitors deliberately and jointly refuse to serve more customers.

If you study other markets, most cartels have a nefarious objective. Cartels typically want to create artificial scarcity of the product they sell. Artificial scarcity is desirable for suppliers because when demand for a product far outstrips that product's supply, then the suppliers have all the power. Suppliers can convert that power into higher prices. In desperation, people will pay far above what they would in a competitive market where that same product is plentiful.

It is an undisputed fact that elite colleges admit too few students, as there are far more students who can handle the rigor at elite colleges than are accepted at those colleges. It is an undisputed fact that this is a market failure. It is an undisputed fact that elite colleges have become drastically more rejective since the start of US News' college rankings regime. Until this book, no one has really been able to provide a structural explanation for all these undisputed facts. Why do elite colleges reject virtually everyone? Why do elite colleges act as if they are in a cartel?

There are only two possible explanations for elite colleges' high rejection rates. The first explanation is the accidental cartel theory. The accidental cartel theory holds that elite colleges behave exactly as if they are in a cartel but that elite colleges didn't set out to create a cartel. This explanation holds that an incentive structure has evolved naturally such that each elite college pursuing its individual best interests leads to our anti-social and anti-competitive outcome of limited enrollment and limited competition. Once the cartel naturally emerged, elite colleges have merely kept it going.

The second explanation is the deliberate cartel theory. The deliberate cartel theory holds that the elite colleges behave exactly as if they are in a cartel and that one, a few, or all the main actors have deliberately designed and upheld this cartel.

The difference between these theories can be explained through metaphor. Some people believe that our solar system works because a creator designed the universe to work through natural laws. Other people believe that natural laws emerged from chaos and that randomness produced our solar system. No one disputes the mechanics of the solar system. No one says the Earth doesn't orbit around the Sun or that gravity isn't real. The dispute is merely about whether our solar system works by design or by accident.

I can't confirm which of these two competing theories is true. I can't tell you if output restrictions are deliberately designed or collateral damage, and it's not because I haven't tried to find out the truth. My issue is that to know the truth about how the elite college seats cartel got started, I would need deep access to the email and communication records of the elite colleges. I would need to know what administrators spoke about between themselves and what they spoke about with US News. Elite colleges have absolutely nothing to gain and everything to lose by handing over that information to me. I can't persuade them to do it. Importantly, I can't force them, either. I have nothing to threaten them with. I have nothing to offer them. I have no legal standing to subpoena the records. For this reason, I can't tell you the whole story. Further, the point of this book isn't to have all the answers. It is to get us to start asking the right questions. My hope is that after this book is published, legislative or legal actors will ask for records, and the elite colleges will have to hand them over. Congress should hold hearings on this subject. If it does, we shall have an answer soon enough.

Despite that disclaimer, there is sufficient evidence to prove that there is an output-reducing market structure. The actions of the elite colleges are public. The elite colleges voluntarily publish their admissions rates and enrollment numbers. The elite colleges are forced by law to publish their budgets and their endowments. US News voluntarily publishes some insight into its ranking system. Furthermore, economists have published numerous studies confirming what the actions of elite colleges imply about their incentives and motivations. The clear implication of this evidence is that elite colleges are organized in what resembles a cartel that restricts output. It is the nature of this market structure and the relationships within it that we will describe in the rest of this chapter.

Creatively, the elite colleges have deviated from how cartels normally fix output. For clarity, let's compare the elite colleges to the Organization of the Petroleum Exporting Countries, or OPEC. OPEC is a generic example of an output-restricting cartel. Specifically, OPEC is composed of major oil-producing nations like Saudi Arabia, Venezuela, and the UAE. Through OPEC, these nations collude on their overall output level of oil. Recognizing that all colluding countries will be better off if a stable cartel can create an artificial scarcity of a needed product, these petro-states use OPEC to reach agreements on supply restrictions. Structurally, OPEC is organized horizontally. By horizontal, I mean that the competitors directly collude with each other.

Unlike OPEC, the college cartel doesn't collude on output horizontally. Instead, the college cartel is organized in a hub-and-spoke cartel. In such a cartel structure, the hub is an actor who orders and then enforces output restrictions. The spokes are all the actors who follow the hub's directions. Since I don't like speaking in economic jargon, let's examine these structures through diagrams.

The Hub-and-Spoke Structure of The College Cartel

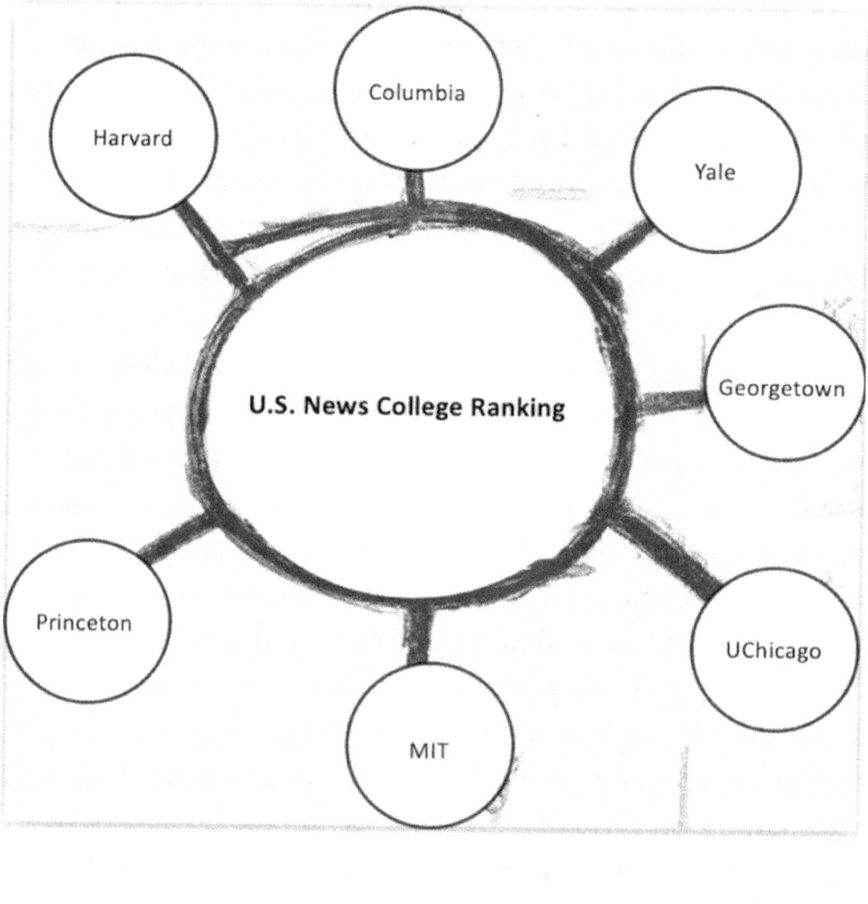

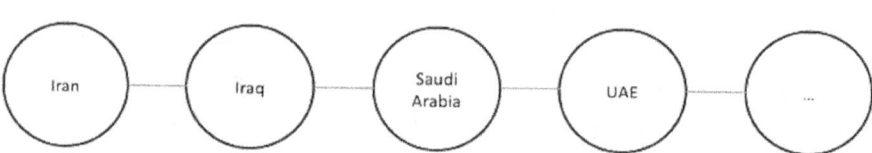

The Horizontal Structure of OPEC

It is intellectually useful to think of the hub-and-spoke structure of the college cartel as an octopus. US News is the head of the octopus. The various elite colleges are the tentacles. In this metaphor, the head of the octopus coordinates the actions of all the tentacles. If any tentacle goes rogue, the head punishes that tentacle, reasserting control. Unlike the college octopus, OPEC's horizontal structure is better described as a snake. Each nation in OPEC links together to form the body of the snake. For the snake to move, each part of its body must move in unison. If any part of its body goes rogue, the collusive scheme falls apart.

This hub-and-spoke structure only works because the elite colleges have a hub in common. This hub is their upstream supplier: US News. It might seem weird to think of US News as a supplier for elite colleges. Yet, on deeper examination, this relationship becomes explicitly clear. Harken back to earlier chapters. Remember that students go to college to acquire skills and a signal of ability. The strength of the signal a student inherits from his college is directly related to that college's prestige and relative position compared to other colleges. Ultimately, it is US News' college ranking that provides each college with that positional ranking and corresponding level of prestige. Thus, US News provides a key input to all elite colleges.

In practice, US News coordinates supply restrictions through its ranking formula. This is because the US News' rankings openly reward rejectivity and low enrollment. An expert in college admissions practices, Stanford sociologist Mitchell Stevens, explicitly calls US News' rankings "the machinery that organizes and governs" the elite college market.[160]

Crucially, if any elite college acts against what the US News ranking formula encourages, that elite college will accrue less prestige as it will be ranked lower. As a result, in the minds of students, that college will be perceived as a worse product. Since no college wants to be perceived as inferior, there is little incentive to deviate from what US News encourages. US News rankings are powerful as a coordinating tool because they explicitly outline what each college ought to do.

What does US News receive in exchange for creating the rules through which prestige is allocated and artificial scarcity is maintained? It receives credibility and access to unique data. This exchange allows US News to dominate the winner-takes-all college rankings market.

For the hub-and-spoke structure of this cartel to work, the hub must maintain a dominant position in its market. Otherwise, why would elite colleges be afraid of dropping in the US News' ranking? If there were other ways in which the public formed its impressions of relative prestige, then colleges would focus on those mechanisms instead of the US News' ranking. However, because of the credibility that elite schools lend to US News, the ranking service can maintain an overwhelming market share. As a result, US News can coordinate its spokes in turn. This give-and-take, the scarcity of seats in exchange for market share in the rankings market is the implicit bargain between elite colleges and US News. This cynical arrangement structures the output cartel.

The hub-and-spoke structure of the college cartel produces more stable collusive results than a horizontal structure could. This is because, in a horizontal structure, competitors must enforce restrictions against each other. Yet, since competitors have naturally divergent interests, it can be hard to get them to cooperate without any of them cheating. Furthermore, to sanction others, each member of this horizontal cartel must hurt itself. Thus, there is less credibility when it comes to enforcement because each member of the cartel might think that they can overproduce a little and get away with it since it would hurt others to punish this cheating. As a result, OPEC sometimes has trouble enforcing commitments from its members.

On the other hand, the elite college system is far better positioned because elite colleges don't have to hold each other accountable directly. Instead, the upstream US News coordinates and enforces artificial scarcity. Since US News is in a different business, its interests don't directly clash with the spokes it controls and coordinates. As a result, the threat of sanction is credible and clear. The elite colleges fall in line. To see how the ranking formula specifically encourages output restriction, let's break down the current US News ranking methodology:

US News' ranking works by crunching a variety of metrics to create a single number through which it can compare one school to another. For example, student selectivity, which used to receive a 12.5 percent weightage, today still receives a 7 percent weightage.[161] However, instead of directly measuring things like acceptance rate, proxy measurements such as test scores and percentage of students in the top 10 percent of their respective high schools are used. Of course, to maximize their scores in these areas, elite colleges are incentivized to be very rejective, naturally capping the number of students they want to accept.

Beyond "student selectivity," there are other strong incentives in the US News rankings to enroll few students. For example, the class-size index has an 8 percent weight. The student-faculty ratio has a 1 percent weight. Financial resources per student has a 10 percent weight. Thinking about all these weightings logically, if you rank colleges on ratios, then there are two ways for the colleges to respond. The first is to maximize the numerator. The second is to minimize the denominator. Elite colleges do both. For example, the 10 percent weight on financial resources per student means that to climb the rankings, an elite college will want to increase financial resources and decrease the number of students who share those resources. They will want to minimize enrollment! The same holds true for the student-faculty ratio and class-size index. All these metrics are stealthy proxies for exclusivity and limited enrollment. If we sum up all the weights of the metrics in which minimizing the number of students enrolled is incentivized, we arrive at the fact that at least 26 percent of the weighting of these influential rankings currently incentivizes low enrollment.

Yet this is not all. In fact, there is a mechanism for more direct enforcement of norms built into the rankings themselves. Exactly 20 percent of the weight in the rankings is given to "peer assessment." In other words, colleges rate other colleges on how well they are doing, and these assessments are then heavily weighted in the ranking. If any elite college tried to upset the status quo of artificial scarcity, not only would that college be tanked in the rankings because of numerical metrics, but other colleges could also retaliate through the "peer assessment." Because of the "peer assessment," elite colleges are incentivized to get along, not only on enrollment but also on a whole host of other norms.

Even beyond any conscious enforcement of norms, unconscious bias also encourages rejectivity in the "peer assessment" category. In practice, college administrators don't know that much about other schools. As a result, much of the peer assessment is based on the general reputation of a college. Of course, much of that general reputation is formed by where they have ranked historically. Therefore, there is a reinforcement of prior rankings in the current rankings. Up until 2018 the acceptance rate was still factored in. The result is that colleges that were formerly incentivized to be rejective continue to dominate. Others proceed to imitate them.

The internal logic that keeps the whole system ticking is the certainty that elite colleges will always try to maximize their prestige. Empirically, elite colleges have been consumed by increasing prestige. Economists Peter Blair and Kent Smetters confirmed just that in a study they published in 2021.[162] These economists built a model which found that the only way to explain the bafflingly high rejectivity of elite colleges is by adding prestige consideration into their economic model. As long as colleges continue to maximize their individual prestige and the metrics for achieving that prestige are implicitly agreed upon, artificial scarcity will continue. Power will continue to accumulate at the top. Implicit collusion will reign.

Elite colleges might dispute this entire narrative. The elite colleges might claim that it's true that they don't increase enrollment that much but that they don't do this to create artificial scarcity or even to maximize prestige. These elite colleges might even rage at the allegation that they curtail enrollment for selfish motives of prestige. Instead, elite colleges might claim that instead they are faced with genuine limitations that don't allow them to expand enrollment. Elite colleges might argue that there are physical, structural, or economic constraints on their ability to expand enrollment. Georgetown might complain that it would like to expand but that its local neighborhood would never allow new construction of facilities to expand. Harvard might explain that it would like to enroll more students but that not that many students can handle the workload at Harvard. Yale might allege that each student admitted into its class strongly influences all the other students precisely because its class size is so small. Accordingly, perhaps if Yale increased class size, it would reduce quality.

I don't buy any of these explanations. Of course, expansion comes with a set of challenges, but these challenges are not insurmountable if there is a will to face them. Upton Sinclair famously observed, "It is difficult to get a man to understand something when his salary depends on his not understanding it." I think a corollary of that sentiment can be ascribed to elite colleges. It's difficult to get an elite college to accept the plausibility of expansion when its power depends on its objections.

Firstly, many elite colleges assert that physical barriers to increased construction limit their ability for expansion. This might be somewhat true for city schools like Columbia or Georgetown, which are subject to strict zoning and neighborly considerations. However, this is certainly not true for a school like Dartmouth, which is in the middle of nowhere. It's not true of Cornell. It's not true of Duke. It's true of neither Michigan nor the University of Virginia. So at the very least, we should see these schools pushing for an expansion of enrollment. Yet, they don't. Furthermore, even for the city schools, I find the excuse of physical barriers to be unpersuasive because, with even a slight amount of imagination, any of these elite colleges can solve this problem. For example, Yale is located in New Haven. They might argue that zoning restrictions limit their expansive potential. However, within 2 miles of Yale are the following colleges: Southern Connecticut State University, Albertus Magnus College, and the University of New Haven. It is entirely unclear why Yale can't buy out these colleges' campuses. Any other business with 40 billion-plus dollars in the bank would use that money to make strategic acquisitions to grow. Yale uses it to invest in the money market. Why is that the case?

More generally, Georgetown, NYU, and other schools have started satellite campuses in the Middle East or in Europe. Why can't they do the same thing here in the United States? Whether that means acquiring existing campuses or building new ones in geographically diverse locations, there is nothing stopping elite schools from building in different locations, even locations very far from the original campus. If NYU can build a campus in Shanghai, I refuse to accept that they can't build one in Savannah. The physical restrictions that elite colleges allege melt away when you take this more zoomed-out view.

Secondly, sometimes elite schools argue that they don't increase enrollment because there aren't that many students who can handle the workload and intellectual rigor at elite colleges. These elite colleges argue that if you expand enrollment, there will be a mismatch whereby newly admitted students won't do well academically. This mismatch theory is just not true. As economists Peter Blair and Kent Smetters concluded in a 2021 study, if elite colleges had kept the same admissions standard since 1990, enrollments would have increased by 300 percent. As applications have increased from all over the world, the number of qualified applications has also increased. Just keeping the standard the same would have led to a radical expansion in seats.

In fact, the mismatch theory can be turned on its head. The secret truth is that mismatch at elite colleges largely occurs when these schools admit scores of spoiled brats who have no interest in learning. This isn't just one or two students. There are a lot of spoiled brat students admitted to elite schools. At worst, these are students who got into it through bribery, whether legally or illegally conducted. At best, these are students that elite colleges judged to be worthy because of metrics that favor rich kids, like admissions essays. Perhaps this is why so many current students at Harvard quip, "The hardest part of Harvard is getting in."

Sometimes, elite colleges move beyond the mismatch idea, and instead, they emphasize a need to maintain the "look and feel" of the campus. These words mean nothing, literally. As far as the "look and feel" of the campus is concerned, elite colleges salivate over multi-million dollar donations so that they can quickly tear down old buildings and put up new buildings with a rich donor's name on them. Yet, when it comes time to increase enrollment, they can't jeopardize the "look and feel" of the campus.

Some elite colleges argue that they don't expand enrollment because fewer people on campus are better for the quality of education. Elite colleges might try to quantify this argument by citing the relationship between smaller class sizes and better student academic performances. Of course, it is unclear why an elite college cannot have more students on campus and still maintain small class sizes by simply hiring more professors. For example, while tenured professors are relatively expensive, adjunct or part-time professors are relatively cheap to add. Yet, elite colleges don't hire as many adjuncts as they could. What explains that fact? Certainly, undergraduate students don't seem to prefer one type of professor to the other. Most undergraduate college students don't even know which professors are tenured and which are adjuncts.

The reason elite colleges choose not to hire more adjuncts is that the rankings disincentivize hiring adjuncts, proving once more that elite colleges are hyper-fixated on maximizing prestige.

The most direct and straightforward harm of artificial scarcity is that many students who want an elite college degree and are qualified to study at elite colleges are not let into elite institutions. The result is a massive loss in consumer surplus for customers who are forced to secure less prestigious education. This massive consumer harm shows up in the desperation of students who plagiarize papers, bribe sports coaches, and participate in all types of nefarious activities to secure admission. It shows up in the bitterness people feel toward elite colleges, which foreclose opportunities to ambitious and bright children. It shows up in the price premium people are forced to pay because of the scarcity of seats.

It is undeniable that artificial scarcity raises the price of an elite college degree. For students whose parents can afford to pay sticker price, this has been directly borne out by the steep rise in sticker tuition over the last thirty years at elite colleges.

The parents who can afford sticker tuition are not the only ones affected by the impact of artificial scarcity on the price of tuition. It affects all students. Because elite colleges have so much market power, they can price discriminate. In other words, they can charge different people different amounts of money based on their ability to pay. Accordingly, elite colleges also collect a massive amount of money from students whose parents cannot afford sticker tuition. For example, when a student only gets into one prestigious college and no peer schools, such a student is in a very poor position to negotiate with elite colleges on financial aid. Yet, even for students like Craig McFarland who get into more than one prestigious school, through collusion elite colleges can recreate an anti-competitive market. Sadly, artificial scarcity makes that type of collusion easier. We explore this practice in more detail in the chapter on price-fixing.

Beyond price harms to consumers, the concentration of market power allows elite colleges to manipulate the political process to maintain policies that benefit themselves. Because market power has allowed them to capture so much money, they have a tremendous amount of leverage with politicians. This is because they can deploy their resources on lobbying, and they often do. The net result is regulatory capture.

There are so many examples of this regulatory capture. For example, we have already reviewed how elite colleges lobbied to destroy whatever teeth President Obama's college scorecard could have had. Yet, this is not all. Every year, elite colleges spend millions of dollars lobbying Congress to maintain a high level of research spending, expand financial aid programs like Pell grants, and increase the amount of credit available to students. By manipulating the political process, concentration on the supply side of the higher education market allows elite colleges to influence the demand side of the market. By driving the amount of demand even higher while holding supply essentially stagnant, they accrue even more power for themselves. A vicious cycle develops as an increase in political power translates into even more influence on the policy-making apparatus. As we explore later, this stranglehold on Congress allows elite colleges to lobby for more federal aid to offset increased prices. Regulatory capture also allows elite colleges to push for insane antitrust exemptions which have historically allowed them to fix prices on financial aid.

Our national experiment in artificial scarcity has failed. The flip side is that if artificial scarcity can be attacked directly, all the anti-competitive behavior that flows from market power will also fall. This is what I call the domino theory of elite college reform. If we can increase supply at elite colleges, the entire market will change for the better. We explore this idea in later chapters.

CHAPTER 7

PRICE-FIXING

My trip had been weeks in the making. It had been a logistical nightmare. Nevertheless, I was finally at the station. This protest was actually happening. On May 19th, 2022, I boarded a train going north in high hopes. I was headed straight for Yale, and I didn't think they would see me coming.

It was a five-hour train from Washington DC to New Haven. I had a lot of time to kill, but I was too nervous to sleep. I didn't know what to do. Midway through, I decided to go through my checklist again. I still needed to pick up a helium tank. I still needed to print out my permits. I still needed to send texts to the people coming to the protest. I still needed to do a lot of things. I was going crazy.

Suddenly, my phone started ringing. The call was from a number I didn't recognize. My service was spotty, but I picked up anyway. As I reflect on it now, I wish I hadn't. The person on the other end of the phone introduced himself. His name was Ed Stannard. Ed was a reporter with the New Haven Register. He had a few questions for me about the protest I was staging at

Yale the coming Monday. The protest was scheduled for Monday morning. It was already Thursday, and time was of the essence.

The call was short, and my service was terrible. I asked Ed if I could call him back, but he wasn't available later. It was now or never. So, I stayed on the line. The audio cut in and out. The train kept rumbling along toward New Haven. To minimize the background noise, I headed towards a less crowded part of the train as the train's forward motion lurched me back and forward. Despite the inconvenient surroundings, I stayed focused on the call.

The reason Ed Stannard was calling me was that I was organizing a protest scheduled to take place at Yale's graduation. Ed asked me about the protest I was staging. He asked about the air blimp I was planning to fly over Yale's campus. However, as the call went on, my words were less clearly making it to Ed Stannard. Instead, I felt as though a lot of what I was saying was being lost on the spotty connection.

In talking to Ed, there was one thing I was worried about. I knew how powerful Yale was. This protest was meant to take the administration by surprise. If Yale knew about it, there was a lot Yale could do to derail the whole thing. So, I asked Ed to hold off asking Yale's communications team about the protest until after it was done. Ed said it was too late. He'd already sent Yale an email asking for comment. Suddenly, almost as soon as I first picked up, the call was over.

The next day, May 20th, Ed Stannard published his article.[163] It was a Friday, and Ed Stannard fully previewed the protest set to take place on Monday. Not everything about the article was perfect. In fact, Ed Stannard had even spelled my name wrong. Still, I was glad at least someone was noticing the protest and the issue that inspired it. For nearly three decades, the media had completely ignored a critical story. That story was about how elite colleges like Yale, Georgetown, Columbia, and others collude to fix prices on financial aid. It is a story we can no longer afford to ignore.

When I first started writing this book, I had absolutely no idea that elite colleges were fixing prices. I thought the worst of elite college misconduct was seat scarcity. But I was wrong. I don't want to be too harsh on myself. I'm not the only one who was completely ignorant about price-fixing by elite colleges. Instead, most people, including some of the most renowned experts on college pricing, were completely in the dark. For decades, no major media outlet had bothered to cover it. I still remember when I first figured it out. I couldn't believe it. How could this scheme have gone on for so long? Why had it been ignored?

It was a late night in October 2021, and I was Googling some combination of words that included "elite," "college," "cartel," and "price-fixing." Through the miracle of internet search, I stumbled across an obscure article published in The Nation, written by a lawyer I had never heard of.[164] I read the article. I read it all the way through. At first, I didn't believe what the article said. The article alleged that seventeen elite colleges were operating a price-fixing cartel. It couldn't be true. I read it again. I read it a third time. I started doing more research. Surely someone else must have written about a scheme this corrupt? Yet, apart from this one article, the next most recent mention of elite college price-fixing in a major media source dated back to the 1990s.

Fast forward again to May 19th, 2022. Right after my call with Ed Stannard of the New Haven Register, I sat back down in my train seat. The train continued to rumble toward Connecticut. An hour later, my phone started ringing again. Again, it was a number I didn't recognize. Again, I picked up. This time the call was even less welcome.

The man on the line was a captain of Yale's police department. He asked me if I could meet with him. I asked him why. He mentioned that he wanted to make sure that the protest I had planned would be conducted in a safe way. He wanted to go over my plans. I said I could meet him the next day. He asked me to meet him outside of Yale's campus. I said I would. The call ended.

After speaking with Yale's police chief, I became slightly nervous. I had a good reason to be nervous. If Yale killed my protest, weeks of preparation would have been for nothing. If Yale had killed my protest, Congress might not act in time. On the other hand, if I could pull it off, Congress could be jolted into action. If I could pull it off, we could finally see progress on the issue I had come to care so deeply about. We'll explore the Congressional angle later in this chapter, but just know that the protest's success was important. There was a lot at stake.

Essentially, the protest I had planned for the coming Monday was admittedly audacious. I had hired a man named Larry to bring one of his proprietary airships to New Haven. Larry's blimps were like miniature Zeppelins. Ranging from ten to fifteen feet, one could put messages on these blimps and fly them over the air. The message I asked Larry to prepare was simple: Yale Stop Fixing Prices! My plan was to have Larry fly his biggest blimp over Yale's graduation ceremony. In a moment of shock and novelty, I wanted to get a message across to parents, the media, and the broader public. I wanted this audience to ask the question: is Yale fixing prices?

When I finally arrived in New Haven on May 19th, I went about checking off my to-do list. I organized costumes for protestors. I made signs participants could hold up. I checked in on the supplier of the extra large helium tank we would need for our airship. Lastly, I printed out all the relevant permits I had secured weeks in advance. I went to sleep knowing I had all the paperwork I needed to sustain any questions from Yale's police captain. I was determined that he wasn't going to stop the protest.

The next morning I arrived at the location Yale's police captain had asked me to meet. Except, it turned out I wasn't only meeting with Yale's police captain. Instead, it was a gaggle of New Haven officials, including members of the fire department, members of the main police department, members of random agencies, and even an official from an obscure body called the Department of Emergency Management and Homeland Security. I immediately realized that this was going to be much tougher than I thought.

These officials grilled me on the permits. So, I showed them all the paperwork. I had secured all the relevant permits weeks prior. As far as the air blimp was concerned, I had previously called the New Haven Police Department and made sure that no local authorization was needed. Then, I asked Larry to secure all relevant FAA authorization. I was good to go.

Except... the Department of Emergency Management and Homeland Security didn't seem to see it that way. An official named Rick Fontana told me point blank, "That blimp isn't flying." He showed me a paper copy of a permit he said was necessary to fly. I asked him why I hadn't been notified of this permit earlier and why I hadn't found it anywhere. He said it was on the website. I later looked for it online, but I still couldn't find it. Nevertheless, I asked Rick Fontana what we could do to accommodate his safety concerns without neutering the protest. He didn't really have any particularly compelling ideas. In the end, I asked if I could at least fly a balloon instead of an airship. He agreed to that.

I was incredibly annoyed after that meeting with Rick Fontana and those other New Haven bureaucrats. I had been preparing this surprise protest for weeks. This protest was meant to start a bigger debate about how elite colleges were taking advantage of students. Didn't these bureaucrats get why I was doing this? More than anything, I was annoyed with myself. This was my fault. I shouldn't have leaked my protest plans to the press so soon. I should have waited until the moment of the protest. Now my tactical blunder was going to ruin the protest's effectiveness.

Coming away from that meeting, I was shocked. With Ed Stannard's one request for comment, a chain reaction had been set off whereby Yale's communication department got Yale's police department to lean heavily on New Haven officials. I'm not in an objective position to evaluate whether these government officials' security concerns were legitimate. But I do know that until Yale got involved, I didn't have a single problem with permits. This sequence of events made me realize that I had underestimated Yale.

I now suspect that this wasn't the total extent of Yale's interference with my protest. In fact, I was scheduled to give a radio interview to a local New Haven radio station on the day of the protest. Then, the day of the protest approached, and the radio interview was surprisingly canceled. I'm not alleging that Yale intervened to kill the story, but neither am I ruling out that possibility. Essentially, in a town like New Haven, Yale is the center of a lot of economic activity. As the wealthiest organization in the city, Yale has an unbelievable grip on the various levers of power there. In some ways, Yale is the head of a fiefdom.

Right after my meeting with that massive gaggle of New Haven bureaucrats, I called Larry, the air blimp operator. Larry was the one who had designed the blimp we were going to fly at the protest. On our call, I told Larry that the plan would have to be changed. The local bureaucrats were denying us. Larry listened carefully, and I told him exactly what they said. Larry waited for a beat. Then he said, "I'm kinda libertarian." I paused. What was Larry trying to say?

I didn't have to wait long to find out. Instead, "Libertarian" Larry then suggested that he would be willing to fly the blimp anyway. He felt that New Haven didn't have the actual authority to ask for a permit. I told him I'd have to think it through. I emailed some lawyers I knew socially to ask them for an opinion about what would happen if "Libertarian" Larry and I flew the blimp over Yale's graduation over the express objection of New Haven's bureaucrats. My question was effectively this: would we go to jail? I waited for an email response from anyone for hours. The clock was ticking; I needed an answer.

While I waited, "Libertarian" Larry had posed this same question about legal consequences in a Facebook group of drone operators. His Facebook group seemed to be reacting pretty positively to the idea of just flying anyway. As I spoke to Larry on the phone that weekend, I realized that if Larry was willing to take the risk, I should be too. I told him that if we could guarantee everyone's safety, I would be willing to just do it. I was down to roll the legal dice.

As the weekend ended, it was game time. I drove my uHaul truck with all the protest materials to a parking spot right next to Yale's campus. I had previously hired some people from Craigslist to help with logistics, and they slowly started to arrive early in the morning. Then another twist changed the course of the protest. One of the big assumptions behind the air blimp idea was that the weather would cooperate with the protest schedule. If it rained or stormed, the air blimp would have to be grounded. If it was too windy, the air blimp could spiral out of control. As Larry sized up the surroundings, we came to a sad realization.

The weather wasn't cooperating. It was too windy to fly as high as we would have needed to. We wouldn't end up assuming legal risk after all. The weather had foreclosed that option.

Despite these roadblocks, the protest continued. I handled it as stoically as I could. We came up with solutions, and we did what we could. Around 9 AM, Larry tied the smallest blimp he had to his waist, and he walked it around like a balloon with a harness. Around 9:30 AM, other undergraduate students from various schools who were deeply opposed to high tuition costs came to join the protest. My sister and a family friend were also mobilized in the effort. In total, some thirty people dressed up as monopoly men and respectfully protested on Yale's campus. As parents passed the protest by, they took photos, but without the blimp flying over the graduation, the protest had less impact than I would have liked. In terms of media coverage, after the radio interview was canceled, we were limited to Ed Stannard's effort in the New Haven Register.

I won't lie to you. The failure of the protest to attract more media attention was personally disappointing. However, it wasn't a total loss. Instead, a short video about the protest achieved thousands of views on Twitter. My thread about the elite college price-fixing conspiracy was retweeted by prominent personalities like Ian Madrigal and Matt Stoller. In fact, the targeted traction on Twitter helped me later get on the phone with some of the same Congressional movers and shakers that I had wanted to reach in the first place.

Furthermore, the article that Ed Stannard published about the protest was also interesting in its own right. It was particularly interesting because it included a response from Yale spokesperson Karen Peart. When Ed Stannard asked her for a response to our protest about Yale's price-fixing practices, Karen pointed him to a statement that read: "Yale's financial aid resources meet <u>the full demonstrated need</u> of every undergraduate."

The phrase "full demonstrated need" is actually a secret password. Understanding what those words mean unlocks the economic logic of the entire elite college price-fixing scheme. These words also allow one to understand why the media has ignored the story. This is the story we focus on in this chapter.

"Full demonstrated need" is a phrase from a George Orwell novel. After all, George Orwell warned us about double-speak. He told us that when people want to do something bad, they'll frame it as something good. He taught us that sometimes war would be described as peace, as the very opposite of what it is. We didn't listen closely enough, and the elite colleges have taken advantage of that fact.

As you read this chapter, I want you to recognize that elite colleges have cunningly used double-speak to mislead us into thinking that their collusion is for our benefit. Language like "financial aid" and "demonstrated need" distorts more than it describes. In any other context, we wouldn't call price flexibility "financial aid." Instead, we would call it perfect price discrimination. Elite colleges use words as their shield. Deploying them strategically, they've avoided scrutiny brilliantly. This is one of the reasons why the media hasn't held elite colleges accountable.

As we explore in this chapter, "demonstrated need" doesn't mean what you might think it does. After all, who determines how "needy" someone is? How is "need" defined and "demonstrated"? If you can control definitions, you can frame something exploitive as something beneficial. This is what elite colleges do today. In fact, it's something elite colleges have done for many decades.

To understand elite college price-fixing, we need to fully consider the term "financial aid." Essentially, the real price, or net tuition, for a student is determined by a simple equation. Real price = (sticker price) - (financial aid). Fiddling with either of the variables on the right side of the equation changes the real price students pay. But price-fixing is far more likely to go undetected if you fiddle with financial aid, which differs from person to person, instead of sticker price, which is the same for everyone and publicly available. Empirically, this is what elite colleges have done. If you want to understand how elite colleges fix prices, you need to understand how they collude on financial aid offers.

The history of elite college price-fixing is as long as it is dark. This economic dark art began with the Ivy League and MIT. Starting in the 1950s, representatives from the Ivy League universities and MIT started meeting and colluding on financial aid offers for admitted students. The objective of these meetings was simple. These representatives would look through each other's admitted students lists. If a student overlapped or was offered admissions by more than one of the Ivy League schools or MIT, then the representatives of those schools would collude on financial aid for that overlapping admitted student. This is why the meeting was called the Overlap meeting.

At these Overlap meetings, the agenda was clear. Representatives from the participating elite colleges first shared information about the family incomes of applicants. Together, the elite colleges then decided what they thought they could reasonably squeeze out of the applicant's family. The colluding schools then agreed on how much financial aid they would each offer that student. The collusion was precise. As two scholars quantified in a study of the Ivy Overlap cartel, when tuition bids among schools differed by more than $500, Overlap members pledged to charge 'approximately the same amount,' thus fixing the price.[165]

This price-fixing cartel was known as the Ivy Overlap group. Plainly, the Overlap Cartel conspired to take away students' bargaining power. For students that paid the full sticker price or got a full scholarship, the Overlap cartel didn't increase costs. But, many middle-class students didn't pay the full cost, nor did they get a full ride. Instead, for middle-class students that paid some of the tuition and relied on some financial aid, net prices were inflated artificially.

Two economists summed up the Ivy Overlap scheme in a 1991 paper. Essentially, "if the admissions officers agreed that a student could afford to pay $4000 per year, then a college whose total annual costs were $20,000 would offer $16,000 in aid, while a college whose total costs were $25,000 would offer $21,000 in aid."[166] The net price the student paid would often stay the same regardless of which of the Ivies or MIT the student was admitted to. The Ivy Overlap cartel sustained this anti-competitive conduct for decades.

This Overlap Cartel was different in structure from the hub-and-spoke seat cartel we detailed in an earlier chapter. The Overlap Cartel was a horizontal cartel instead. By horizontal, I mean a cartel where the colluders were direct competitors with each other. Indeed, the Wall Street Journal concluded in May 1989, "The Ivy League schools are part of a price-fixing system that OPEC might envy."[167] I'm bringing up this horizontal cartel structure to make one simple point. Unlike their more passive participation in the hub-and-spoke seat cartel, elite colleges had to actively collude with their competitors to fix prices. This created legal vulnerabilities. The elite colleges exposed themselves to antitrust lawsuits by choosing to collude actively.

The Ivy Overlap group was ridiculous from the start. I don't think you could find a better textbook example of active price-fixing. As tuition costs started to spiral out of control in the 1980s, sometimes increasing by 10 percent a year, it was only a matter of time before someone finally took the Ivy Overlap cartel on.

That, someone was Attorney General Richard Thornburgh. Under his leadership, in the late 1980s and early 1990s, the Department of Justice caught onto the Ivy Overlap price-fixing scheme. The DOJ launched an investigation, and suddenly the entire atmosphere changed. The heightened legal scrutiny caused some Ivy League schools to reevaluate their practices. Yale didn't attend the Overlap meeting in 1990 because it knew that the DOJ was watching. But, sitting the cartel out for one year wasn't enough, especially when Yale had sat in for the four decades prior. A reckoning was coming for everyone.

Richard Thornburgh is one of those quietly great men who is slowly lost to history. Few people today probably remember who he was or what he accomplished. But, this book seeks to remedy that error of social memory. Richard Thornburgh was born in 1932 in Pittsburg, Pennsylvania. He grew up during the Great Depression but came of age during the boom times of the 1950s and 1960s. His later life was similarly full of ups and downs.

Richard Thornburgh first went to Yale University to get a degree in engineering because he wanted to be a civil engineer like his father. Yet, when he really weighed his options after his graduation from Yale, he decided to go to law school instead. After law school, he went to work for a private firm and married his childhood sweetheart in 1955. But, a few years later, in a stroke of misfortune, Richard Thornburgh's life changed forever.

By 1960, Richard and his wife had a large, vibrant family which included three boys. Then, one day, Richard's wife died in an automobile accident. His son was badly injured in the same accident. Richard's whole life came apart. He felt pain like never before. He faced an internal crisis.

With his whole world looking dimmer, Richard Thornburgh spent a lot of time thinking deeply about what he wanted to do with the rest of his life. What would his mission be? What would his legacy be? Eventually, Richard Thornburgh got more serious about public service. As time passed, Richard began to heal. In 1963, he remarried. In 1966, he ran for Congress, but fate had long ago decided that things weren't going to be easy for Richard Thornburgh. He lost his race for Congress.

Possessing an uncommon resilience, Richard Thornburgh got back on his feet. He kept working. He looked for other ways to serve the public. Finally, in 1969, Richard got his big break. That year President Nixon appointed Richard Thornburgh as the US Attorney for the Western District of Pennsylvania. The appointment changed the trajectory of his life.

As US Attorney, Richard Thornburgh took on big risky cases against big powerful opponents. He got tough on organized crime. Most importantly, Richard prosecuted big steel companies for polluting the water in Pennsylvania in a case that predated strong environmental laws. With his impressive track record, President Gerald Ford eventually promoted Richard Thornburgh. He suddenly became the Assistant Attorney General for the Criminal Division of the Department of Justice.

Richard continued to excel at the DOJ, but Richard Thornburgh eventually decided he wanted to serve the public from a higher perch. In 1978, Richard Thornburgh began his campaign for Governor of Pennsylvania. He won this time. But, almost as soon as he entered office, Richard had to face a crisis unlike anything any American Governor had faced.

That crisis was the 1979 partial meltdown of a nuclear power plant at Three Mile Island in Harrisburg, Pennsylvania. Whereas other leaders might have panicked, Governor Thornburgh showed nerves of steel. With a stiff upper lip and determined frame of mind, he coordinated clean-up efforts. He met the moment. The federal government, working with Pennsylvania, was able to contain the nuclear meltdown problem. Governor Thornburgh was widely lauded for his leadership, and Pennsylvania voters reelected him in 1982.

After eight successful years in office, Governor Thornburgh stepped down. In 1987, Richard Thornburgh went to teach at Harvard. Yet, public service wasn't done with him yet, and in 1988 it came calling again. This time the call came directly from President Reagan.

After the Iran Contra scandal, President Reagan was already hurt politically. The 1986 Wedtech scandal only hurt President Reagan even more. His administration was seen as steeped in illegal maneuvering. President Reagan's Justice Department was seen as unethical. President Reagan needed help. He needed someone with credibility and honor to step in as his Attorney General. He asked Richard Thornburgh if he would help him. Richard Thornburgh answered the call.

After the Reagan reign came to an end, and George H.W. Bush was inaugurated, Thornburgh was asked to stay on as Attorney General. From 1988 to 1991, Attorney General Thornburgh would have a dramatic impact.

In those three years, Thornburgh had the DOJ bring cases against corrupt officials, white-collar criminals, wall street fraudsters, and even Exxon for the Valdez oil spill. But while all of this is incredibly impressive, it's not exactly relevant to this book. What is relevant is the case that Attorney General

Thornburgh's Department of Justice filed against the Ivy Overlap cartel.

Attorney General Thornburgh showed leadership on the Ivy Overlap case all the way through. He oversaw an aggressive investigation that started in 1987. During the course of the DOJ's investigation, only twenty elite colleges were asked for documents. Then, the circle was expanded to thirty. In the end, fifty-seven colleges were asked for documents.[168]

Under Attorney General Thornburgh's leadership, the DOJ ignored all the political squirming that investigating elite colleges was causing on both sides of the political aisle. After all, the colleges being investigated were the alma mater of many prominent politicians, including AG Thornburgh himself. Adding to the pressure, at the time, some in the media criticized the legal scrutiny of elite colleges as a political witch hunt. Nevertheless, displaying some of the steel that saw Thornburgh through a personal crisis and nuclear meltdown, the DOJ was directed to continue investigating.

After studying the price data for a few years, the DOJ finally launched a legal challenge against the nine members of the Ivy Overlap cartel in 1991. On May 23rd, 1991, Attorney General Richard Thornburgh called a press conference where he declared that "students and their families are entitled to the full benefits of price competition when they choose a college. This collegiate cartel denied them the right to compare prices and discounts among schools, just as they would in shopping for any other service."

In its case, the DOJ alleged that the Ivy Overlap cartel was in violation of the Sherman Antitrust Act. Even though Yale had tried to sneak out of the cartel towards the very end, it was included as a defendant in the suit.

The basis for the DOJ's legal challenge was the Sherman Antitrust Act. The Sherman Antitrust Act has been interpreted in a variety of ways. Yet, even the softest judicial interpretation of the Act has found that <u>an attempt to fix prices</u> is instantly illegal. The only exception to this general rule is if a cartel has an explicit exemption from the Sherman Antitrust Act. Such an exemption can only be provided by Congress. From the 1950s to the 1990s, elite colleges didn't have such an exemption. Instead, elite colleges were in open violation of the Sherman Antitrust Act.

The colleges were offended by the investigation and subsequent legal challenge. In response to the Overlap investigation conducted by the DOJ, a Dartmouth official complained, "schools like ours should not be seen as competitors in the same way that toaster manufacturers are."[169] Dartmouth was far from the only school to take this position. Instead, annoyance was the consensus.

The reason elite colleges are annoyed whenever the cost of attendance is discussed is that elite colleges think about cost the same way the 19th-century Earl of Downton Abbey would. Ensconced in snobbish attitudes, elite colleges, like old-world aristocrats, look down upon those who complain about the expense as lower-class, tasteless, and uncultured. The underlying attitude of the elite colleges is that what they produce is of such value that they should not be asked to account for its price. In fact, elite colleges have even made the argument that they are doing students a favor by allowing them not to have to choose on the basis of price between competing schools! Instead, these overlapping students could be "free" to choose on the basis of educational considerations alone.

Yet no amount of snobbery can remake a basic reality. Prices matter. Beyond snobbish annoyance, the elite colleges tried a principled justification for their price-fixing practices. Harvard's general counsel claimed that "our practices served the good social purposes of making sure that a limited amount of financial funds went to the neediest students." In other words, the Overlap Cartel tried to explain away the price-fixing by saying that in a competitive market, elite colleges would give away too much money to middle-class students and not enough to the neediest ones.

Of course, Harvard's justification didn't make any sense, especially when coming from Harvard. Harvard, the richest of the Ivy League schools, had more resources than the others. As a proportion of income, Harvard spent less on financial aid than other schools in the cartel. What the cartel basically allowed Harvard to do was spend more resources on itself as opposed to attracting students with lower prices. Harvard's argument was total bull, and Harvard knew that it was going to get killed in court.

This is why when push came to shove, the Ivy League schools, including Harvard, folded. Instead of dragging out a fight in the courts, all eight Ivy League schools settled with the DOJ. I thought that one New York Times headline from 1991 was a perfectly funny synopsis of the legal settlement: "Ivy Universities Deny Price-Fixing But Agree to Avoid It in the Future."

Yet, almost as soon as the case was settled, elite colleges were back to their dirty tricks. Columbia University said in a press statement in May of 1991 that it would be lobbying Congress to change the antitrust laws to allow elite colleges to fix prices again. Columbia University clearly had no interest in adhering to the spirit of the legal settlement. Far from being embarrassed or chastened, Columbia University was now on the warpath.

One school from the Overlap Cartel went even further. That school, MIT, didn't even sign the settlement. Apparently, MIT's

President Charles Vest took great personal offense for being called a price-fixer. So, unlike the Ivy Leaguers, MIT decided to take a more muscular approach to fight the DOJ challenge. MIT went to court. Once the dice were rolled, MIT President Charles Vest commented, "MIT has a long history of admitting students based on merit and a tradition of ensuring that students receive full financial aid <u>based only on need</u>. Our financial aid process has been very effective for many years in helping talented students from low-income families attend MIT. We are confident in the integrity of our processes."[170]

While framed as a moral crusade, the real reason MIT was so desperate to keep the price-fixing cartel alive was that MIT was more reliant on tuition revenue than other elite colleges. As MIT's President Paul Gray explained in a 1989 interview, "MIT's endowment is substantial in absolute terms, but it is not large in the context of MIT. In absolute terms, the size of MIT's endowment ranks around 7th. Harvard has the largest at $4 billion; MIT has about $1.2-1.3 billion. However, you must relate absolute endowment to the size of the institution. Taking the number of faculty members and graduate students, MIT is 20th-30th."[171] More competition would mean less tuition revenue, and MIT didn't want less tuition revenue because it lagged the others in alternative revenue streams. So, MIT selfishly proceeded to trial against the DOJ.

At trial, the DOJ attempted to demonstrate how collusion raised prices by comparing MIT to another elite college, albeit one that didn't collude on financial aid. By the 1990s, Stanford University was routinely ranked as one of the most prestigious schools in America. Uniquely, Stanford was also very generous with financial aid. In fact, by the 1990s, the collusive MIT expected families to contribute an average of $2,521 more than the competing Stanford.[172] In a cynical effort to suppress competition, Stanford was even invited to join the Ivy Overlap cartel. Thankfully, Stanford declined the offer to collude.

Stanford served as a strong example for the DOJ. It was a school every bit as prestigious as the Ivy Overlap schools, but it was also a school choosing to compete. As a result, students were getting a better deal. Imagine what would happen if all the other schools competed too.

In court, MIT had two main arguments in pushing back against the DOJ. The first was an economic one. Essentially, MIT argued that its price-fixing had beneficial effects. MIT asserted that "the overlap meetings served a public purpose by assuring students were admitted on merit and that available financial aid funds - both the colleges' private funds and government monies - were awarded on the basis of need only, thereby serving the largest possible group of eligible students. They enabled the participating colleges to preserve a need-blind admissions system and avoid the potentially costly results of a bidding system for relatively affluent students who did not need assistance in order to attend college."[173] In other words, MIT argued that price-fixing on students who could "afford" to pay more let MIT offer more aid to students who needed the money more.

When framed in this zero-sum way, it might seem as though MIT and other elite colleges have a point. Why should they waste limited resources on bidding for students who can afford an education to the detriment of students who can't? Viewed from this lens, perhaps price-fixing is more akin to a wealth redistribution scheme that takes resources from the rich students to give resources to the needy ones.

There were a few big flaws in MIT's argument. Firstly, an important assumption in MIT's argument is that the financial aid budget was limited to begin with. Was there really a tradeoff between giving more financial aid to middle-class students and the poorest ones?

The tradeoff wasn't true. Financial aid budgets don't have to be zero-sum or fixed, and certainly not at the wealthy colleges involved in the Overlap case. Financial aid budgets are constituents of larger university budgets. In 1992, MIT spent $29 million on undergraduate financial aid. For context, MIT's spending in 1992 was $1,083,360,000. As a proportion of the total budget, the undergraduate financial aid budget was a tiny fraction. Even if it had been doubled, it still would have been a tiny fraction of the total budget. Obviously, the argument that financial aid was necessarily scarce was an implausible one. If financial aid was scarce, it is because it has not been made a priority, not because it was impossible to offer more.

Importantly, there was a lot of fat at MIT and other elite colleges that could be cut to free up resources for financial aid, and this is really an important point. The whole justification for having competitive markets is that competition forces institutions to cut costs and increase efficiency. Competitive markets force obese institutions to lean out. After all, was the extra revenue raised by colluding being redistributed from rich students to poor students, as MIT claimed it was? Or was MIT's price-fixing loot going into needlessly extravagant dining halls, expensive buildings, and unnecessary administrators? Was the loot being invested into improving education, or was it being invested into optimizing for MIT's US News ranking? In truth, instead of redistributing from rich to poor, colluding schools were instead redistributing from rich to richer, aka themselves. Since the extra money MIT extracted by fixing prices was going into things that made the college more expensive without making the college better at educating students, MIT's justification of redistribution fell flat.

Beyond just MIT, we should ask a more general question. Is the problem in elite education that the elite colleges don't spend enough on education? I don't think anyone really believes that. Past a certain level of spending, does a nicer building really facilitate better learning, or is it just gratuitous? Framed another way, Pythagoras taught his students by drawing with a stick in the dirt. Yet, he and his students mastered the mysteries of the triangle. Good teaching doesn't always need expensive facilities. More money expended doesn't necessarily mean better education. If the extra money is being spent in ways that improve the inputs of education but not the actual education, then there might be no effective redistribution of resources. Instead, extra money is merely being taken from the wealthier students and wasted by the college.

This description of extravagant spending was closer to the mark. As one economist explained in his analysis of the Overlap cartel, "The cartel profits made on excessively high tuition charged to some students may provide a cross-subsidy to other students in the form of altruistic financial aid. However, the money might also be spent on teacher salaries, football stadiums, lawn care, or wasteful expenditures. Thus, the fact that universities spend all their revenues does not show that they do not exercise cartel power."[174] Plainly, a lot of money was being wasted. Elite colleges like MIT didn't need to fix prices. They needed to cut costs so that they could better compete on financial aid offers.

The Overlap Cartel's other main defense against the DOJ was not an economic one but rather a legal one. They held that the education sector was meaningfully different from other economic sectors and, therefore, should be held to a different standard. In effect, MIT said that because non-profit colleges were not motivated by pure profit, they should be exempted from antitrust laws. The lawyer representing MIT in the case said, "MIT's function is to teach, to discover, and to build. It is to leave to the next generation a better and more knowledgeable world. Yet in the eyes of the Antitrust Division, such an institution is indistinguishable from a manufacturer of toaster ovens or porcelain fixtures."[175] His logical implication was that competition law was not relevant in an industry outside the capitalist paradigm of profit and loss. But this argument was also a stretch. The courts had long ruled that antitrust laws apply to non-profit organizations engaging in commerce. MIT's undergraduate program was obviously a form of commerce.

While the idea that elite education should be treated just like other sectors of the economy might seem intuitive, elite colleges are very hostile to it. This is because elite colleges have an inherent desire to escape not only regulatory laws but also the pressures of the competition itself. This is what motivates them to frame themselves as different from other firms, with more enlightened motivation than other actors. Further, this desire to escape competition is what might encourage elite colleges to besmirch competition as wasteful or harmful to students.

The question we must ask is simple. Why should we believe in competition in every other sector of the economy apart from this one? The point of markets is to create incentives to do more with less, and quality doesn't need to drop with the price. In fact, the history of competitive markets points to outcomes where the price goes down but quality goes up.

For all these reasons, as the Overlap case finally came before a judge, the verdict was definitive. A federal district court in

Philadelphia found the collusion to be unlawful. The judge rejected the Overlap Cartel's reasoning on both the economic justification and the legal one. Yet, unwilling to accept defeat, The Overlap cartel changed its strategy.

Having lost a battle in the Judicial branch, elite colleges decided to win the war in the Legislative one. Lobbying Congress, elite colleges were able to get a two-year exemption from antitrust laws. For the next two years, until 1994, the Overlap cartel was free to practice their price-fixing collusion. MIT rejoiced. They posted a statement that read: "Finally, in the wake of the trial, Congress passed, and President George Bush signed, a bill that permits colleges for the next two years to agree with one another to award financial aid only on the basis of 'demonstrated financial need.'"

Instead of relying solely on the legislative hall pass, MIT further appealed the judicial decision made in the Federal District Court. For context, in the federal legal system, if you don't like the decision a court makes, you can appeal the decision to a higher court. If you appeal the decision enough times, then the case can arrive at the Supreme Court, but the Supreme Court's verdict is then final. MIT didn't like the decision made by the Federal District Court, so when MIT appealed, the case went one level up.

That's how the case came before the Court of Appeals for the Third Circuit. In this second court proceeding, the arguments were largely legal. The questions were procedural. MIT asked the judges to adjudicate whether it was fair to hold them to a strict standard of antitrust scrutiny. Essentially, MIT wanted the court to allow them to be judged based on a "rule of reason" standard. This is fancy legal talk that just means that MIT wanted a more lenient standard. Under this more lenient standard, MIT would be allowed to painfully and slowly go through a list of pros and cons to show that price-fixing was net beneficial for students. Basically, MIT wanted a more technical and complicated trial that would last longer and cost more.

Surprisingly, the judges on the 3rd Circuit Court of Appeals ruled for MIT. The court basically concluded that while it was certainly true that MIT was fixing prices, MIT deserved this more lenient standard through which it could calculate all the pros and cons. Therefore, the Court of Appeals for the Third Circuit ordered a retrial in Federal District Court under a "rule of reason" standard. The case was going to be retried in a more technical and complicated way that would be full of expert testimony and complicated statistical modeling.

I believe that this appellate court proceeding was wrongly decided, but decided it was. This decision by the Court of Appeals was a blow to the DOJ. In essence, the DOJ now had three options. The first option was that the DOJ could appeal the Appeals Court decision to the Supreme Court, where the DOJ could argue for a more strict standard in evaluating MIT's price-fixing. The second option was that the DOJ could go back down to the district court for a retrial and spend years before reaching a decision in a complicated, technical, and expensive trial. The third option was that the DOJ could try to settle with MIT.

This aggressive litigation posture from MIT began to create political pressure on the newly inaugurated Clinton administration. The political figures in the Clinton White House didn't want the case to go to the Supreme Court.[176] The Supreme Court was a wild card. After all, while there was every chance that the Supreme Court could agree with the DOJ, there was also an outside chance that the Supreme Court could do something weird, like create an antitrust carveout for elite colleges the way it had for Major League Baseball in 1922. If the Supreme Court went in that direction, this type of weird outcome would become permanent. The DOJ didn't want to take that risk.

Going back for a retrial didn't make much sense, either. The trial was going to be expensive and drag out for years. Elite colleges had already been exerting pressure on Congress to create an antitrust carveout for them. What if the DOJ invested all these resources in a legal case that ended up not mattering because of Congressional interference? This, too, was an unpalatable risk.

There was a cultural aspect to this also. After all, the Clinton administration had a cozy relationship with elite colleges. This coziness, combined with the lobbying and legal firepower that MIT and other elite colleges were deploying, created a lot of political pressure. All that political pressure was being felt deeply by a DOJ lawyer named Robert Litan. Many years after the case was settled, Robert recalled, "During my first week on the job, I was assigned the (thankless) task of figuring out what to do. Ultimately, higher-ups in the department gave me strong signals to find a way to settle with MIT."

As the political pressure grew to settle the case, DOJ lawyer Robert Litan acquiesced. A settlement was reached with MIT in December 1993. The government's case ended in compromise, and the settlement was fundamentally disappointing. MIT had beaten the DOJ at the political game, and MIT knew it. In fact, two analysts described the settlement as one "that allows MIT to engage in most of the conduct that the Government had challenged."[177] The elite colleges had somehow won, and they weren't done yet.

With the judicial proceedings ended, the Overlap cartel next lobbied Congress to make the two-year legislative exemption that they had received in 1992 more permanent going forward. Elite college lobbyists advocated for a new law that would grant broad price-fixing powers to elite colleges. Led by Senators Howard Metzenbaum of Ohio and Ted Kennedy of Massachusetts, this is precisely what Congress did by passing Section 568 of the Improving America's Schools Act of 1994.

The passage of Section 568 was an unqualified victory for the Overlap cartel. This is because Section 568 was a more permanent exemption from the nation's antitrust laws. With this antitrust exemption made long-term, the Overlap cartel was in a stronger position than it had been prior to the initial DOJ challenge. To understand why you need only read the brief but powerful text which made up Section 568:

(a) Exemption.—It shall not be unlawful under the antitrust laws for 2 or more institutions of higher education <u>at which all students admitted are admitted on a need-blind basis</u>, to agree or attempt to agree—

(1) to award such students financial aid only on the basis of demonstrated financial need for such aid;

(2) to use common principles of analysis for determining the need of such students for financial aid if the agreement to use such principles does not restrict financial aid officers at such institutions in their exercising independent professional judgment with respect to individual applicants for such financial aid; or

(3) to use a common aid application form for need-based financial aid for such students if the agreement to use such form does not restrict such institutions in their requesting from such students, or in their using, data in addition to the data requested on such form.

As you can read from the text, Section 568 made it legal for colleges to jointly agree to <u>only</u> award financial aid based on "demonstrated financial need." Furthermore, Section 568 made it legal for colleges to agree on a common formula to jointly calculate that "demonstrated financial need." Lastly, Section 568 made it legal for every college to settle on one common form so that all of them had access to the exact same data about an applicant's financial situation. In sum, Section 568 made it possible for elite colleges to fix prices by jointly determining how much "need" had been demonstrated.

After my protest at Yale in May of 2022, Yale's spokeswoman was telling the truth when she said that "Yale's financial aid resources meet <u>the full demonstrated need</u> of every undergraduate." However, there was a statement within her statement. What the Yale Spokeswoman failed to mention was that the collusion on prices occurs in jointly determining how much need has been demonstrated in the first place.

After its passage in 1994, Section 568 resurrected the Ivy Overlap cartel and made it even stronger. Whereas before, elite colleges operated outside the law, elite colleges had now redrawn the law itself. Section 568's passage was a testament to the political power of elite colleges. After all, few other cartels would have been brazen enough to lobby Congress into protecting its monopoly power in the face of a legal challenge. Even fewer would have been able to successfully turn lobbying into legislation.

In the Overlap era, elite colleges used to discuss each individual overlapping admitted student, but legal challenges made the elite colleges adapt. However, they refused to give up on collusion. Once Section 568 became law, elite colleges were able to practice more abstract collusion. Instead of colluding on each individual student, elite colleges now used a common formula to determine how much financial aid they would offer. The outcome is virtually the same. If you use the same formula to determine price, and you plug in the same data into that formula, then you end up offering a ridiculously similar price. For decades, elite colleges often used the same formula with the same data and therefore offered similar prices.

The passage of the Improving America's Schools Act of 1994 led to tangible increases in the monopoly power of elite colleges. After the approval of Section 568, more and more elite colleges gorged themselves. Whereas the Overlap cartel was limited to a few elite colleges, Section 568 opened the doors wide open for many new elites to join the action. Once legal immunity was fully granted in 1998, a much bigger "consortium" of colleges practicing "need-blind admissions" was formed. This cartel called itself the 568 Presidents Group. One estimate from 2022 finds that colleges in the 568 Cartel control 74 percent of the seats in the elite college market.[178]

The 568 Presidents Group's website described its origin story as follows: "In late 1998, an ad hoc group of college and university presidents met to discuss their shared belief in the primacy of need-based financial aid and their common concern about restoring public confidence in a financial aid system that aspires to be both understandable and fair. At that time, they committed to the development of a common methodology based on recommendations that had already been developed by participating institutions for further consideration. On April 18th, 2000, the 568 Presidents appointed a group of eight campus-based senior financial aid professionals to serve on a Common Standards Subcommittee and to report back to them on ways to improve the financial aid system so as to better serve the needs of families in their efforts to pay for college."

If you read between the lines and replace the warm phrases with cold facts, you arrive at a simple question. Doesn't this conduct sound familiar? Isn't this almost exactly what the Overlap representatives used to do? As of January 2022, members of the 568 Presidents Group included: "Amherst College, Boston College, California Institute of Technology, Claremont McKenna College, Columbia University, Cornell University, Dartmouth College, Davidson College, Georgetown University, Grinnell College, Johns Hopkins University, Massachusetts Institute of Technology, Middlebury College, Northwestern University, Pomona College, Rice University, Swarthmore College, University of Notre Dame, Wellesley College, Williams College, Yale University."

You might recognize some of these names. In fact, the 568 Presidents Group was the Overlap group reincarnated. Yet, like the Hydra of Greek mythology, this cartel came back stronger than ever. Colleges like Johns Hopkins, which was never part of the original cartel, made the market even more collusive by joining the 568 Presidents Group.

However, in the interest of fairness, it must be noted that not everyone that participated in Overlap joined the 568 cartel. For example, Harvard, which was a key member of the Overlap cartel, decided to decline participation in the 568 cartel. Sally Donahue, Harvard's former Director of Financial Aid, "said in 2008 that Harvard never joined the 568 Cartel because its financial-aid formula would have yielded financial-aid packages that were smaller than what Harvard wanted to award."[179] Nonetheless, Harvard serves as the exception that proves the rule. When a cartel controls 74 percent of the market share, it's clear that the majority of important players participate in the cartel. That level of price-fixing cannot help but raise prices.

Because of the moat that prevents competitors from entering the elite college market, which we discussed in a previous chapter, the threat of entry from a cheaper competitor didn't dissuade elite colleges. Furthermore, because of the artificial scarcity of seats, few applicants get into many different top colleges anyways. Yet, for those lucky few, because of the Section 568 antitrust exemption, even students who had multiple offers of admission were deprived of the true benefits of competition. If a qualified student applied to college before 2022 and got into a few different elite schools, there is a high likelihood that all or most of those elite schools colluded on price.

Importantly, even schools that don't join the 568 Presidents Group stood to benefit from the market collusion. Because elite seats are artificially made scarce, there are far more qualified students than there are seats. As a result, competition to fill one's class isn't so intense anymore amongst elite colleges. In the absence of any particularly vigorous competition on quantity or quality of students, if all your competitors are jointly offering higher prices, then you can independently raise your prices also. As a result of Section 568, prices went up at non-568 Presidents Group colleges also.

For nearly 25 years, from the foundation of the 568 Presidents Group in 1998 to 2022, the 568 Cartel operated virtually unchallenged. In this period, elite college price-fixing was the norm. Not coincidentally, rising tuition greatly exceeded the cost of inflation at these elite schools.

Late in the Summer of 2022, I ran into a Republican Congressman, Ken Buck, at a bar in Washington, DC. I hadn't met him before, but I've always found Congressman Buck to be quite interesting. He and I disagree on probably every single issue apart from one. That one issue of agreement is antitrust.

As soon as I recognized him at the bar, I realized that I had the opportunity to make a case against Section 568. I seized my opportunity.

I opened the conversation by telling Congressman Buck how much I supported his position on antitrust. When he told me he appreciated my comment, I immediately pivoted to how he should investigate the monopoly power of elite colleges. Congressman Buck started listening closely. I kept going. He kept listening. Finally, I started talking about the Section 568 issue. Congressman Buck immediately sensed the political potential of what I was telling him. He pulled me aside to introduce me to his staff. He had me connect with his Deputy Chief of Staff. His Deputy Chief of Staff and I scheduled a meeting for an in-depth briefing on the issue. I dusted off my suit. I was headed to Capitol Hill.

In the paragraphs that follow, I'll tell you what I told the Congressman and his staff. But, to understand what I told the Congressman's staff in the richest way, we must start with a class-action lawsuit working its way through court right now. After all, that lawsuit framed my conversation with the Congressman and his staff. Frankly, the way elite colleges respond to the lawsuit will determine the future of elite college price-fixing.

On January 10, 2022, I remember waking up to texts from all my friends. The texts were all worded differently, but in their essence, they were alike. Each one linked to the same article in that morning's Wall Street Journal. There was breaking news. A class-action lawsuit had been filed against Georgetown and other elite colleges for fixing prices on financial aid offers. The lawsuit plainly stated that the 568 Presidents Group was in violation of the Sherman Antitrust Act. On January 10th, I'm sure the elite colleges had a sense of deja-vu.

Yet, there is something meaningfully different this time. Unlike the DOJ's case against the Overlap Cartel of the late 1990s, this lawsuit wasn't brought by any government authority. Instead, the lawsuit is a private antitrust class action that sought to recover damages on behalf of exploited students. Essentially, the plaintiffs, or the people doing the suing, are a group of students who sought admission and then financial aid from some of the colleges in the 568 Presidents Group. These named students represent a broader class of people who all sought admissions and financial aid from 568 Presidents Group colleges. The defendants, or people being sued, are all of the elite colleges that have ever participated in the 568 Presidents Group.

Class-action lawsuits are a bit weird because those named students represent far more students than they could even imagine. In total, the lawsuit alleges that the 568 Presidents Group overcharged <u>over 170,000 students</u> with its price-fixing scheme. If the named students win their case, all those others will also be entitled to compensation. Furthermore, those named students are suing colleges they never attended on behalf of others who did and were squeezed by the collusion and conspiracy. That's a lot of people squeezed out of a lot of money, and if the courts side with the students, the damages will likely be in the billions of dollars. This case is a big deal.

The magnitude of this case might be why elite colleges seem to be back to their old tricks. Elite colleges have hired some of the fanciest lawyers money can buy to fight the class action suit. In fact, UPenn has hired Seth Waxman, the former Solicitor General of the United States. Unfortunately, no lawyer will be able to get the elite colleges out of this bind so easily.

Still, these fancy lawyers will certainly try. In August of 2022, Seth Waxman, representing the elite college defendants, tried to get the judge to throw out the class-action case. The elite colleges failed. US District Judge Matthew Kennelly told the elite colleges to buck up instead.[180] The elite colleges were ordered to respond to the lawsuit by September 9th, 2022. As things stand now, we're headed for a titanic trial in the courts sometime in 2023 or 2024. Any college that has ever been a part of the 568 Presidents Group is going to get dragged to the stand.

Of course, this class action might strike you as doomed to failure. After all, wasn't the entire narrative of this chapter about how elite colleges persuaded Congress to give them an antitrust exemption? If elite colleges have immunity from the antitrust laws, then how could they be liable for breaking them?

Go back and read Section 568 more closely. I included part of the statute earlier in this chapter. In the very first sentence of Section 568, there is a conditional: "It shall not be unlawful under the antitrust laws for 2 or more institutions of higher education <u>at which all students admitted are admitted on a need-blind basis</u>, to agree or attempt to agree…"

This underlying conditional is the beating heart of the entire class action lawsuit. The plaintiffs, the students suing the schools, believe that not all students offered admission at these schools are admitted on a need-blind basis. Importantly, if even one student is not admitted on a need-blind basis, then the college doesn't qualify for the antitrust exemption. If that school doesn't qualify for the antitrust exemption but fixes prices by participating in the 568 Presidents Group anyway, then it is in violation of the Sherman Antitrust Act. Any school that colludes with any other school that hasn't qualified for the antitrust exemption is also in violation of the Sherman Antitrust Act.

In theory, if even one kid at even one of the schools in the 568 Presidents Group got in because of his wealth, then all of the colleges in the 568 Presidents Group are liable for breaking the law. More generally, this entire legal case will hinge on whether elite colleges practice need-blind admissions or not. In court, there might be some debate about what need-blind means. But there shouldn't be. Section 568 defines the term. As the statute holds, "the term 'on a need-blind basis' means without regard to the financial circumstances of the student involved or the student's family."

Under this definition of "need-blind," there are all sorts of ways in which elite colleges aren't need-blind in the admissions process. We devoted a whole chapter of this book to discuss all the ways in which admissions are biased toward the wealthy. In that earlier chapter, we observed the curious case of Jared Kushner and the despicable practice of "development lists." We observed how biased the practices of legacy admissions and early decision admissions are. We even observed that sports recruiting is biased toward the rich.

The lawsuit basically claims that while Section 568 made price-fixing legal in theory, the elite colleges named in the suit have not been eligible for the Section 568 exemption in practice. The US District Court judge assigned to this case seems to agree with the students. As US District Judge Matthew Kennelly wrote in a recent decision allowing the lawsuit to continue, "the plaintiffs must plausibly allege that the defendants consider some applicants' need for financial aid in their admissions decisions. The plaintiffs have met this burden."[181]

I personally think that elite colleges are legally screwed. If they're going to beat this lawsuit, they're not going to do it in court. Instead, they're going to do it in the halls of Congress. The same branch of government that bailed them out of the Overlap case will probably be the one that will bail them out of this legal jam.

Such a looming political bailout is why I protested at campuses like Yale and Georgetown last summer. Its why I launched an online petition on Change.org to stop the renewal of Section 568. Frankly, it's one of the reasons that I've published this book. I feel an urgent need to sound the alarm bell. I want to explain this story to the broader public. This is a critical moment.

If the public doesn't pay attention to the exemption, the lobbying power of elite colleges might overpower any resistance from Congress. Elite colleges might lobby to not only renew the antitrust exemption but also amend the exemption to patch any conduct that might have been illegal the first time around. Moreover, the elite colleges might even push for an amended exemption to be made retroactive. If this happens, a multi-billion-dollar legal case would die not in court but in Congress.

The day after my protest at Yale in May of 2022, I got a bit of traction on antitrust Twitter. Quite frankly I have virtually no Twitter following, so any attention to me feels like "traction." However, the antitrust world is a small and insular community, and my tweet seemed to be getting retweeted by heavy hitters in that world, like Matt Stoller and Ian Madrigal. Finally, I noticed that a prominent person in the Democratic party liked one of my tweets. I followed up with him on Twitter. We scheduled a call.

An interesting quirk of Section 568 is that it required renewal every seven years from Congress. Following the lawsuit, the next time Section 568 came up for renewal before Congress was on September 30, 2022. On my call with a prominent person in the Democratic party, I was told that elite colleges were holding off on lobbying on Section 568. I was told that elite colleges might try to stuff the renewal into a bigger spending bill that was needed to fund the rest of the government. In other words, I was told that the elite colleges might try a QB sneak.

In the end, the QB sneak never materialized. Instead, the 568-exemption lapsed in 2022, after Congress didn't renew it. However, that doesn't mean that these price-fixing practices are over. With the grip that elite colleges have on Congress, that exemption could come back at any time.

If the public knows and cares about the antitrust exemption, Congress probably won't renew it. The issue is the wider public still doesn't know much about this antitrust exemption. Frankly, it is a bit complicated. After all, you need to understand that price is dependent on financial aid, and you need to know that elite colleges collude on how to calculate financial aid offers. How many people know all those things? Yet, if it was easy to figure out how elite colleges were screwing the public, then the elite colleges would have been forced to stop a long time ago. Their power is derived from the public's confusion. That is what this book hopes to remedy.

I think that one of Aesop's fables applies to elite colleges. Once upon a time, a scorpion wanted to cross a river, but the scorpion couldn't swim. This stranded scorpion cried for help, and a nearby frog answered the call. The scorpion asked for help. The frog said that he would be willing to help the scorpion but only if the scorpion promised not to sting him. The scorpion readily agreed. Then the scorpion climbed on the frog's back and the frog jumped across the river. Once across, the scorpion dismounted and immediately stung the frog. Betrayed, the frog asked why the scorpion did it. The scorpion had a simple response to the frog. He said, "it was in my nature."

Just as the scorpion couldn't help himself, elite colleges will always jump to squeeze more money out of students. They simply cannot change their nature. So, if an opportunity to extract money from middle-class students under the pretense of cross-subsidy is offered to colleges, they will take it, but the money will never be spent on effective cross-subsidy programs that redistribute income from rich students to poor students.

What should we do in response? Should we allow elite colleges to continue to discriminate and price fix in the hope that colleges will reform their nature? If we do that, we have learned nothing from the fate of the frog in the fable.

Instead, we should leave the cross-subsidization to other actors, like state and federal governments, which are better equipped to handle that role. Elite colleges should be subjected to as much competition as possible in the hope that such competition will drive them to cut costs and teach more efficiently.

The ending of this chapter is a plea. If you're an American citizen, please pay attention to whatever Congress does on this issue of price-fixing by elite colleges. If Congress tries to renew Section 568, please hold them accountable. If Congress goes further and uses legislation to kill the legal case, please hold them accountable. Tell everyone you can about this antitrust exemption. Change begins with you, and we're in desperate need of change.

CHAPTER 8

SUBSIDY CANNIBALS

I'm not Senator Chuck Schumer's biggest fan, but I have valid reasons for not liking him. Senator Schumer is weak on antitrust. He's weak on Wall Street. He's weak on crony capitalism. So, when I heard that Senator Schumer allowed Harvard's President Lawrence Bacow to personally lobby him for a subsidy, I was disappointed, but I wasn't surprised. Of course, Lawrence Bacow would go see Senator Schumer.[182] It's Senator Schumer.

The meeting I'm referring to took place in Washington DC, in May 2022. Importantly, the meeting had a specific purpose. Harvard President Lawrence Bacow wanted a particular subsidy, and he felt that the political environment was ripe to get it. Senator Schumer certainly went into the meeting with an open mind.

As the two powerful men sat down face to face, President Bacow made his ask. President Bacow explained to Senator Schumer that he wanted a repeal of a recently enacted endowment tax on Harvard and other universities with gigantic endowments. In that particular meeting with Senator Schumer, President Bacow didn't mince words. He asked Senator Schumer for a repeal openly. In 2022, the exact same year that Harvard's endowment grew by 33 percent to be worth a total of $53.2 billion, Mr. Bacow felt that paying a proportionally microscopic $50 million towards the endowment tax was too high a price. The average person might think President Bacow was joking. He wasn't.

For context, the endowment tax that President Bacow hates so much is relatively new and microscopic in magnitude. Signed into law by President Trump in 2017, the endowment tax applies only to university endowments which are worth more than $500,000 per full-time student. Importantly, the tax levied is a puny 1.4 percent on endowment gains. Essentially, the tax is a penny on each dollar that the endowment grows. Moreover, it only applies to the world's wealthiest universities—those same universities which annually reap billions in federal subsidies and pay virtually no other federal taxes.

The Senator Schumer meeting and other lobbying pressure exerted by the elite colleges must have had some impact because, in an early draft of what eventually became the Inflation Reduction Act, there was a provision included which authorized the repeal of the endowment tax. The only reason it didn't make it into the final bill is that Senator Manchin gave a hard no to the elite college giveaway provision. Since Senator Manchin wielded an all-important vote in an evenly divided Senate, the repeal didn't pass.[183] But why were elite colleges even able to get so far? Even without the repeal, why do elite colleges pay so little in taxes?

Senator Schumer isn't the only person that Harvard President Lawrence Bacow went to see in Washington DC that May. Instead, President Bacow also stopped by the Economic Club for a public conversation with local billionaire David Rubenstein.

The conversation was an absolute gem. It highlighted the line of argument that President Bacow made to Senator Schumer and any other lawmakers with a receptive ear.

As private-equity billionaire David Rubenstein and Harvard President Lawrence Bacow made their way on stage, the auditorium at The Economic Club filled up. It was a members-only event. Contextually, membership dues cost at least $2,500 a year, so you can imagine the types of people in attendance. As President Lawrence Bacow sat down, he sat to applause. This was a room that revered him.

Fairly early in the conversation, billionaire David Rubenstein brought up the question of the endowment tax. As David posed, "Now, historically, the endowments were tax-free. You get money from them, and you don't have to pay taxes to the federal government. A number of years ago, some members of Congress thought it would be a good idea to tax the endowments. What was the theory behind why that's a good idea for the country?"[184]

President Bacow was seemingly waiting for this question. He had an answer that was bursting to come out. He responded, "I think this is bad public policy. You know, we're a charitable institution. To put it in context, Harvard this year will pay more in federal tax than General Motors, more in federal tax than Ford, more in federal tax than Chevron." President Bacow took a beat, but he couldn't sit still for long. President Bacow immediately followed up, "there was the view that we lean too far to the left, and the tax was constructed disproportionately to tax institutions in liberal states." In plain English, Lawrence Bacow framed the tax as a culture war measure with no basis in moral or economic reasoning.

The conversation at the Economic Club was interesting because the interviewer, billionaire David Rubenstein, is no stranger to the workings of elite colleges. For one, David Rubenstein serves on the boards of elite universities like UChicago and Harvard. David Rubenstein is also a massive donor to elite universities and has donated over $100 million to Duke alone.[185] For another, David Rubenstein separately spends a lot of time interviewing other wealthy people for The David Rubenstein Show, his Bloomberg Television program. Elite colleges serve as a major talking point on David's show. For example, David Rubenstein often asks people about the schools they graduated from and about the donations they make to those schools. Obviously, David Rubenstein understands these institutions quite well.

Still, despite David Rubenstein's intimate knowledge, he provided no follow-up to President Bacow's argument that the endowment tax was a culture war exercise. Instead, David Rubenstein moved onto other topics like the faculty strength at Harvard and drug use on campus. Why did he do that? Is there no substantive case for the endowment tax? Let's go back in time to find out.

In 2016, I was a senior in high school. It was an electric year. The autumn of college anxiety soon blossomed into a spring of academic sabbatical. With college admissions wrapped up, my entire senior class shifted its attention to a more vicarious topic. That topic was the Presidential election of 2016.

We were fairly convinced of the outcome. Everyone at my high school seemed to think that Democratic nominee Hillary Clinton had the election won. Every poll I read only increasingly confirmed that belief. Almost everyone in my neighborhood in suburban Virginia was planning on voting for Hillary Clinton. The vast majority of my high school teachers leaned Democratic. So, why would I, or anyone else, have any reason to think that Trump had a chance?

As we got closer to election day, my confidence in the prevailing consensus only grew. In the fall of 2016, I moved into my dorm at Georgetown. At Georgetown, virtually everyone I talked to increasingly confirmed my prior beliefs. We didn't pay much attention to the specific arguments laid forth by the Trump campaign. Safely ensconced in our bubble, why would we?

To be fair to us, Republican nominee Donald Trump didn't make it easy to follow his campaign. His speeches were disorganized. His arguments were often personally motivated and chaotic. It was hard to decipher the signal in all his noise. Accordingly, most liberals just stopped trying to decipher him. Generally, many journalists stopped paying close attention to his substantive arguments because it was easier to condemn his style. This response was to the ultimate detriment of the Democratic party. Because of this attitude, one of the substantive Trump arguments that most liberals missed was his critique of elite colleges. As it turns out, even a broken clock can be right twice a day.

It was September 2016. Republican nominee Trump stepped on stage at a rally in the all-important state of Pennsylvania. If Trump wanted to win the Presidential election, he had to win this state. The clock was ticking. Virtually every poll showed Hillary Clinton winning the state mostly because of her strength in Philadelphia and its surrounding suburbs. So, when Trump stepped on stage, he needed to project beyond the audience and into the broader public. He needed votes desperately.

Trump's broader campaign theme in 2016 was that the American taxpayer was getting ripped off. That was his critique of NATO. That was his critique of the forever wars in the Middle East. That was his critique of environmental policy. But suddenly, Trump applied that same theme to an unsuspecting target—the elite colleges. At that rally in Pennsylvania, Trump complained, "These huge multibillion-dollar endowments are tax-free, but too many universities don't use the money to help with tuition and student debt."[186] The public responded with a roar. Trump went on, "Instead, they use the money to pay administrators or put donors' names on buildings."

It was ironic that Trump was willing to make this argument. As we explored in an earlier chapter, Trump's own son-in-law, Jared Kushner, was accepted at Harvard largely because Jared's family donated millions of dollars. Further, all of Trump's children went to either Penn or Georgetown, sometimes both. Trump himself graduated from Penn. Elite Ivy League degrees were customary for the Trump family. Why hadn't any of this criticism come out before?

Still, valid criticism is always better late than never, and on this issue of elite college endowments, Trump was right. As Trump was swept into office in a political upset, he turned these campaign critiques into substantive policy changes. In 2017, President Trump's wide-ranging tax bill included a provision that taxed the endowment gains at only the wealthiest elite colleges. I disagree with almost everything else in that tax bill, but the right policy was implemented on this issue of endowment taxes. Obviously, elite colleges fought it all the way, but the Republican Congress wouldn't budge. The tax made it into the signed bill. In 2017, the Tax Cuts and Jobs Act became law.

So, was President Lawrence Bacow right when he said that the endowment tax only passed because of culture war considerations? He probably is. I'm sure Republicans enacted the tax because they don't like the liberal lean of the faculty and administrations at elite colleges. Yet, that has nothing to do with whether the endowment tax is a good policy. After all, legislation passes all the time for bad reasons. But the real question we ought to ask is this: regardless of why it passed, is the endowment tax a good policy?

Of course, prior to 2018, there was no tax levied on endowments. So, what happened in all the many decades preceding? Why did we need a tax? In the preceding decades, endowments grew completely tax-free. From 1996 to 2007, endowments at the top 5 percent of research universities grew at an average rate of 30 percent![187] During that time, elite colleges went from colleges with hedge funds to hedge funds with colleges. In 1994, Columbia had an endowment of approximately $2 billion. In 2021, that endowment had grown to approximately $14.4 billion. In 1994, Duke had an endowment of $699 million. In 2021, Duke's endowment totaled $12.7 billion. This is the story across the industry.

All that concentration of resources has gone to a narrower band of already wealthy students. In the chapter on artificial scarcity, we explored how undergraduate enrollment has been stagnant at elite colleges. In the diversity paradox, we explored how admissions are fundamentally biased to privilege the wealthy. Well, when you add those two trends together, a dark picture emerges. As University of California professor Charlie Eaton quantifies: "private institutions in the 99th percentile for endowment wealth per student increased their annual spending per student from endowments by 751 percent from $9,724 in 1977 to $92,736 in 2012. At the same time, these wealthiest schools have kept flat the overall number of undergraduates and the share of undergraduates from low-income households." There's more money than ever before. Proportionally less of it goes to those who need it most. The endowments are doing nothing for social mobility in America. They might actively be harming it.

Of course, one of the broader theses of this book is that it doesn't make sense to think of elite colleges as an association of charities anymore. The only frame that makes sense is that of a cartel. The question emerges, why do we directly subsidize a cartel? If we're not going to break up the cartel, then why aren't we taxing its gains?

The tax-free status that elite colleges have so fiercely lobbied to protect for all these years has amounted to a massive subsidy for the colleges. In a study on the topic, Charlie Eaton found that in 2012 alone, the tax exemptions amounted to a $19.6 billion subsidy. As gains have grown, that subsidy has only gotten larger. What are we getting in return for the tens of billions of dollars that elite colleges get in tax-exempt status? Is social mobility increasing? Are more students getting a world-class education?

This subsidy gravy train is the backdrop which incentivized an endowment tax to be enacted. The specific structure of the endowment tax was also meant to tackle the problem of artificial scarcity. After all, the tax only kicked in for endowments that were worth more than $500,000 per full-time student. Therefore, if you wanted to avoid the tax, you could always enroll more students. Unfortunately, elite colleges haven't done that. Instead, they've ponied up the tax money for a few years and spent a lot of resources lobbying Congress to get rid of it forever.

All of this leads me to believe that the tax rate of 1.4 percent is too low. The problem with the endowment tax isn't that it exists. The problem with the endowment tax is that it doesn't go far enough. If the tax rate was jacked up, the government could impose enough of a cost on artificial scarcity that schools would voluntarily break the seat cartel. This is an idea we explore in a later chapter.

Of course, tax exemptions aren't the only subsidy that elite colleges reap. Instead, they also get outright subsidies. To understand a few of the largest, let's travel back to 1987. On February

18th of 1987, President Reagan's Secretary of Education William Bennet penned an op-ed in The New York Times titled Our Greedy Colleges.[188] His central argument was a controversial one, especially at that time. Essentially, the common narrative for why college tuition was getting more expensive in the 1980s was that the government was not doing enough to subsidize costs. In his op-ed, William Bennet came out swinging against that narrative. His explanation was simpler. According to Secretary Bennet, the colleges were too greedy.

When Yale's president complained that the government wasn't giving Yale enough subsidies, Bennet directly refuted Yale's facts in his Op-Ed. As he wrote: "This assertion flies in the face of the facts. Since 1982, money available through Federal student aid programs has increased every single year. Overall, Federal outlays for student aid have been up 57 percent since 1980. Since 1980, inflation has been just 26 percent."

Then, Secretary Bennet wrote something that shocked the education world. To quote him exactly: "If anything, increases in financial aid in recent years have enabled colleges and universities blithely to raise their tuitions, confident that Federal loan subsidies would help cushion the increase. In 1978, subsidies became available to a greatly expanded number of students. In 1980, college tuitions began rising year after year at a rate that exceeded inflation."

Bennet's op-ed created heated controversy in academic circles. His thesis that college was becoming more expensive because of subsidies became hotly debated on campuses around the country. Many decades later, what do we think now? Was he right?

Secretary Bennet was partly right. But Secretary Bennet missed an important part of the story. He completely ignored the role of market power and how market power can influence precisely how much aid and credit an institution can capture. As a result, Secretary Bennet generalized the lessons applicable to a handful of elite schools to the broader college system. This book supports a sharper but narrower version of his argument. My thesis is that colleges with market power deliberately raise prices or decrease their own aid when their students receive expanded credit and federal financial aid. In doing so, these elite colleges expose themselves as greedy beyond belief.

This issue of elite colleges capturing federal help for the needy doesn't get nearly enough attention. Part of the reason is that the economists who study the linkage between aid and tuition use jargon like "tax incidence" to describe what elite colleges are doing. I won't make the same mistake of using confusing and soft language. Let's call it what it is. Elite colleges are stealing money from students who have very little. Increasing tuition, or decreasing institutional aid, to capture federal credit or aid is subsidy cannibalism.

In studying the greed of elite colleges, we can first start with the cannibalism of the Pell Grant program. The Pell Grant is a program meant to give money to the neediest students. Pell Grants are direct subsidies to poor kids in the form of grants to pay for college tuition. In 2011, the Pell Grant program gave 9.5 million low-income students grants worth over $35 billion.[189] The Pell Grant has been incredibly popular politically. This is why the maximum Pell Grant award went from $1400 in 1975 to $5,775 in 2011. In 2023, the maximum Pell Grant award was raised again to $7,395.[190] Yet, during this time, the purchasing power of the Pell Grant has declined, particularly at many elite colleges. At many of these elite schools, the college has captured more and more of the Pell Grant, so let's explore how exactly they do that.

A lot of this story has to do with who has access to what information and when. Part of this story starts in 1992. That year, the same year Ivy Overlap colleges were being sued by the DOJ for price-fixing, Congress created a form called FAFSA to streamline the government financial aid programs. FAFSA stands for Federal Application for Federal Student Aid. The FAFSA form has changed over the years, but when it was first created, students were asked over a hundred questions on the form about topics like their family incomes and assets. The set of questions has since been consolidated to thirty-six. But the main point of FAFSA is that it collects a tremendous amount of information, fact-checks it against government records, and then gives all that information to colleges you apply to. I was talking to one of my friends at law school about his experience with FAFSA, and he told me something funny. He said, "Filling out the financial aid form taught my family more about our financial situation than we had ever known." Just think about how much information the form must collect for that statement to be semi-plausible.

The original logic behind giving the FAFSA information to colleges was simple. Policy makers hoped that elite colleges could use the FAFSA information to price-discriminate between the rich and poor. Policy makers thought colleges would redistribute wealth towards working and middle-class students by charging the rich more. I guess policy makers got what they wanted. They at least got half of it. Colleges use the FAFSA information to charge more from some students. Whether that money leads to less cost for others is an entirely divergent story. As a study by economist Ian Fillmore concluded: "Of the student surplus they extract by virtue of the FAFSA information, colleges only transfer 22.2 percent to other students."[191] Off the bat, it's clear that FAFSA hasn't always done what it was supposed to.

This information being handed to elite colleges makes an impact in other ways too. As a student, the total amount of financial aid you receive is the financial aid you receive from the government plus the financial aid you receive from the college itself. The financial aid you receive from the college itself is called institutional aid. So, the total price you pay is equal to the sticker price of tuition minus the federal aid you receive and minus the institutional aid you receive. In mathematical form: Amount owed = (Sticker Price) - (Federal Aid) - (Institutional Aid). As you might infer from this formula, colleges can cannibalize the aid you receive if they decrease institutional aid in response to your level of federal aid. Or they can cannibalize your federal aid by increasing their sticker price tuition. Through these two mechanisms, colleges can steal the government subsidy meant for you. Empirically, they do both.

Elite colleges already set sticker prices incredibly high. As a result, their more pernicious practice is cannibalizing your federal aid by reducing their institutional aid in response. However, colleges need two things to cannibalize your government aid by reducing institutional aid. First, they need artificial scarcity. Importantly, without artificial scarcity, if one college raises its price, a student can just go to someone else who won't. However, if a college has market power, you have few reasonable options to turn to in the face of blatantly anti-competitive conduct like cannibalism of aid. Second, to cannibalize Pell Grants, colleges need information. They need to know exactly how much you can afford. Plus, they need to know exactly how much government aid you receive. Unfortunately, elite colleges have access to both prerequisites. They have artificial scarcity, and they have access to your financial information.

One of the reasons students don't realize that elite colleges are cannibalizing their outside aid is that they have access to very little information, while elite colleges have access to a lot of information. Plus, very weirdly, elite colleges get to give you a price quote at the very end of the admissions process. As economist Lesley Turner describes in her study on the topic: "a school observes the student's FAFSA, EFC, and outside aid before deciding the level of its own discount, which it provides via institutional aid. Students receive a financial aid package from each school specifying federal, state, and institutional grant aid and loans. Students do not observe their Pell Grant award until this point, where it is included as a component of the final price displayed in their financial aid package."[192]

Allowing the college to see exactly how much aid is being doled out to any given student before letting the college decide how much that college will provide in institutional aid is a rigged game. Elite colleges know how much aid the government gives a student, and then they can skimp out on their fair share. Of course, the potential for theft doesn't always result in theft. I often leave my gym bag in a gym locker without locking it. There is potential for theft. Yet, to date, I've never once lost something at the gym. Unfortunately, in the case of elite colleges, the potential for cannibalism is often taken full advantage of.

In fact, economist Lesley Turner estimated in 2012 that selective non-profit institutions cannibalize 79 percent of their students' Pell Grants. Imagine that. For each dollar the government gives to low-income students to go to elite colleges, only 21 cents make it to those kids. It is an unbelievable statistic. This type of cannibalism is pure class war. Importantly, this cannibalism doesn't occur at less elite colleges with far less market power. Lesley Turner's study found that non-elite public colleges didn't cannibalize Pell Grants in the same way. Essentially, the elite colleges with the billion-dollar endowments steal eighty percent of the aid meant for the neediest, while far less wealthy public schools don't. It's an absolute scandal.

This type of cannibalism is possible because of the extreme market power concentrated in elite colleges. Take away their market power through competition, and they won't be able to price discriminate in this way. This is one of the reasons we need to break artificial scarcity at elite colleges.

I want to add a caveat to this point about Pell Grant cannibalism. While I've been quite critical of schools like Princeton, Harvard, and Yale throughout this book, Pell Grant cannibalism is a practice they refrain from. Instead, some of the wealthiest schools where endowments are solidly in the tens of billions give most or all Pell Grant students full scholarships. At these schools, the issue isn't that they charge too much for Pell Grant students. Their issue is that they don't accept enough such students. Further, just because the wealthiest schools refrain from Pell Grant cannibalism doesn't stop them from cannibalizing other types of government aid.

The elite schools who do practice Pell Grant cannibalism are the schools that want to catch up on their endowments. Schools like Georgetown and NYU have smaller endowments compared to their peers. These are the schools that are trying everything they can to catch up. That "everything" includes cannibalism of Pell Grants.

Of course, this type of subsidy cannibalism doesn't just happen on Pell Grants. Instead, any direct subsidy to students, such as tuition tax credits, can be exploited the same way the Pell Grant subsidy is exploited. No one really talks about it, but tuition tax credits for middle-class and upper-middle-class families are huge aid programs. In fact, tuition tax credits give students over $20 billion dollars in annual aid.[193] The issue is that the elite colleges cannibalize that aid the exact same way they might cannibalize Pell Grants. After all, the FAFSA forms give elite colleges all the information they need to know who is going to qualify for tuition tax credits and who isn't. They adjust the pricing accordingly.

Beyond Pell Grants and Tuition Tax Credits, the federal government also provides subsidized loans. These subsidized loans are loans with favorable interest rates and deferred payments. Those loan benefits can be thought of as a subsidy, just like the Pell Grant or the tuition tax credits. Importantly, because of the information colleges have, colleges can easily identify whether an applicant will receive subsidized loans. Further, just as colleges can decrease their own institutional aid and increase their own sticker prices in response to increased aid from other sources, they can do the same with regard to subsidies in the form of subsidized loans. Empirically, this is what colleges have done. A study conducted by the Federal Reserve Bank of New York found that whenever subsidized loan maximums went up by a dollar, colleges raised prices by sixty cents.[194] Elite colleges, with more market power, captured even more than sixty cents on the dollar.

On all these subsidy programs meant for students, the story is basically the same. The public does its job. A tremendous amount of money is spent, but in the elite college market, the schools end up capturing most of it. The question is, why haven't we stopped them?

One reason might be the extreme control elite colleges exercise on Congress. Harvard routinely spent over half a million dollars lobbying each year.[195] The other Ivy League schools aren't far behind. According to Open Secrets, the higher education lobby spent an aggregate of $86 million lobbying in 2021.[196] That, of course, completely ignores the big campaign donations made by the trustees and alumni of these schools. It ignores the revolving door between elite colleges and top jobs in administrations. The simple fact is that elite colleges have successfully captured the federal government. This is why the endowment tax is so slight, why FAFSA is how it is, why artificial scarcity isn't attacked, why antitrust exemptions are passed, and why elite colleges can cannibalize subsidies meant for students. If we want to break the college cartel, we must break its grip on Congress.

CHAPTER 9

CONTAGION

When the movie King Kong first came out in 1933, it was an absolute sensation. For those who haven't seen it, the basic story is that a giant ape, the last of his species, is found by a film crew who are shooting a film on this ape's distant and exotic island. While filming, the crew decides to capture Kong and bring him back to New York City to show him to the world. Yet, on his arrival in New York, King Kong, the giant ape, escapes and climbs to the top of the Empire State Building. At this point, fighter jets are scrambled to shoot him down. The fighter jets eventually succeed, and the film ends on the melancholy note of King Kong's death.

Perhaps the most striking scene of the entire movie is when Kong first reaches the top of the Empire State Building. Having ascended to the top, he now must fight off fighter jets sent to dislodge him. In doing so, Kong begins to destabilize the very structure on which he is perched. That scene of Kong destabilizing the structure can be interpreted as a metaphor. Just like Kong, the elite schools are perched atop a larger structure. Just like Kong, elite schools have to fight off those who are trying to dislodge them. Just like Kong, the way they go about it is deeply destabilizing to the entire structure which supports them. The metaphoric implication is that one of the ways to stabilize the higher education structure is to reduce the destructive power of the beast atop it.

Framed differently, we've spent some chapters of this book talking about how the broader higher education system doesn't exert much competitive influence on the college cartel, and this is true. However, this does not mean that the college cartel doesn't exert influence on the broader higher education system. In fact, the college cartel exerts tremendous influence on the schools below it in the prestige hierarchy. It distorts these less prestigious colleges in terrible ways, and this knock-on effect might be the most objectionable and harmful aspect of the elite college cartel.

For context, it's important to note that only 2.7 percent of undergraduates in America attend selective private colleges.[197] Instead, four times as many students attend public flagship universities as attend selective private colleges. Even more broadly, roughly 79 percent of undergraduates attend public colleges across all levels of prestige. This distribution of students means that when the elite college cartel distorts the incentives of the less prestigious schools below it, an astonishingly greater scope of students is affected.

Just as the 2008 financial crisis began in a small circle of elite financial institutions but ended up destabilizing the broader economy and impacting people entirely disconnected from Wall Street, so too does the elite college cartel destabilize the broader higher education sector. Specifically, the elite college cartel destabilizes less prestigious colleges in three main ways. First, through its cultural control over the acceptance of a rankings regime in higher education, the elite college cartel applies ranking pressure on less elite colleges. Second, through anticompetition, the elite college cartel exerts a tremendous amount of market pressure on the less elite colleges. Third, through the elite college cartel's control of the federal government, policies are enacted that have massive implications for other schools. Through this combination of rankings pressure, market pressure, and regulatory capture, less-elite colleges have increasingly become corrupted with the same squeeze and spend pathology which prevails at the elite schools. As a result, the elite colleges are destabilizing the elite market and the broader superstructure of higher education on which they are perched. I call this the King Kong theory. We can see one aspect of the King Kong theory in action by examining the life of one of this country's former Presidents.

Lyndon Johnson had a financially challenging childhood, and so did most of the people around him. Part of it had to do with geography. Another part of it had to do with the era in which he lived. Born in 1908, Lyndon Johnson grew up in the Texas Hill Country, and when Lyndon Johnson was a boy, the Texas Hill Country was ravished with poverty. The area didn't yet have electrification. It didn't have much plumbing. It didn't even have well-made roads. Sadly, the Texas Hill Country of Lyndon Johnson's childhood was underdeveloped and tough. The people who lived there were quite poor. After all, agriculture was one of the area's main industries, and agriculture was notoriously difficult in the water-poor Hill Country.

Nevertheless, American pioneers made a go at life in the Hill Country. They faced poverty with sheer will. If you weren't willing to work exceptionally hard in the Hill Country, you couldn't survive there. Yet, plenty of people survived. Indeed, they grew strong. Some of them, like young Lyndon Johnson, even grew ambitious.

Early in his childhood, Lyndon Johnson decided that his life would be grander and more prosperous than that of the average Hill Country resident. Years later, Lyndon Johnson would recall, "When I was fourteen years old, I decided I was not going to be the victim of a system which would allow the price of a commodity like cotton to drop from forty cents to six cents and destroy the homes of people like my own family."[198] Instead, Lyndon's eventual plan was to work his way through college. College was both his way out and his way up. Accordingly, in 1927, Lyndon Johnson enrolled at Southwest Texas State Teachers College in San Marcos, a public college.

Yet, misfortune soon struck Lyndon Johnson. After completing his freshman year, Lyndon ran out of money. He couldn't afford his tuition for the next year. As a result, Lyndon was forced to temporarily drop out to support himself. Still, he hoped he might one day reenter the college. For now, he needed a job. Thankfully, he found one.

In his gap year, Lyndon Johnson became a teacher at an under-resourced school in Cotulla, Texas. The children at this school were mostly Mexican immigrants, and few people seemed to care about them. There were only five other teachers at this school, all of them Cotulla housewives who skimped on any extra duties.[199] But Lyndon wasn't like these other teachers. Lyndon never skimped. Instead, Lyndon Johnson took everything he learned during his first year at college and transmitted it right back to the students he was now teaching. As Lyndon later described in a speech, "I often walked home late in the afternoon, after the classes were finished, wishing there was more that I could do. But all I knew was to teach them the little that

I knew, hoping that it might help them against the hardships that lay ahead. And somehow, you never forget what poverty and hatred can do when you see its scars on the hopeful face of a young child."[200]

Lyndon Johnson changed the lives of some of the children at that school. He made them believe that they could become something through grit and will. Coaching the debate team, Lyndon helped some students at the school become expert debaters. These debaters even won statewide competitions. Perhaps most revealingly, Lyndon even taught people who weren't students. For example, Lyndon would often sit on the steps of the school to teach the janitor English in his free time. Lyndon was one of the few people who actually made a difference in the poverty-stricken Cotulla. When his year of teaching came to a close, fortune smiled on him once again.

In his year in Cotulla, Lyndon Johnson stabilized his finances and was able to reenter Southwest Texas State Teachers College in San Marcos. Back at school, Lyndon rushed through his coursework and graduated in 1930. He might not have known it then, but completing his education at a public college changed the course of his career.

Importantly, whatever impact college had on Lyndon's life trajectory, it was not because Lyndon's degree served as some hyper-prestigious credential. Maybe, the degree had some limited signaling benefits, but the overwhelming value of Lyndon's college education came from the specific and substantive skills he developed during his time at San Marcos. The real value came from his trips to the Texas Legislature with the President of the college. The real value came from his experience as the chief editor of the college newspaper. The real value came from his experiences in organizing campus politics. The real value came from his opportunity to teach what he had learned to students in Cotulla. Importantly, all these experiences were affordable. Lyndon Johnson paid yearly tuition that totaled hundreds of dollars. Even adjusted for inflation, Lyndon Johnson spent a fraction of what a student today would spend on even just one semester at an elite private college.

Lyndon Johnson later ascended to Congress, became a Senator, and was even elected President. Public education was an engine of social mobility for Lyndon Johnson, and Lyndon Johnson became an engine of social mobility for the nation. He gave back to the country at many points in his life. He gave back as a public-school teacher in Cotulla. He gave back as a Congressman who brought electrification to the Texas Hill Country. He gave back as a Senator who passed critical legislation that moved the country forward. He gave back as President when he developed the most substantive record of policy accomplishments since FDR. There's a lesson we ought to learn from this story.

It might seem obvious, but we obviously want as many Lyndon Johnsons as possible to take up education, as affordably as possible, at our state-funded public colleges. We want every school filled to the brim with ambitious, smart, hardworking young people. We want these students to develop substantive skills as cheaply as possible. Yet increasingly that isn't happening. Instead, because of the rankings regime that elite colleges have empowered, the admissions incentives have become completely warped at public colleges.

Furthermore, because of the artificial scarcity of elite seats, more and more spoiled rich kids are trickling into public colleges instead, taking away seats from ambitious but poor or middle-class students. In fact, basically, everyone but the next Lyndon Johnson is increasingly inhabiting our best public universities. As a result, social mobility in America is fading away. To see how far we've strayed, we need only explore a recent anecdote from the University of Michigan.

In 2018, the student government at the University of Michigan had a clever idea to put out a guide about "cost-effective" living.[201] The student government probably had the right intentions. After all, the cost of living at public colleges has drastically increased. Yet, almost as soon as the guide was published, it became a campus-wide joke. It's easy to see why. After all, the guide included suggestions like not doing a weekly manicure and doing one's own laundry instead of hiring a service or maid. The guide was totally out of touch. Clearly, so was every student in student government who read and approved the guide. The gilded guide was a massive indictment of Michigan. The whole episode was incredibly cringe.

Most of the students at Michigan made their jokes and moved on, but two students went beyond laughs when they read the clueless guide. After reading it, students Lauren Schandevel and Griffin St. Onge decided to do something. These two students decided to speak up for a silent demographic at the University of Michigan. That demographic was working-class students. Accordingly, Lauren and Griffin took it upon themselves to write a 115-page document titled Being Not Rich at UM- A Guide.[202]

The document offered practical advice to lower and middle-income children on how to adapt to life on campus. In an interview with NPR, Lauren explained what motivated her to write it: "I had been warned about it a little bit, but I had never met the kind of wealth that some of the students have here by the time I came to university." Similar guides have popped up in recent years at the University of Texas at Austin, University of Georgia, University of San Francisco, University of Iowa, and many others. What does it tell you about the demographics at our flagship public colleges that these guides are both so necessary and also so subversive? What does it tell us that the guides are framed in the negative as if being rich was supposed to be the default at public colleges? Why isn't being working class more common at our flagship public colleges? Where have all the Lyndon Johnsons gone?

The broad thesis of this chapter is that the elite college cartel has played a large role in distorting public colleges. However, that narrative isn't the whole story. Instead, our tragedy has many villains. Yes, elite colleges are destabilizing public colleges, but they aren't the only ones. Part of it is the fault of state legislators too. To understand how state legislators have completely fumbled policy, we actually have to go back to the Great Financial Crisis of 2008.

By September 2008, the American economy was in total collapse. President George Bush, in his final months, was increasingly fearing a Great Depression. The economic damage would be generational if the federal government didn't do something. In essence, a Wall Street dominated by a small number of big banks had given the American public only two options: bailout or murder-suicide. While a bailout was deeply unfair, President Bush decided he couldn't choose the second option. In a race against time, the Bush administration asked Congress to approve hundreds of billions of dollars in government spending meant to counteract the financial meltdown.

Although the Bush administration threw its weight behind a bailout, the Republicans in Congress were a tough sell. They saw this bailout as socialism. Accordingly, if the bailout was going to pass in Congress, it would need heavy Democratic support. Without the Democrats, the financial markets would melt. Credit would freeze. Banks would fail. Unemployment would spike. In short, the banks had become "too big to fail." Therefore, President Bush, and the whole country, needed Democratic votes.

To get it, President Bush deployed his Treasury secretary, Hank Paulson, to convince key Democrats to support a bailout. Essentially, it was Hank Paulson's job to get House Speaker Nancy Pelosi on board. Her support was critical, and Hank Paulson was determined to get it. At one meeting in late September, Hank Paulson got on one knee to beg. He literally begged Speaker Pelosi not to "blow it up," referring to a bailout deal. To see a cabinet secretary on the floor begging was something Speaker Pelosi had never seen before. She was shocked. Yet, she kept her cool. To diffuse the tension in the room, Speaker Pelosi responded, "I didn't know you were Catholic."[203] It was a joke meant to poke fun at Hank Paulson's kneeling.

In the end, a bailout happened. Democrats voted with the Bush administration. Plus, when President Obama was swept into office, more bailouts were authorized. Yet, no amount of government spending could undo the deep damage the big banks had inflicted on the American people. Perhaps the bailouts helped us avoid a Great Depression, but the economy still went into a Great Recession. Tax revenues collapsed at both the federal and state level.

With busted state budgets post-2008, governors and state legislators needed to cut costs desperately. Public universities were the easiest target. State legislators deserve blame because state governments have quasi-privatized their public colleges in the last decades. Policymakers were savage, and once they made cuts, the funding almost never came back. While less state funding has been a long-term trend, the fatal trigger-pull came in 2008. Empirically, in 2018, states spent an average of 13 percent less per student on higher education than they did in 2008. In some states, like Pennsylvania and Arizona, per-student spending fell by more than 30 percent in this period.[204] The long-term drawdown in state funding caused a massive shock to the system.

Put yourself in the role of a university president. What would you do if your budget was getting slashed? Would you fire people? Would you downscale? What do you think your trustees would want you to do? I'm not sure what you would have done, but I do know what happened. Public colleges became increasingly desperate for revenue. Therefore, they became hypersensitive to market incentives. They changed.

Throughout this book, we've explored exactly what the market incentives in higher education are. We've explored how students want prestigious signals for the job market. We've previously concluded that US News' rankings regime allocates prestige only to very rejective colleges that spend as much as possible. Therefore, we've already established that the market incentives are always to maximize recruitment of rich students, those students who can pay a lot in tuition and donations and reject most other students.

In cutting state funding, lawmakers have fundamentally changed the incentive structure of public colleges. Today, public college administrators increasingly go after wealthier but less impressive applicants, those students who can pay more in tuition but who can't get into the most elite colleges anymore. Instead of enrolling more students who resemble Lyndon Johnson, public colleges today want more students who resemble George Bush. For example, let's explore an embarrassing admissions scandal at UVa.

In 2017, author Jeff Thomas filed a Freedom of Information Act request for access to documents pertaining to admissions decisions from the University of Virginia's advancement office.[205] The advancement office at the University kept a "watch list" of wealthy alumni and donors. That "watch list" was routinely used to pressure the admissions office. Quite clearly, the University of Virginia would have preferred to keep this a secret, but under legal scrutiny, they had to cave. Grudgingly, the University of Virginia handed the files over, although the files that were received were significantly redacted. Even so, Jeff Thomas had accidentally uncovered a goldmine. He soon handed the documents over to The Washington Post, which made the documents publicly available.

There's too much juicy content in the files to cover, so instead, I'll just give you a taste. In the 2011 admissions list, one applicant was initially marked as denied. Then an advancement officer wrote "$500k" next to his name. Suddenly, "must be on WL" and "if at all possible A" appeared on the file. It is unclear who the student is, but we can all guess what the final decision was. This was at the University of Virginia, a school partly funded with taxpayer money. Yet somehow stories like this aren't even surprising anymore.

It's almost common knowledge that public colleges are increasingly motivated by the same desperation for resources that characterize private colleges. What's less well understood is how elite private colleges have infected them with that desperation. That's the story of contagion.

Administrators at elite colleges might push back on this point. How is it Harvard's fault that UVa wants to get in on the action? Why should Stanford be held responsible for Michigan's greed? It might seem counterintuitive to blame elite private colleges for decisions made by lawmakers and state governments. I sympathize with that view. Certainly, other actors like state governments are also to blame. However, a big part of the blame also must go to elite colleges.

Blame must go to elite colleges because while public colleges are independently responding to market incentives, not all those market incentives are natural. Those incentives didn't all just emerge from the sky as an act of God. Instead, many market incentives are a crown of thorns pressed upon public colleges by the elite colleges higher on the prestige ladder. Specifically, the way prestige is allocated by the rankings regime, and the glut of wealthy students applying to public colleges are both the fault of elite colleges. Two all-powerful trends of the last few decades, more exposure to rankings pressure in the public college market and increasing artificial scarcity in the elite market, have created a deeply toxic combination.

After all, it was the elite colleges that have lifted up US News' rankings into the dominance it now enjoys. It was the elite colleges that lobbied to kill President Obama's college scorecard effort. It is the elite colleges that continue to participate in a hub and spoke cartel. Intentional or not, the collusive hub that elite colleges have empowered has externalities on all colleges, not just elite ones. In legitimizing US News' rankings, elite colleges have condemned not only themselves to competing on that particular rankings criteria but also the rest of the college market. This is mostly the fault of elite private colleges alone.

In the fall of 2016, I remember getting a phone call from a friend from high school. My friends had just settled in at the University of Illinois, and I was settling into life at Georgetown. As we chatted on the phone, I went for a walk around campus. Naturally, we started talking about our experiences at our respective colleges. Soon, the conver-sation turned to demographics. I asked him what the students at the University of Illinois were like. He then said something that shocked me. My friend explained to me that a drastically large proportion of the class was composed of international students, largely from Asia. I remember thinking that was odd but made nothing of it until I started researching this book.

Apparently, in 2017, 22.6 percent of the student body at the University of Illinois Urbana-Champaign was made up of international students.[206] That number was almost one in four. There is actually a simple economic logic as to why that number is so high. It isn't just random. Instead, while state governments often regulate and cap prices for in-state students, they let the colleges charge as much as they can for out-of-state or international students. In practice, out-of-state students tend to pay 2 or 3 times as much as in-state students.[207] Therefore, from a financial point of view, international students and out-of-state students are the ones you want to increase your revenues.

If the total amount of enrollment increased enough so that these richer out-of-state students didn't take spots from hard-working and ambitious local students, there would be no problem with more out-of-state students. But this is not what has happened. Instead, out-of-state students have largely displaced hard-working and ambitious local students. One study on the topic found that of all the growth in seats at flagship public universities from 2012 to 2015, more than 57 percent of new seats went to out-of-state students instead of in-state students. Campuses like the University of Michigan, UC Berkeley, or UVa are flush with international students. Accordingly, there are far fewer Lyndon Johnsons at those types of flagship public schools today than there should be.

Maybe the argument that we should have more American students at American public colleges strikes you as xenophobic. I certainly don't mean it that way. My own parents are immigrants to this country. I would never support slamming the door in the face of someone who has something positive to contribute to America, but there shouldn't be a tradeoff. If more seats are made available to everyone, we can accommodate more international students and domestic students. This isn't what public colleges have done. Instead, public colleges have tried to maximize stats like spending per student to climb the rankings. As a result, they've displaced poor local students with rich global ones. It's wrong. What's worse is that no one is holding the public colleges accountable for it. Instead, the main critique of colleges seems to be cultural. Recently, we've best seen this broken dynamic most obviously play out in Florida.

In April of 2022, Governor Ron DeSantis of Florida ushered in a law titled the Stop WOKE Act.[208] The basic rationale of the law was to ban things like diversity training sessions which can cause "psychological distress". The law itself is only one of many fronts on which Governor DeSantis has litigated a culture war. It is a culture war that is seemingly never-ending, and increasingly Governor DeSantis' culture war is being waged against the state's public universities, the professors who work there, and the students who study there. Let's explore one example from the University of South Florida.

Sam Rechek isn't your normal student. For one, Sam Rechek wants to be known as the "free speech guy." Presently a student at the University of South Florida, Sam Rechek is a prominent campus leader. One example of his leadership is that Sam recently founded a student organization called the First Amendment Forum. His goal with the organization was simple. Essentially, the mission of The First Amendment Forum is to promote free speech and debate on campus. It's a mission that has put Sam

Rechek on the warpath with Governor DeSantis. Indeed, Sam feels that the Governor wants to suppress speech with legislation like the Stop WOKE Act. This is why Sam recently sued the state of Florida.

The genesis of the lawsuit is intriguing. To protect free speech, Sam teamed up with a history professor at the University of South Florida. That professor, Adriana Novoa, teaches at least three courses which are affected by the Stop WOKE Act. If the law is enforced, Professor Novoa will be forced to change her syllabus to avoid certain ideas and topics. Professor Novoa doesn't want to do that. This is why she and Sam have filed a pending lawsuit against the Stop WOKE Act. Their basic argument is that the legislation is a violation of the Constitutionally protected right to free speech. As Professor Novoa recently said in an interview, "I know indoctrination. I've seen indoctrination. And indoctrination isn't coming from my classroom—it's coming from a law intended to limit the freedom to think and express these thoughts, which is the foundation of a good education."

While I wish Sam and Professor Novoa the best, the legal battles around the Stop WOKE Act aren't directly relevant to this book. Instead, I'm bringing up the fight between Governor DeSantis, Sam Rechek, and Professor Novoa as negative proof. Florida's governor is about as critical of institutions of higher education as anyone in the country. He almost sees himself in opposition to the universities. If anyone is going to bring up much-needed critiques of public colleges, it's him. Therefore, I want you to ask the question: what's missing from this picture? What is Governor DeSantis not saying that he should be?

In September of 2022, around the same time, Sam and Professor Novoa's free speech lawsuit was making the news, the University of South Florida was in the news for another reason too. When the University of South Florida climbed in US News' newest ranking, the President of the University, a woman named Rhea Law, gave a nice and long statement. As President Rhea Law confidently proclaimed, "The University of South Florida is proud to achieve our highest-ever position in U.S. News & World Report's rankings and to once again be recognized as America's fastest-rising university."[209] Excitedly, President Rhea didn't stop there. Instead, she continued her ode to the rankings when she said, "USF's standing in the rankings is a testament to the hard work and success of our faculty, staff and students, who make an impact in our communities every day. We will continue to help shape the future for our society as we pursue our goal of becoming a top-25 public university."

When I first read President Rhea Law's statement, I immediately went to Google to see what Governor DeSantis had to say in response. I expected him to critique using US News' ranking regime as a north star, even if on cultural grounds. Instead, what I found was deeply disappointing. Around the same time as President Law's statement, Governor DeSantis said: "Florida schools are some of the best in the nation, and these rankings show that our investments in higher education and our focus on providing an affordable, quality education are paying off."[210] Even worse, Brian Lamb, Governor DeSantis' appointed chair of the Board of Governors for the University of Florida system, said: "The hard work of our Board, university leadership, faculty and students, reflects in the improvement and prominence rankings of all of our state universities released today by the U.S. News and World Report."[211]

Governor DeSantis takes great pride in his ability to win culture wars against opponents of conservative culture. He takes on Disney. He takes on professors. He takes on students.

He takes on Governors from other states. Oftentimes, he wins these culture wars. But, in the case of Governor DeSantis versus elite colleges, Governor DeSantis has totally lost. Essentially, the credibility that elite colleges have given US News over the years has been so powerful that even a notable higher education critic like Governor DeSantis hasn't tried to reevaluate using US News' ranking as a metric to optimize around. Of course, Governor DeSantis isn't alone. At public college after public college, in state after state, blind adherence to US News' ranking is standard practice.

Huey Long, the former Governor of Louisiana, used to tell an anecdote when campaigning. Once upon a time, said Long, there was a traveling salesman who sold two different medicines. One of the medicines was called Low Popahirum. Low Popahirum was made by skinning the bark of a tree from the bottom up. The other medicine was called High Populorum. High Popalorum was made from skinning the bark of the same tree from the top down. As Long finished, "The only difference I've found in Congress between the Republican and Democratic leadership is that one of them is skinning us from the ankle up and the other from the ear down." Can't this same critique be applied to the breadth of American colleges today? Public flagship schools and elite private colleges have become as indistinguishable as Low Popahirum and High Populorum.

So far, we've explored how elite colleges transmitted bad incentives to public colleges through the empowerment of US News' ranking regime. However, this isn't the only way the elite college cartel has distorted other markets. Instead, the artificial scarcity of elite college seats also destabilizes public colleges. We've explored in previous chapters how expensive it has gotten to gain admission into the top elite colleges today. We've seen some people respond to the scarcity with illegal maneuvers like Varsity Blues. We've seen others up the bid price on donations to the various development offices at elite colleges. However, there's a growing number of wealthy kids who just turn to public colleges instead. Again, in desperation for resources, public colleges are only too happy to oblige. A scarcity of seats at the top creates a mismatch where the wrong kids take up seats at the wrong schools. That's how we get something like the completely out-of-touch 2018 University of Michigan guide on affordable living.

If the most private, elite colleges didn't have a hub-and-spoke cartel, the seats at elite colleges would have doubled or tripled since just 1990.[212] As a result, more wealthy international students and out-of-state kids would have gone to those schools, opening more slots for ambitious students at flagship public colleges. Instead, the opposite has happened. The elite colleges have become more rejective. The public colleges have absorbed the leftover loafers. We've observed a crowding out of local talent at public colleges by the global inheritance class.

Of course, the way scarcity at the very top affects public colleges is more subtle than my rather simple description. It's not that Harvard increasing its class size would automatically suck wealthy international students out of the University of South Florida. Instead, the process would be more of a trickle-up. Harvard tripling enrollment would pull students out of Georgetown. Georgetown tripling enrollment would pull students out of George Washington University. George Washington University opening up seats would pull students out of the University of South Florida. A more stable equilibrium would result.

The last area where elite colleges impact public colleges is through control over the federal government. What's particularly important to note is that the elite college cartel seemingly has control over all three branches of government. We can see just how extensive their reach is through an anecdote.

When the class-action price-fixing lawsuit against the seventeen elite colleges was first filed in January of 2022, it hit the elite colleges like a slap in the face. No one had come after elite colleges like this, not since the early 1990s. In fact, the whole reason elite colleges had gone to Congress in the first place was to prevent this from ever happening again. Yet soon confusion turned into focus. The elite colleges lawyered up.

As soon as they were notified of the complaint, the elite colleges called up their fancy big law firms for help. Columbia University called in a partner from Skadden. MIT went with a partner from Freshfields Bruckhaus Deringer, one of the world's oldest law firms. Yet, the University of Pennsylvania out-classed its peers. Penn brought in partner Seth Waxman from Wilmer Hale.

Seth Waxman is interesting because his resume perfectly points in one main direction. That direction is up. Born in 1951 in Connecticut, Seth Waxman first matriculated at Harvard University in 1969. After graduating from Harvard with honors, Seth then won the prestigious Rockefeller Fellowship. After he finished the Rockefeller Fellowship program, Seth finally enrolled at Yale Law School. He again distinguished himself academically and graduated in 1977.

After his schooling, Seth made quite a name for himself in private practice before he then joined the Department of Justice in 1994 during the Clinton administration. At the Department of Justice, Seth Waxman took on more and more responsibility as the years went by. Then the inevitable happened. In 1997, Seth Waxman was appointed by President Clinton to be the 41st Solicitor General of the United States. He stayed in the position until 2001.

Seth Waxman now works at the fancy big law firm Wilmer Hale, and when his client Penn was sued for price-fixing in January of 2022, it was Seth Waxman who stepped in to handle the situation. In fact, when all the fancy lawyers who represented all the various respective schools had to decide who among them would take the lead in arguing a joint motion to dismiss before a Federal District Judge, it was Seth Waxman who was chosen.[213] He was rendered to be the best of the best.

At court, the legal team that Seth Waxman led offered a variety of creative arguments. For example, one argument the defense team tried was that "need-blind" shouldn't be taken at face value because to do so would lead to "absurd" conclusions. While the argument failed to persuade the judge, it was a creative argument nonetheless. It served as only further proof that the elite colleges had the best legal talent in the world on their side.

The broader point is that because of the number of resources elite colleges have, whether the venue is the Judiciary, Congress, or a Presidential Administration, elite colleges have deep access to work those institutions to their advantage. When the venue is the Judiciary, elite colleges walk into court with the former Solicitor General. They walk in with a number of appeals planned. They walk in with every advantage.

When the venue is Congress, the advantage is even deeper. According to Open Secrets, the higher education lobby spent an aggregate of $86 million lobbying in 2021.[214] Dumping those kinds of resources into lobbying Congress clearly makes a difference. For example, in the chapter about price-fixing, we saw how a price-fixing cartel of nine schools expanded into a cartel of seventeen schools once Congress stepped in to protect the original nine. For another, in the chapter about subsidy cannibalism, we saw how FAFSA's design helps elite colleges capture subsidies and tax credits. All these policies that elite colleges push for in Congress end up having massive consequences for the roughly 97 percent of undergraduates who don't attend elite schools. For example, there is some evidence that FAFSA's design helps other less-elite colleges collude on prices too.[215]

When the venue is a Presidential Administration, elite colleges also have deep access. In the chapter about artificial scarcity, we saw how elite colleges lobbied to kill President Obama's ranking reform. More generally, the Department of Education weirdly often makes decisions that clearly benefit the elite colleges. Frankly, it's beyond the scope of this book to examine all the ways in which federal policy distorts incentives at public colleges. Other books and experts can do a far better job of analyzing those things than I can.

Instead, the important point I want to make is that when power is centralized by elite colleges, they use it to capture parts of the federal government. The subsequent policies that emerge from the captured parts of government have implications for the rest of the higher education sector. Through rankings pressure, market pressure, and government capture, elite colleges distort the rest of the market. When we're thinking about the impact of the elite college cartel, we must recognize that it's much wider in scope than one might first think. That's why this is such an urgent problem to solve.

CHAPTER 10

SOLUTIONS

In 2018, two young women named Alex Cooper and Sofia Franklyn launched a podcast. Their podcast, Call Her Daddy, was an immediate hit. Starting from scratch, within two months, Call Her Daddy had two million downloads. By the middle of 2018, virtually every student at Georgetown had become a listener.

Part of the reason Call Her Daddy was so successful was the salaciousness of its content. Essentially, the content of the podcast was "locker room talk" but from a woman's perspective. For context, these are the slightly outrageous titles of some of the earliest Call Her Daddy episodes: You're Just a Hole, Stop Nutting Early Please, and Welcome to Slut Camp. Episode after episode, Alex and Sofia told taboo stories about relationships, sex, and debauchery. Episode after episode, they kept going viral.

Alex and Sofia were cynical on their podcast. The two hosts were often telling stories about people cheating on their partners and also stories about people getting cheated on by their partners. In fact, Call Her Daddy originated a catchphrase: "cheat or be cheated on!" Absurdly, Alex and Sofia would repeat that maxim all the time as they encouraged listeners to cheat first. In fact, Cheat or Be Cheated On was even the title of one of Call Her Daddy's earliest Youtube videos.

Obviously, with messages like "cheat or be cheated on", Alex and Sofia attracted a lot of criticism. Even among their listeners, not everyone got on board with the cheat first message. In fact, if you visit their Youtube video titled Cheat or Be Cheated On, the top comments are mostly salty. As one of the top comments reads: "Don't be a cheater. Be a goddamn grown-up and just break up with your significant other before hooking up with someone else. It's not hard. Don't cheat, just don't."

I think that particular commenter might have missed the joke. Still, you can imagine why that commentator might feel that way. Maybe he or she has been cheated on. Therefore, the depravity of the cheat-first mindset might have reopened an old wound. Nevertheless, that commenter isn't alone. Instead, many of the top comments are equally salty. I remember when I first saw how salty the comments were. I thought to myself: It's just a joke! Why are they taking it so seriously?

Of course, if we analyzed the mantra "cheat or be cheated on" more seriously, we'd quickly realize that it's a logical fallacy. Indeed, "cheat or be cheated on" is a classic example of a false dilemma or a logical error where two options are presented as the only two possibilities. In truth, no one has to really only choose between cheating or being cheated on. There's always that third possibility of not cheating and not being cheated on.

I'm bringing up this clearly irrelevant anecdote about Call Her Daddy to concretely illustrate a more relevant point. Essentially, "cheat or be cheated on" is a whimsical example of a far more dangerous trend. That trend is the proliferation of false dilemmas in the public discourse. Indeed, false dilemmas are increasingly posed to the public, often quite seriously. For example, we're periodically told we can either bail out the banks or collapse the economy. Other times we're told we can either vote for one party or help the other party get elected. Sometimes, we're even told that we must either let in every immigrant or no immigrants at all. Since we're so constantly bombarded by false dilemmas, we frequently forget we have other options.

In the case of elite colleges, there's a new false dilemma brewing. Throughout this book, you've become acquainted with the general sentiment of doing nothing to check the power of elite colleges. We've seen this do-nothing policy time after time on issue after issue, from antitrust exemptions to low endowment taxes. But that do-nothing policy has sparked a potent backlash. Increasingly, there's now a second alternative to do nothing. Unfortunately, that second alternative is on the other extreme. That alternative is destroying the elite colleges. Dangerously, these two options, do-nothing and destroy totally, are being sold as a false dilemma.

For example, in 2021, a Yale student named Caleb Dunson wrote the following in an article published by the Yale Daily News: "Greed and elitism are embedded in Yale's DNA — they are what keep the university running. Its "tax-exempt status" has been in the state constitution since before America's founding. Its labor practices began with_enslaving people and now include union-busting. It started off excluding women and people of color from its student body and now parades them around for diversity photos and social justice brownie points. Changes might be made at the University's margins, but Yale's fundamental nature will, in all likelihood, remain the same. Since we can't change Yale, we have to tear it down."[216]

It's not just Caleb Dunson who feels this way. This broader destructive sentiment is injecting itself into the mainstream. Besiege The Ivy League was a recent headline in the American Prospect.[217] Further, the calls to abolish elite colleges are not limited to the left. I've heard from conservative activists that one policy solution for the decadence at elite colleges is merely seizing their entire endowments. I don't agree.

The public is being sold a false dilemma once more. Essentially, the options are now framed as do-nothing or destroy totally. It's the same fallacy as "cheat or be cheated on." Or, as Caleb Dunson puts it: "since we can't change Yale, we have to tear it down."

I understand the impulse. "Cheat or be cheated on" feels sensible, especially if you've only ever been cheated on in relationships. Similarly, if you've never seen Yale change, maybe tearing it down is the only alternative. But are decay or death our only two options? Is there nothing better?

The people who want to tear down elite colleges tend to believe that there is something inherently wrong with elite colleges. Caleb Dunson seems to believe that the problem of extreme exclusion is seared into Yale's genetic makeup. But what if it's not? What if Yale's environment is the real problem? What if the problem is the way we've nurtured Yale?

The thesis of this book is that the problems with elite colleges aren't inherent. Instead, their problems are structural. The problems we face are not problems of providence or personality. The problems we face are the result of market and political structure. Plainly, our problem is the cartel, not the college. We don't need to kill the bad guy. We need to break the cartel.

In Shakespeare's Julius Caesar, Cassius says to Brutus, "The fault, dear Brutus, is not in our stars, but in ourselves, that we are underlings." Cassius was right. There was nothing inherently better about Caesar. He was a man like any other. What made Caesar powerful was the behavior of the people who surrounded him, men like Cassius and Brutus. What made Caesar truly powerful was the structure of Roman society. Essentially, what allowed Caesar to become powerful was everything but Caesar. Today, we might similarly conclude that the fault is not in our schools; it is in our system. Our problems actually arise from the way we've allowed the elite college market to concentrate and monopolize.

I'm as populist as anyone in either major political party, but we're not a nation in need of demagoguery. We're a nation in need of discipline. We don't need to sack the elite colleges. We need to save them. That's the point of this book. It's a point I feel very strongly about, and I'll tell you a story from my own life that illustrates why I believe it.

It was a random night during the second week of my freshman year at Georgetown. I was in my dorm room playing Xbox with some other kids. I don't remember now, but I might even have been vaping. In other words, it was a classic weekday at college. Suddenly, my roommate handed his controller to someone else. He then got up and told me he was going to a talk by an economics professor. I was engrossed in the video game, but I subconsciously replied, "Nice, who's giving the talk?" My roommate replied, "It's George Akerlof, I think." I paused the Xbox as the other players groaned. I promptly replied, "Wait up, I'm coming."

As we walked to the talk, I asked him why he was going to this talk. He mentioned he needed to go for class credit. He asked why I wanted to go, and I responded, "George Akerlof is a major legend. Haven't you heard about information asymmetry?" Of course, what I was referring to was an economic concept from a paper George Akerlof published in the 1970s. The name of the paper was The Market for Lemons, and decades later, that paper won him a Nobel Prize. Having taken AP Economics courses in high school, I had learned all about Akerlof's contributions to the area of information economics. I was quite excited to meet him.

When we arrived at the classroom where the talk was to take place, I was shocked by how few other people had shown up. It was a room with maybe thirty people in the audience. As Professor Akerlof got up to speak, my roommate and I sat down in a middle row. Shortly, the talk began.

Professor Akerlof's talk was about identity economics. In 2010, he published a book on the subject with Rachel Kranton, an economics professor at Duke University. The thesis of the book flew in the face of common economic assumptions that people were generally rational agents. Instead, Akerlof and Kranton argued that people are actually motivated by protecting their sense of identity. His talk progressed along a similar theme. After he finished, I immediately got up to ask him a question. Afterwards, we took a photo.

The talk had taken place on a Wednesday, but on the Monday that followed, I sent Professor Akerlof an email. I'd been stewing on something Professor Akerlof had mentioned in his talk, and in my email, I asked him if we could chat. He responded quite kindly. He told me he was free the next day. He asked me to stop by. On November 8, 2016, we had our first meeting.

As time went on, I stopped by his office quite a few times. Later in my freshman year, I proposed an experiment to him, which he encouraged me to pursue. When I launched a startup in college, he sat down with me to think about the economics of the business. When I wrote my first book, he was willing to give me a quote for the back of the book. When I started this book, he gave me pointers on which questions to start with. When I applied to law school, he was kind enough to write me a letter of recommendation.

I wanted to include this story in this book because a lot of this book has been critical of elite colleges. I characterize elite colleges as greedy, collusive, and corrupt. I malign the intentions of the boards of trustees and even presidents of most elite colleges. Yet, all of that aside, there is a lot these institutions have to offer to students. I wouldn't have met George Akerlof, but for Georgetown, and although we often go years without speaking, he has had a profound impact on my life both by his example and his advice. Some of my other professors and peers have had just as big an impact. I am different from having met them, and I was lucky to get that chance.

As I hope my relationship with Professor Akerlof demonstrates, elite colleges can foster special opportunities. They can uniquely uplift people, which is why I believe that despite their collusion, there is something to the elite colleges that is worth saving. Despite their corruption, there is something about the elite colleges worth reforming. There is a new ambition buried and burning within the hallowed halls of elite colleges. It's time to let it free.

Undoubtedly, there are things to admire about elite colleges. The faculty is often world-class. One's peers are quite impressive. The entrepreneurial communities are strong. Most importantly, the signaling aspects of the school can be very helpful when offered to the right students.

Take my case as an example. George Akerlof's letter of recommendation, combined with Georgetown's strong reputation, gave me a unique signal which helped me get into Columbia

Law School. Of course, it's not just me who has benefited from elite signals. For another, President Barack Obama benefited from prestigious educational signaling, which helped him overcome racial bias to win the Presidential election in 2008. More generally, prestigious signals empirically increase career earnings and opportunities for students from poor or working-class backgrounds whose parents haven't received a college education. Destroying the elite colleges totally would limit this benefit. Far better would be to offer these benefits to more people.

There's a lot that elite colleges do right. What's wrong with elite colleges isn't everything about them. The critique of this book is far narrower. What's wrong with elite colleges is that they're too expensive, and too few students get in. My argument isn't that we need to destroy elite colleges. My argument is that we need to grow them.

During his Presidential debate with Vice President Nixon in 1960, Senator Kennedy famously observed, "This is a great country, but I think it could be a greater country; and this is a powerful country, but I think it could be a more powerful country." Just because something was good for me doesn't mean it can't be better for others. I had an amazing experience at Georgetown, and I'm having an amazing experience at Columbia Law. But that doesn't make it hypocritical for me to speak up. After all, I just want more students to have the same opportunities I did, for an affordable price. If there's a cartel preventing that, I want to break that cartel. It's really not that radical a vision.

So why haven't these problems been fixed already? If these ideas are so common-sense, why isn't anyone proposing them? My explanation is that part of the reason that this market has gotten so dysfunctional is that, before this book, few others correctly identified the collusive behavior of elite colleges as one that resembles that of a cartel. Instead, the elite colleges have been wrongly understood as charities.

To be fair to others, it's easy to miss the fact that elite colleges are organized as a cartel. It's a cartel that camouflages. To produce seat scarcity, the elite college cartel resembles a weird hub-and-spoke structure. Even weirder are the "non-profit" labels attached to the schools. The confusing language, the weird market structure, and a general lack of scrutiny are all reasons why competition amongst elite colleges has decayed and why seat scarcity has festered.

The other reason for our elite college dysfunction is politics. The political dynamics surrounding the elite colleges are extreme. Some on the left want to "tear down" Yale. Others on the right want the exact same, but for very different reasons. Yet, within the governing wings, neither party nor leadership has a credible plan to reform elite colleges. So, we're stuck between a discourse of "tear it down" and keeping it exactly the same. It's not good enough. We need to break through politics where our only two options are death or decay. Instead, we need restructuring and rebirth. That's what I hope this chapter will sketch out.

We can start sketching out that alternative vision by retracing the argumentative path we took in this book. This book began by admitting that employers are looking for skills and signals from young people and therefore talented young people are looking for a prestigious signal from prospective colleges. This book then described how the higher education industry has rushed into a wasteful equilibrium where more money is constantly spent on creating a prestigious signal in ever more frivolous ways. We further described the cynical bargain between the elite colleges and US News' ranking, which allocates prestige to reward ever more expensive and rejective colleges. Lastly, the book describes how the elite college cartel abuses market power and political power to squeeze more money out of students and the broader public, which has distortive effects on many of the other colleges in the higher education sector.

This book breaks down the market dynamics into both the demand side and the supply side, as we can observe from this book's argumentative path. In the first chapters, we described the demand side or the dynamics that explain why students want to go to elite colleges in the first place. In the middle chapters, we described the supply side, or why there are so few elite colleges and why there are so few seats at those elite colleges. In the later chapters, we explored the interactions between students and colleges in the marketplace and how elite colleges use their market power in abusive ways.

Historically, those who have criticized elite colleges have often made demand-side critiques. When Peter Thiel offers students money to drop out of elite colleges, he is implicitly saying that people shouldn't want to go to those schools. When Mike Rowe tells young people to go to vocational school, he too is offering a demand side critique. This book doesn't offer a demand-side critique. My focus isn't on why students should give up their demand for prestigious signals. Instead, I focus on how we can reform the supply side or how the system currently allocates prestigious signals and to whom.

There are a couple of reasons for my focus on supply-side reform. First, the supply side problems at elite colleges have been dangerously under covered by the media. Second, it's far easier to change the behavior of a few dozen elite colleges than hundreds of thousands of students and many thousands of employers. I generally agree that employers shouldn't make employment decisions based on the hollow prestige of signals, but that's outside the scope of this book. I'm skeptical about our ability to fundamentally change the behavior of employers. Therefore, I leave such criticism to others.

Instead, the reforms I propose are on how we allocate prestigious signals and to whom. Mechanistically, elite college reform can work through one of two paths. Either a policy intervention can change what an elite college wants, or a policy intervention can restrict an elite college's ability to do something that society doesn't want. Essentially, policy intervention can either reform what an elite college wants or its capability to achieve whatever it wants. For example, by changing how we allocate prestige to colleges, we change what elite colleges want to do. At present, elite colleges want to enroll a few students and spend a lot of money to score higher on the rankings. In an alternative rankings regime, elite colleges may well want to expand enrollments and spend less per student to be ranked more highly. Further, by stripping elite colleges of market or political power, we can reduce elite colleges' ability to distort the market in ways detrimental to society. This is an example of a policy intervention reducing capability.

Regardless of the mechanism, we mostly care about results. Broadly, the results we want are three. First, we must expand the supply of elite seats. Second, we must increase price competition and quality competition between elite colleges. Third, we must end the regulatory capture of elite colleges. In the rest of this chapter, I offer proposals for a policy that can accomplish all three goals. I hope others will study these policy directions in much further detail than I can within the context of this book. I hope real reform of elite colleges enters the political agenda in both political parties.

INCREASE THE NUMBER OF ELITE SEATS

The most fundamental problem in the elite college sector is the artificial scarcity of seats. This scarcity is what gives elite colleges the market power that they can abuse through higher prices and lower quality. The gains from that market power are what allow elite colleges to afford regulatory capture. Therefore, artificial scarcity is the most important problem to solve. After all, most other problems flow from artificial scarcity. In this book, I propose two government interventions that can eradicate scarcity and sweep in abundance.

My first proposal is that the federal government should buy US News. Essentially, the government should nationalize and reform the US News' ranking. This is a very feasible proposal. US News would be super cheap to buy, as US News is valued in the low hundreds of millions. If the government offers Mortimer Zuckerman a premium on anything the private market would, I assume he'd take it. He's a businessman.

Once the government owns US News, the Department of Education should do a detailed analysis of all the criteria used in the US News ranking that incentivizes more spending and fewer seats. It should then invert those criteria to drive more expansion and less spending. In the earlier chapter on artificial scarcity, I detailed how a variety of US News' rankings criteria have the number of students as a denominator. For example, the class-size index has an 8 percent weighting in the US News rankings calculation. More impactfully, financial resources per student have a 10 percent weight. Further, the student-faculty ratio of a university has a 1 percent weighting. Obviously, if you want to score highly on these criteria, the fewer the number of students enrolled, the better. In a hyper-intense competition for prestige, minimizing undergraduate enrollment is exactly what elite colleges are incentivized to do.

These are precisely the types of criteria that need to be removed from the ranking regime. Further, they should be replaced by criteria that create incentives for growth. Elite colleges should score higher in the ranking for enrolling more students than the year before. By buying US News, the federal government can make sure such changes are made.

I recently mentioned this proposal to a university professor who fairly countered, "why buy US News when the government can just make its own ranking from scratch?" It's a fair question. I have three answers in response.

First, the government is inefficient at building websites. Anyone who remembers the Healthcare.gov fiasco knows this. According to The Atlantic, the federal government spent $150 million just on cost overruns when it tried to launch its own website for healthcare exchanges after the passage of Obamacare.[218] The total development cost of the entire website was estimated at nearly a billion dollars. Any Silicon Valley type would tell you that such cost overruns are ridiculous. Better to spend the money buying a system that already works than to spend much more than that developing one.

Second, the government, in developing its own ranking product, would have to beat US News anyway. As we explored in earlier chapters, college ranking is a winner-takes-all market. While I'm almost always in favor of vigorous competition, in this one narrow instance, I believe that it is better to just nationalize the current monopolist than laboriously win a monopoly by competition.

Third, we've seen the elite colleges beat back a government effort to develop their own rankings before. When President

Obama tried to implement a college rankings system in the 2010s, elite colleges lobbied the administration into a retreat. Some even argued that rankings were something best left for US News. So, what if you could take away that excuse from the elite colleges?

Of course, nationalizing US News would not be without its own challenges. What if elite colleges try to create a new hub-and-spoke cartel with a different private ranking, say Forbes? This is a valid concern. However, there are ways to prevent that from happening. First, the government can tie public subsidies to unique participation with a government-owned US News. For example, each elite college might be offered a year-long waiver of endowment taxes if it moves up in the government-owned US News ranking. Other substantial subsidies like research funding could also be tied to US News participation. Second, if elite colleges switch whom they cite and uplift in public, there might be a serious antitrust challenge that can be made against them. After all, this time, the formation of a hub-and-spoke cartel conspiracy will be more obvious.

In truth, I'm skeptical the federal government will actually buy US News. They should, but I'm not sure they will. So, I'll offer an alternative solution. This solution is less than ideal but better than the present. If the federal government doesn't buy US News, I believe that some altruistic billionaire should buy US News from Mortimer Zuckerman. If you are a billionaire reading this, consider buying US News from Mortimer Zuckerman and do everything the government ought to. Invert the rankings criteria and fix the elite college market.

Getting the rankings regime into the right hands is also important because rankings are one of the primary mechanisms that lead to contagion at less-elite colleges. If we fix the ranking in the elite college market, the spill over into the non-elite market will be massive. Therefore, nationalizing the rankings might be my most important proposal in this book.

My second proposal to end seat scarcity draws inspiration from something the federal government already does. Namely, the federal government should tax the endowments of colleges that don't grow enrollments. But this time Congress should make the tax high enough to shift behavior.

To refresh your memory, in 2017, a 1.4 percent tax on net investment income was implemented on colleges with mega-endowments worth more than $500,000 per student. One objective of the tax was to encourage these institutions to admit more students so that the institutions wouldn't have to pay the tax. After all, one way to avoid the tax was to grow one's enrollment so much that the endowment per student came down to below $500,000 per student. Empirically, this didn't happen. Instead, these elite colleges have just paid the tax instead of expanding enrollment. Essentially, it was more lucrative to keep the seat cartel running and throw the government a penny than to defect from the seat cartel unilaterally.

The current endowment tax rate clearly hasn't been high enough to encourage expansion. So, Congress should move the tax rate closer to 30 percent, akin to the tax rate on corporations, and if the elite college cartel persists in hoarding seats, then Congress should go back and raise it more. The tax needs to be raised until it is more lucrative to defect from the seat cartel than continue to participate in it. I'm not sure exactly what that number will be. I'm hoping some economist can figure that out.

FIX PRICING NOT PRICES

Elite college pricing is broken in all sorts of ways. There's legalized price-fixing. Even without collusion, there is limited price competition. Worse, there is rampant subsidy cannibalism. Yet, all these problems are fundamentally related to a bigger problem. That problem is high barriers to entry. In an elite college market with lower barriers to entry, there would be far more pricing pressure from ambitious entrants looking to gobble market share. These entrants would always be trying to quickly climb the rankings by offering unbelievable deals to well-qualified students. However, because of the moat protecting the incumbents in the elite college market, these entrants never get that chance to compete. Therefore, the most powerful way to spur price competition in the elite college market is to break the moat which forecloses the entry of new colleges into the most prestigious elite echelon.

At present, entry into the elite college market is impossible. So, how do we break the moat? How do we lower those barriers to entry? One answer is breaking up elite college endowments.

Remember, in an earlier chapter, we described how the biggest barrier preventing ambitious lower-ranked universities from competing with established elite universities is the massive endowment gaps that separate school from school. We studied the example of John Doerr's donation to Stanford as emblematic of the problem. Essentially, schools like Harvard, Stanford, and Yale have so much money that they will always be near or at the top of the prestige competition. As a result, they will always attract future donations from big billion-dollar donors who want to associate themselves with some of that prestige. Therefore, elite endowments correspondingly grow more than others. The result is that resources agglomerate towards the top. Plainly, the rich colleges keep getting richer.

This extra capital becomes a powerful barrier to entry as endowments get bigger, but schools like Harvard see no reason to expand enrollment. As these endowments grow disproportionately, other colleges can't afford to compete on rankings and prestige, they just get out-spent on the criteria. Students respond in turn. To try and get those prestigious signals for themselves, students do everything possible, including paying over-the-top prices. It's monopoly power at work.

The endowment moat is also bad for innovation. Harvard, Yale, and other top schools don't have to do anything particularly special to attract new capital. They don't have to innovate in teaching. This might be why we've seen so little innovation in teaching methods in higher education for centuries. Essentially, lecture halls, exams, and midterms are all centuries-old methods. They don't have to do anything apart from harvest their old brand names for new money. Competitive markets don't stagnate in the same way.

Now just imagine a world in which the resource gaps are small enough that a university ranked in the thirties can potentially break into the twenties or tens by doing something innovative or offering lower prices to attract the best students. There will be much more competition for meritorious students. After all, in a truly competitive market, attracting marginal meritorious students will be the best way to climb the rankings. A fierce competition will begin. That competition will play out in two ways. First, universities will compete more vigorously on price. Second, universities will compete more vigorously by cutting costs. Rebalancing the elite college market to open up entry would be the most vigorous way to breathe new life into elite education.

My proposal for breaking the endowment moat is simple. The federal government should break up the massive elite college endowments. This solution is a throwback to old-school trust-busting. It's long overdue, and it's also feasible. Breaking up elite endowments is actually quite easy. You don't have to file an antitrust suit or rely on the courts to mandate it. Instead, all you need to do is pass legislation. Congress could just massively tax large endowments. It could then take those resources and support public colleges to increase competition in the elite market. For example, if you assessed a one-time 100 percent tax on every dollar above 10 billion dollars at every single elite college endowment, you could plow billions into dozens of public colleges, leveling the playing field in the elite college market and introducing new public challengers into the elite market. For example, Harvard's endowment is worth something around 50 billion dollars. If you assessed a tax on Harvard for 40 billion dollars, you would leave Harvard with a 10 billion dollar endowment and enough money to invest in four public colleges with 10 billion dollars each. Instead of just one Harvard, we would now have five. You could repeat the process with Yale, Stanford, Princeton, MIT, Penn, and others too. Dozens of elite public colleges would emerge. This project could instantly reawaken a vigorous competition for students, professors, and new programs.

Of course, the 10 billion dollar endowment number is an arbitrary bright line. You could draw the line higher or lower. If you wanted to break up endowments into more pieces, you could set the line at 5 billion. If you wanted to break up endowments into fewer pieces, you could set the line at 15 billion. This book takes no position on specifics. Instead, this book takes a position on the principle that endowment breakups can be positive.

On May 31, 2022, I proposed a version of this breaking-up endowments idea on my Substack blog, The Muckrake. The idea instantly got traction. For context, my Substack has fewer than two hundred followers. On a good day, an article of mine usually gets a hundred views or less. However, this article got tens of thousands of views. It went nerd viral on a forum called Hacker News. When I woke up the next day, some professor named Peter Shulman from Case Western Reserve University had started a Twitter thread attacking my blog post. The fight was on.

Professor Peter Shulman's basic argument was that my blog post wasn't detailed enough on specifics to be doable. For example, one critique Professor Peter Shulman made was that what we call elite college endowments are actually thousands of smaller funds committed to a specific purpose. It is much harder to tax all these small funds, Professor Peter Shulman argued. For do-nothings like Peter, everything is too difficult. Why even try?

What Professor Peter Shulman obviously missed is that my article was a blog post. The point of blog posts is to get people talking about big ideas. I didn't have the resources or the time to commit to writing up a white paper on exactly how to logistically tax the elite college endowments to break them up. I'm also not going to do that in this book.

The important point is that breaking up endowments is doable. For example, take Peter Shulman's point about the hundreds of small endowments. Well, the government could just tax every single endowment fund at a university at 100 percent, and then give the university back a 10 billion check for a new unrestricted endowment. There are common sense ways to structure reform if you want to do something.

On his Twitter thread, Professor Peter Shulman also argued that an endowment breakup would blow up operating budgets at elite colleges that had grown used to the money. The best version of this argument is that elite colleges would need time to adapt to shrinking endowments. I'll concede that. Therefore, an endowment could be broken up over the course of a few years to give the university the time to wean itself off.

Lastly, one critic made the point that some university budgets have grown up in such a way that they could never adapt to less money. This is a ridiculous assertion. I will never concede the point that 10 billion dollars isn't enough for an elite college to run a robust undergraduate program. I know this because Cornell University currently has an endowment that totals nearly 10 billion dollars. Dartmouth, Brown, and Vanderbilt have endowments of a similar size. In fact, some elite colleges have far smaller endowments. Georgetown's endowment is in the low single-digit billions. Ten billion dollars isn't an unfair breakup. It might still be too big. Again, the question is not whether a breakup is possible to do. The question is whether we have the will to do something.

It wasn't easy when the government broke up Standard Oil in 1911 or AT&T in 1984. But it was both possible and necessary. We can't be afraid to take decisive action because it seems scary. Teddy Roosevelt didn't back down when he went after the big railroad trusts. Franklin Roosevelt didn't back down when he enacted social security. John Kennedy didn't back down when he plowed billions of dollars into a race to the moon. The greatness of America has always been in our ability to back decisive change at moments of national need. We shouldn't forget that.

I will never concede that we shouldn't do anything because it's hard. However, I will concede that breaking up endowments with a one-time tax isn't a total solution. After all, there is a structural problem in the elite college market that makes it winner-takes-most. Namely, that structural problem is the zero-sum nature of prestige. Essentially, if one college permanently displaces another in a rankings regime, then it's unclear if the total number of competitors meaningfully increased or if one college just took the place of another. We can't solve this zero-sum problem. It is definitional that as one becomes more prestigious, others become less so. The natural implication of this observation is that a new set of winners might re-emerge over time in the elite college market, even if we break up endowments. As those winners get richer, the moat protecting them might re-emerge too. The fly-wheel might kick in again. Some endowments might become outrageously large once more, perhaps over the course of a decade or more.

Still, is that a reason not to break the endowments up? Or is that a reason to break up the endowments more often? Just because one mows the grass doesn't mean the weeds won't come back. Yet, we mow the grass anyway. It's true that we will likely need to periodically intervene in the elite college market to break it up. Once every few decades, endowments will need to be broken up again. Yet, if we do it once, we'll have the confidence to do it again.

Breaking up endowments is a maximalist position on elite college pricing reform, but there are also other less interventionist things that the government can do. In fact, many of these less interventionist policies are low-hanging fruit. Specifically, the federal government should guarantee that an antitrust exemption like Section 568 of Improving America's Schools Act is never enacted again, it should fix bargaining on price, and it should ban restrictive application processes.

In a prior chapter, we already asserted that Congress should keep repealed Section 568 of the Improving America's Schools

Act. The reasons for this are plainly stated in earlier chapters, but to recap, giving elite colleges with market power even more market power through an exemption from antitrust laws makes little sense. During a college affordability crisis, low-hanging fruit like permanently repealing the antitrust exemption should be desperately grasped for.

Similarly, fixing information flows that give elite colleges an unfair bargaining advantage is also obvious low-hanging fruit. For example, one simple fix would be to prevent elite colleges from seeing where else a student applied. This type of information is included in FAFSA forms, and there's absolutely no reason for an elite college to have access to that kind of information. It only bolsters an elite college's ability to negotiate financial aid offers. For example, if an elite college knows that it's the most prestigious college you applied to, that college now has an unfair advantage in negotiations. After all, what's stopping that college from lowballing you on financial aid? Where else are you going to go?

What I'm proposing in this chapter is that there ought to be a complete rethink of who has what information and when. The asymmetric bargaining between students and elite colleges needs to end. The last-mover advantage that elite colleges have in financial-aid negotiations must also change. Information about what government grants a student qualifies for, his or her family's financial situation, and other such details should not be given to elite colleges ahead of time. But how will elite colleges know how much financial aid to offer if they don't have access to their applicants' information ahead of time?

My proposal is that Congress should mandate that elite colleges publish fixed rules for pricing. Just as the federal government publishes the income tax brackets ahead of time, so too should elite colleges publish their prices for students from distinct income brackets. For example, students from families that make less than $50,000 a year might all pay the same price, and students from families that make between $50,000 and $75 000 might be expected to pay more. This type of graduating bracket could continue up the income ladder. Importantly, instead of the awkward dance of sticker price minus financial aid, elite college fixed prices should be converted and displayed as net prices. The rules for qualification into a specific bracket should be fixed. Further, these prices should be public and transparent for all to see and understand. One of the reasons elite colleges can get away with subsidy cannibalism and price-fixing is because pricing is so opaque and weirdly computed. Let's make it much simpler. Let's make it public.

In terms of implementation, the FAFSA forms should be used solely to locate which net price bracket a student falls into. Importantly, FAFSA should not be used to cannibalize government subsidies. Forcing elite colleges to publish fixed rules for pricing would prevent that. After all, if elite colleges increased the prices in the lowest income bracket after the increase in the value of Pell grants, it would now be clear as day. I'd assume that the bad publicity of such cannibalism would prevent elite colleges from even trying it. Yet, I've been wrong before.

If, after such a reform, elite colleges continue to cannibalize subsidies meant for poor students, then I might even be in favor of straight up price-controls in the elite college market. Empirically, prestigious British universities like Oxford and LSE have such price controls. Those universities run fine. If our universities don't shape up, we might have to move in that direction too.

Some pricing reform is necessary because, when left to their own devices, elite colleges use their extracted surpluses to increase their spending instead of offering steeper discounts to needier students. Empirically, as a study by economist Ian Fillmore concludes: "Of the student surplus they extract by virtue of the FAFSA information, colleges only transfer 22.2 percent to other students."[219] We can do better.

Another obvious area for pricing reform is early-decision contracts. What benefit do students gain from an early decision? Students receive a slightly higher chance of admission. Yet, in exchange, students must surrender their bargaining power in future financial-aid negotiations. As such, early decision contracts are nothing more than elite colleges exploiting market power to force students into unilaterally deleveraging their bargaining power. In a world of seat scarcity, elite colleges can get away with it because every small percentage increase in the likelihood of acceptance is viciously competed for by students when seats are scarce. Congress should just ban this exercise of market power. Early decision serves only the schools.

Of course, this chapter is not an exhaustive list of all the various tweaks that must be made in elite college pricing, instead, it's a start. However, the principles articulated in this section are always going to apply. When it comes to university pricing, we should be looking to create more transparency, less unfair bargaining, more price competition, and less barriers to entry.

END REGULATORY CAPTURE

We've touched on how public policy gives elite colleges more power repeatedly in this book. We've also explored how that public policy has often been made. It's often been made in backrooms through extensive lobbying of our most senior politicians. It's sometimes been made by flooding the legal system with appeals. It's even been made by lobbying the administrative agencies or the Presidential administration. There is no way to describe this set of facts without using the words regulatory capture. Let's talk plainly. Elite colleges have captured the government. The main elite college public policy strategy has been to keep the government out of rankings and out of endowments. Mostly, they've succeeded.

The elite colleges have committed serious money to achieve that extensive regulatory capture. Over the last decade, Harvard routinely spent over half a million dollars lobbying each year. The other Ivy League schools weren't far behind. According to Open Secrets, the higher education lobby spent an aggregate of $86 million lobbying in 2021. That, of course, completely ignores the big campaign donations made by the trustees and alumni of these schools. It ignores the revolving door between elite colleges and top jobs in administrations.

The simple fact is that elite colleges have successfully captured the federal government. This is why the endowment tax is so slight, why FAFSA is how it is, why artificial scarcity isn't attacked, why antitrust exemptions are passed, and why elite colleges can cannibalize subsidies meant for students. If we want to break the college cartel, we must break its grip on Congress and also the other two branches of government.

Breaking that grip on the government is super hard. As with any other singular industry, mobilizing the public is difficult because the issues are quite niche. Learning about rankings criteria requires a lot of time. It took me forever to finish this book. Now imagine how hard it would be for the broader public to make that investment. Plus, how many issues are we going to expect voters to be similarly well-informed on? On the other hand, the gains to a handful of monopolists from certain policies are quite large, often in the billions of dollars. The monopolists have every reason to pay attention and make political investments. The public is less so incentivized.

Does this mean nothing can be done? I don't think so. Instead, we need to merge anti-monopoly activism from a whole range of industries into one broader meta-movement that the public can get on board with. After all, the problems with Big Tech are similar in structure to the problems with Big Agriculture, Big Defense, Big Tobacco, Big Telecom, and so many other cartels and monopolies. Anti-monopoly activists should add the college cartel to that list of problem industries. The way we will beat the college cartel is by taking on monopoly in the abstract. We must build a broad coalition and sell the public on the principles we believe in.

Those principles aren't a tough sell. Americans implicitly believe in competitive markets. They implicitly believe in clean government. They implicitly believe in the righteousness of David instead of the oppressiveness of Goliath. Importantly, Americans also explicitly believe that elite colleges have gone too far. The outcry over Varsity Blues proved that. Reform of elite colleges is a potent brew waiting for a real political moment.

Many previous thinkers have already laid out a policy platform to end regulatory capture in the abstract. For example, some have proposed campaign finance laws which restrict unlimited campaign donations by corporate interests. Others have proposed giving citizens restricted dollars that they can only spend on political donations. Some have remarked on the importance of administrative personnel decisions. Others have proposed term limits. This book doesn't take a position on any of these policies. One could write an entire book just on campaign finance and lobbying reform. The main point is that there must be some campaign finance and lobbying reform. If you care about this issue, you ought to propose or support something in that domain too.

CONCLUSION

The proposals in this chapter might seem quite primitive to you. Mostly they are. After all, my goal with this book was to reframe how we see certain institutions and problems. The truth is that no one book can detail how to restructure an entire sector with any precision. No one person has a monopoly on all productive ideas. I hope others can develop these ideas further or propose better ones.

To conclude, the point of this book is to inspire a movement. If you're an academic, please study how high the endowment tax ought to be. If you're a lawyer, please think about what kinds of cases you can bring to curb monopoly abuse by the college cartel. If you're a bureaucrat, please think about what administrative changes you can make to curtail monopoly power. If you're a politician, please think about what laws you can change. If you're a student, please think about how you can bring attention to this issue. If you're a citizen, please pay attention to these issues when you vote.

I end this book with a simple call. Please help however you can. Even something small is better than nothing at all. It was Louis Brandeis who famously observed that: "The most important political office is that of the private citizen." I believe in that sentiment. I hope you do too.

NOTES

INTRODUCTION

1 Shapiro, T. Rees. "Harvard-Stanford admissions hoax becomes international scandal," The Washington Post, June 18, 2015, accessed February 24, 2023, https://www.washingtonpost.com/local/education/harvard-stanford-admissions-hoax-becomes-international-scandal/2015/06/18/4abac970-156a-11e5-89f3-61410da94eb1_story.html.

2 Novinson, Daniel. "Imposter caught," The Stanford Daily, May 24, 2007, accessed February 24, 2023, https://stanforddaily.com/2007/05/24/imposter-caught/.

3 Lumpkin, Lauren. "Former Georgetown tennis coach avoids prison time in college admissions scandal," The Washington Post, October 26, 2021, accessed February 24, 2023, https://www.washingtonpost.com/education/2021/10/26/college-admissions-scandal-gordon-ernst-georgetown/.

4 Massimo, Rick. "Ex-Georgetown tennis coach indicted in admissions cheating scandal," WTOP News, March 12, 2019, accessed February 24, 2023, https://wtop.com/local/2019/03/ex-georgetown-tennis-coach-indicted-in-admissions-cheating-scandal/.

5 Massimo, Rick. "Ex-Georgetown tennis coach indicted in admissions cheating scandal," WTOP News, March 12, 2019, accessed February 24, 2023, https://wtop.com/local/2019/03/ex-georgetown-tennis-coach-indicted-in-admissions-cheating-scandal/.

6 United States Department of Justice, "Indictment - United States v. Singer et al," March 12, 2019, accessed February 24, 2023, https://www.justice.gov/file/1142876/download.

7 Ormseth, Matthew. "Bay Area financier sentenced to 6 months in prison in college admissions scandal," Los Angeles Times, July 29, 2020, accessed February 24, 2023, https://www.latimes.com/california/story/2020-07-29/admissions-scandal-manuel-henriquez-bay-area-financier-sentenced-to-months-in-prison.

8 Olivier, Indigo. "The Columbia University student strike is about far more than tuition," The Guardian, February 18, 2021, accessed February 24, 2023, https://www.theguardian.com/commentisfree/2021/feb/18/the-columbia-university-student-strike-is-about-far-more-than-tuition.

9 Kim, Julianna. "Columbia students go on tuition strike, saying online classes aren't worth full-price." The New York Times, January 29, 2021, accessed February 24, 2023, https://www.nytimes.com/2021/01/29/world/columbia-covid-tuition-strike.html.

10 The Upshot. "Some Colleges Have More Students From the Top 1 Percent Than the Bottom 60. Find Yours." The New York Times, January 18, 2017, https://www.nytimes.com/interactive/2017/01/18/upshot/some-colleges-have-more-students-from-the-top-1-percent-than-the-bottom-60.html.

THE HEAD START

11 Avery, Christopher N., Mark E. Glickman, Caroline M. Hoxby, and Andrew Metrick. "A REVEALED PREFERENCE RANKING OF U.S. COLLEGES AND UNIVERSITIES." The Quarterly Journal of Economics 128, no. 1 (2013): 425–67. https://www.jstor.org/stable/26372502.

12 Avery, Christopher N., Mark E. Glickman, Caroline M. Hoxby, and Andrew Metrick. "A REVEALED PREFERENCE RANKING OF U.S.

COLLEGES AND UNIVERSITIES." The Quarterly Journal of Economics 128, no. 1 (2013): 425–67. https://www.jstor.org/stable/26372502.

13 Cornell University News Service, "New Study Proves that College Rankings Do Matter," Cornell Chronicle, November 18, 1999, https://news.cornell.edu/stories/1999/11/college-rankings-do-matter.

14 Luca, M. and Smith, J. (2013), Salience in Quality Disclosure: Evidence from the U.S. News College Rankings. Journal of Economics & Management Strategy, 22: 58-77. https://doi.org/10.1111/jems.12003

15 Akerlof, George A. "The Market for 'Lemons': Quality Uncertainty and the Market Mechanism." The Quarterly Journal of Economics 84, no. 3 (1970): 488–500. https://doi.org/10.2307/1879431.

16 Dishman, Lydia. "Despite Evidence, Hiring Managers Are Biased Towards Graduates From Top Colleges." Fast Company, August 23, 2016. Accessed February 24, 2023. https://www.fastcompany.com/3060544/despite-evidence-hiring-managers-are-biased-towards-graduates-from-top-colleges.

THE ELITE AFTERGLOW

17 Wai, Jonathan & Makel, Matthew & Gambrell, James. (2020). The Role of Elite Education and Inferred Cognitive Ability in Eminent Creative Expertise: An Historical Analysis of the TIME 100.

18 Harvard Business Review. "Graduates of Elite Universities Get Paid More. Do They Perform Better?" Harvard Business Review, September 15, 2020, https://hbr.org/2020/09/graduates-of-elite-universities-get-paid-more-do-they-perform-better.

19 Page, Clarence. "Biden's remark articulates a gap in understanding." Chicago Tribune, February 7, 2007, sec. News. https://www.chicagotribune.com/news/ct-xpm-2007-02-07-0702070021-story.html.

20 "Obama Comments on Biden Remarks," POLITICO, January 31, 2007, https://www.politico.com/blogs/politico-now/2007/01/obama-comments-on-biden-remarks-000125.

21 Darman, Jonathan. "At War With His Mouth." Newsweek, January 22, 2007. Accessed February 24, 2023. https://www.newsweek.com/war-his-mouth-98197.

22 Patrick Kline & Evan K Rose & Christopher R Walters, 2022. "Systemic Discrimination Among Large U.S. Employers," The Quarterly Journal of Economics, vol 137(4), pages 1963-2036.

23 Patrick Kline & Evan K Rose & Christopher R Walters, 2022. "Systemic Discrimination Among Large U.S. Employers," The Quarterly Journal of Economics, vol 137(4), pages 1963-2036.

24 Stacy Berg Dale, and Alan B. Krueger. "Estimating the Payoff to Attending a More Selective College: An Application of Selection on Observables and Unobservables." The Quarterly Journal of Economics 117, no. 4 (2002): 1491–1527. http://www.jstor.org/stable/4132484.

25 Stacy Berg Dale, and Alan B. Krueger. "Estimating the Payoff to Attending a More Selective College: An Application of Selection on Observables and Unobservables." The Quarterly Journal of Economics 117, no. 4 (2002): 1491–1527. http://www.jstor.org/stable/4132484.

26 Elite Schools and Opting In: Effects of College Selectivity on Career and Family Outcomes
Suqin Ge, Elliott Isaac, and Amalia Miller
Journal of Labor Economics 2022 40:S1, S383-S427

27 Stacy Berg Dale, and Alan B. Krueger. "Estimating the Payoff to Attending a More Selective College: An Application of Selection on Observables and Unobservables." The Quarterly Journal of Economics 117, no. 4 (2002): 1491–1527. http://www.jstor.org/stable/4132484.

28 Stacy Berg Dale, and Alan B. Krueger. "Estimating the Payoff to Attending a More Selective College: An Application of Selection on Observables and Unobservables." The Quarterly Journal of Economics 117, no. 4 (2002): 1491–1527. http://www.jstor.org/stable/4132484.

29 Thompson, Derek. "Does It Matter Where You Go to College?" The Atlantic, December 5, 2018, https://www.theatlantic.com/ideas/archive/2018/12/does-it-matter-where-you-go-college/577816/.

30 "JFK's Harvard essay resurfaces online 87 years later." New York Post. February 3, 2022. Accessed February 24, 2023. https://nypost.com/2022/02/03/jfks-harvard-essay-resurfaces-online-87-years-later/.

31 Carnevale, Anthony P., Peter Schmidt, and Jeff Strohl. The Merit Myth: How Our Colleges Favor the Rich and Divide America. The New Press, 2020.

32 Blair, Peter Q., and Kent Smetters. Why Don't Elite Colleges Expand Supply?. No. w29309. National Bureau of Economic Research, 2021.

33 Blair, Peter Q., and Kent Smetters. Why Don't Elite Colleges Expand Supply?. No. w29309. National Bureau of Economic Research, 2021.

THE COLLEGE OF CARDINALS

34 Korn, Melissa. "Yale, Georgetown, Other Top Schools Illegally Collude to Limit Student Financial Aid, Lawsuit Alleges." Wall Street Journal, December 15, 2021. https://www.wsj.com/articles/yale-georgetown-other-top-schools-illegally-collude-to-limit-student-financial-aid-lawsuit-alleges-11641829659.

35 Stanford University Alumni Association. "Board of Directors: Facts & Information." Stanford University Alumni Association, accessed February 24, 2023. https://alumni.stanford.edu/volunteer/board-facts/.

36 "U-Va. Upheaval: 18 Days of Leadership Crisis," Washington Post, last modified June 30, 2012, https://www.washingtonpost.com/local/education/u-va-upheaval-18-days-of-leadership-crisis/2012/06/30/gJQAVXEgEW_story.html?tid=usw_passupdatepg.

37 "U-Va. Upheaval: 18 Days of Leadership Crisis," Washington Post, last modified June 30, 2012, https://www.washingtonpost.com/local/education/u-va-upheaval-18-days-of-leadership-crisis/2012/06/30/gJQAVXEgEW_story.html?tid=usw_passupdatepg.

38 Rice, Andrew. "Anatomy of a Campus Coup." The New York Times, September 16, 2012, https://www.nytimes.com/2012/09/16/magazine/teresa-sullivan-uva-ouster.html.

39 "U-Va. Upheaval: 18 Days of Leadership Crisis," Washington Post, last modified June 30, 2012, https://www.washingtonpost.com/local/education/u-va-upheaval-18-days-of-leadership-crisis/2012/06/30/gJQAVXEgEW_story.html?tid=usw_passupdatepg.

40 Jones, Paul Tudor II "Op-Ed: Aspiring to achieve greatness," The Daily Progress, October 18, 2021, accessed February 24, 2023, https://dailyprogress.com/news/op-ed-aspiring-to-achieve-greatness/article_be382c81-3059-56a2-81c5-3eb85627c978.html.

41 Jones, Paul Tudor II "Op-Ed: Aspiring to achieve greatness," The Daily Progress, October 18, 2021, accessed February 24, 2023, https://dailyprogress.com/news/op-ed-aspiring-to-achieve-greatness/article_be382c81-3059-56a2-81c5-3eb85627c978.html.

42 Rice, Andrew. "Anatomy of a Campus Coup." The New York Times, September 16, 2012, https://www.nytimes.com/2012/09/16/magazine/teresa-sullivan-uva-ouster.html.

43 Roanoke Times. "McDonnell Threatens to Replace Entire U.Va. Board if Furor Over President's Ouster Lingers," Roanoke Times, June 24, 2012. https://roanoke.com/archive/mcdonnell-threatens-to-replace-entire-uva-board-if-furor-over-presidents-ouster-lingers/article_0b27281a-99f2-52bf-9fbc-fd6773ac90f9.html.

44 Johnson, Jenna. Kumar, Anita. De Vise, Daniel. "U-Va. Board Reinstates Sullivan as President." The Washington Post, June 26, 2012. https://www.washingtonpost.com/local/education/u-va-leadership-crisis-mcdonnell-declines-to-take-sides/2012/06/26/gJQArOHU4V_story.html.

45 Johnson, Jenna. Kumar, Anita. De Vise, Daniel. "U-Va. Board Reinstates Sullivan as President." The Washington Post, June 26, 2012. https://www.washingtonpost.com/local/education/u-va-leadership-crisis-mcdonnell-declines-to-take-sides/2012/06/26/gJQArOHU4V_story.html.

46 University of Virginia. "Teresa A. Sullivan: Biography." Accessed February 24, 2023. https://a.virginia.edu/aboutuva/presidents/sullivan.

47 "Teresa A. Sullivan | Office of the President," University of Virginia, accessed February 24, 2023, https://www.virginia.edu/aboutuva/presidents/sullivan.

48 "College Rankings and UVA," University of Virginia Magazine, accessed February 24, 2023, https://digital.uvamagazine.org/articles/college-rankings-and-uva/.

49 "Shaping university boards for 21st-century higher education in the US," McKinsey & Company, accessed February 24, 2023, https://www.mckinsey.com/industries/education/our-insights/shaping-university-boards-for-21st-century-higher-education-in-the-us.

50 "University Trustees," The University of Chicago, accessed February 24, 2023, https://trustees.uchicago.edu/university-trustees/.

51 Jaschik, Scott. "Author Discusses His New Book, 'Bankers in the Ivory Tower'," Inside Higher Ed, March 1, 2022, accessed February 24, 2023, https://www.insidehighered.com/news/2022/03/01/author-discusses-his-new-book-bankers-ivory-tower.

52 Eaton, Charlie. "Elite private universities got much wealthier while most schools fell behind. My research found out why," The Washington Post, November 4, 2021, accessed February 24, 2023, https://www.washingtonpost.com/politics/2021/11/04/elite-private-universities-got-much-wealthier-while-most-schools-fell-behind-my-research-found-out-why/.

53 Jaschik, Scott. "Author Discusses His New Book, 'Bankers in the Ivory Tower'," Inside Higher Ed, March 1, 2022, accessed February 24, 2023, https://www.insidehighered.com/news/2022/03/01/author-discusses-his-new-book-bankers-ivory-tower.

54 Eaton, Charlie. "Elite private universities got much wealthier while most schools fell behind. My research found out why," The Washington Post, November 4, 2021, accessed February 24, 2023, https://www.washingtonpost.com/politics/2021/11/04/elite-private-universities-got-much-wealthier-while-most-schools-fell-behind-my-research-found-out-why/.

55 Smith, Randall. "Dartmouth Controversy Reflects Quandary for Endowments," The New York Times, January 7, 2013, accessed February 24, 2023, https://archive.nytimes.com/dealbook.nytimes.com/2013/01/07/dartmouth-controversy-reflects-quandary-for-endowments/.

56 Bowen, William. "When a Business Leader Joins a Nonprofit Board," Harvard Business Review, September 1994, accessed February 24, 2023, https://hbr.org/1994/09/when-a-business-leader-joins-a-nonprofit-board.

57 Jones, Paul Tudor II "Op-Ed: Aspiring to achieve greatness," The Daily Progress, October 18, 2021, accessed February 24, 2023, https://dailyprogress.com/news/op-ed-aspiring-to-achieve-greatness/article_be382c81-3059-56a2-81c5-3eb85627c978.html.

58 Bowen, William. "When a Business Leader Joins a Nonprofit Board," Harvard Business Review, September 1994, accessed February 24, 2023, https://hbr.org/1994/09/when-a-business-leader-joins-a-nonprofit-board.

59 John D. Head, "A Study on The Influences of the U.S. News and World Reports: America's Best Colleges Rankings on Policy and Decision-Making at Southern Comprehensive Colleges," PhD diss., University of Tennessee, 2005, accessed February 24, 2023, https://trace.tennessee.edu/utk_graddiss/4302.

60 Vedder, Richard. "Over Invested and over Priced: American Higher Education Today." Center for College Affordability and Productivity (NJ1) (2007).

61 Rivard, Ry. "About-Face on Rankings." Inside Higher Ed, January 6, 2014, accessed February 24, 2023, https://www.insidehighered.com/news/2014/01/06/syracuse-after-refusing-play-rankings-game-may-care-again.

62 Chouinard, Kyle. "SU drops 3 spots in U.S. News' college rankings, climbs up Forbes' rankings" The Daily Orange, September 16, 2022, accessed February 24, 2023, https://dailyorange.com/2022/09/syracuse-university-u-s-news-college-rankings-forbes-rankings/.

63 Kim, Jeongeun. "The cost of rankings? The influence of college rankings on institutional management." PhD diss., University of Michigan, 2015.

64 Rice, Andrew. "Anatomy of a Campus Coup." The New York Times, September 16, 2012, https://www.nytimes.com/2012/09/16/magazine/teresa-sullivan-uva-ouster.html.

65 Gerhard Casper, Stanford University, December 6, 1996, accessed February 24, 2023, https://web.stanford.edu/dept/pres-provost/president/speeches/961206gcfallow.html.

66 McKinley, Jesse. "Student Group Attacks U.S. News College Guide," The New York Times, November 6, 1996, accessed February 24, 2023, https://www.nytimes.com/1996/11/06/us/student-group-attacks-us-news-college-guide.html.

67 McKinley, Jesse. "Student Group Attacks U.S. News College Guide," The New York Times, November 6, 1996, accessed February 24, 2023, https://www.nytimes.com/1996/11/06/us/student-group-attacks-us-news-college-guide.html.

68 Kim, Jeongeun. "The cost of rankings? The influence of college rankings on institutional management." PhD diss., University of Michigan, 2015.

69 Clark, Cole. "Pathways to the university presidency," Deloitte Insights, June 12, 2018, accessed February 24, 2023, https://www2.deloitte.com/us/en/insights/industry/public-sector/college-presidency-higher-education-leadership.html.

70 Rice, Andrew. "Anatomy of a Campus Coup." The New York Times, September 16, 2012, https://www.nytimes.com/2012/09/16/magazine/teresa-sullivan-uva-ouster.html.

71 Rice, Andrew. "Anatomy of a Campus Coup." The New York Times, September 16, 2012, https://www.nytimes.com/2012/09/16/magazine/teresa-sullivan-uva-ouster.html.

72 Berkman, Johanna. "Harvard's Hoard." The New Yorker, 24 June 2001, https://www.nytimes.com/2001/06/24/magazine/harvard-s-hoard.html.

73 "Harvard has a Strong Fundraising Year." Boston Business Journal, September 14, 2006, accessed on March 4, 2023, https://www.bizjournals.com/boston/stories/2006/09/11/daily50.html.

74 Carnevale, Anthony P., Peter Schmidt, and Jeff Strohl. The Merit Myth: How Our Colleges Favor the Rich and Divide America. The New Press, 2020.

75 Yale Daily News, "Former School of Medicine administrator sentenced to nine years in prison for stealing $40 million from the university," October 18, 2022, https://yaledailynews.com/blog/2022/10/18/

former-school-of-medicine-administrator-sentenced-to-nine-years-in-prison-for-stealing-40-million-from-the-university/.

76 Department of Justice. "Former Yale Med School Employee Who Stole $40 Million in Electronics Sentenced to 9 Years in Prison." Accessed on October 19, 2022. https://www.justice.gov/usao-ct/pr/former-yale-med-school-employee-who-stole-40-million-electronics-sentenced-9-years-prison.

77 "How to make college cheaper." The Economist, July 7, 2011, https://www.economist.com/business/2011/07/07/how-to-make-college-cheaper.

78 Austin, Arthur. "Ivy league price-fixing: conflict from the intersection of education and commerce." . John's J. Legal Comment. 21 (2006): 1.

79 Berkman, Johanna. "Harvard's Hoard." The New Yorker, 24 June 2001, https://www.nytimes.com/2001/06/24/magazine/harvard-s-hoard.html.

80 Selingo, Jeffrey. "Are Harvard, Yale and Stanford really public universities?," The Washington Post, April 6, 2015, https://www.washingtonpost.com/news/grade-point/wp/2015/04/06/are-harvard-yale-and-stanford-really-public-universities/.

THE DIVERSITY PARADOX

81 Colvin, Jill and Long, Colleen. "Trump pardoned his son-in-law's dad. Here's what Charles Kushner did." The Chicago Tribune, December 24, 2020, https://www.chicagotribune.com/nation-world/ct-nw-charlie-kushner-pardoned-20201224-6dlgp6ukkzggznmlj7ah3mkg44-story.html.

82 Golden, Daniel. "The Story Behind Jared Kushner's Curious Acceptance into Harvard," ProPublica, November 18, 2016, https://www.propublica.org/article/the-story-behind-jared-kushners-curious-acceptance-into-harvard.

83 Golden, Daniel. "The Story Behind Jared Kushner's Curious Acceptance into Harvard," ProPublica, November 18, 2016, https://www.propublica.org/article/the-story-behind-jared-kushners-curious-acceptance-into-harvard.

84 Newberry, Laura. "The legal way the rich get their kids into elite colleges: Huge donations for years." Los Angeles Times, March 18, 2019, https://www.latimes.com/local/lanow/la-me-ln-college-admissions-scandal-legal-ways-20190318-story.html.

85 United States Supreme Court, "Students for Fair Admissions, Inc. v. HARVARD CORP., 807 F.3d 472 (1st Cir. 2015)." accessed on May 4, 2022, https://www.supremecourt.gov/DocketPDF/20/20-1199/222327/20220502145710361_20-1199%20Volume%20II.pdf.

86 Strauss, Valerie. "The rich have always had a leg up in college admissions. How different then is this new scandal?," The Washington Post, March 13, 2019, accessed on February 26, 2023, https://www.washingtonpost.com/education/2019/03/13/rich-have-always-had-leg-up-college-admissions-how-different-then-is-this-new-scandal/.

87 Sasser, Andrew. "College sued for allegedly conspiring to reduce financial aid offers." The Dartmouth. January 18, 2022. https://www.the-dartmouth.com/article/2022/01/college-sued-for-allegedly-conspiring-to-reduce-financial-aid-offers.

88 Dartmouth News. "Diverse Undergraduate Class of 2026 Takes Shape." Dartmouth News, 31 Mar. 2022, https://home.dartmouth.edu/news/2022/03/diverse-undergraduate-class-2026-takes-shape.

89 568cartel.com. "ECF 266-1 2023-01-03 Second Amended and Supplemental Complaint17318343.1-2." Accessed February 27, 2023. https://568cartel.com/wp-content/uploads/2023/02/ECF-266-1-2023-01-03-Second-Amended-and-Supplemental-Complaint17318343.1-2-1.pdf.

90 Princeton University, "Demographics," Office of Institutional Equity and Diversity, accessed February 27, 2023, https://inclusive.princeton.edu/about/demographics.

91 The Upshot. "Some Colleges Have More Students From the Top 1 Percent Than the Bottom 60. Find Yours." The New York Times, January 18, 2017, https://www.nytimes.com/interactive/2017/01/18/upshot/some-colleges-have-more-students-from-the-top-1-percent-than-the-bottom-60.html.

92 Selingo, Jeffrey. "Are Harvard, Yale and Stanford really public universities?," The Washington Post, April 6, 2015, https://www.washingtonpost.com/news/grade-point/wp/2015/04/06/are-harvard-yale-and-stanford-really-public-universities/.

93 Pollak, Oliver B. "Antisemitism, the Harvard Plan, and the Roots of Reverse Discrimination." Jewish Social Studies 45, no. 2 (1983): 113–22. http://www.jstor.org/stable/4467214.

94 The Crimson Editorial Board, "High Time to End Legacy Admissions," The Harvard Crimson, October 28, 2021, https://www.thecrimson.com/article/2021/10/28/high-time-to-end-legacy-admissions/#:~:text=Between%20 2014%20and%202019%2C%20the,%2Da%2Dmillion%20dollar%20 households.

95 Dicker, Ron. "Lori Loughlin's Daughter in USC Video: 'I Don't Really Care About School'." HuffPost, March 13, 2019, https://www.huffpost.com/entry/lori-loughlin-olivia-jade-dont-care_n_5c88dc34e4b0450ddae5cad2.

96 Spargo, Chris. "COXS-FEIGN Lori Loughlin's daughters' Olivia Jade and Bella seen on rowing machines in photos 'used to scam them into USC'." The Sun, March 12, 2020, https://www.thesun.co.uk/news/11371779/lori-loughlin-daughters-rowing-photos-olivia-bella/.

97 Garrison, Joey. "Lori Loughlin's husband joked about USC admissions process, emails released by feds shows." USA Today, January 15, 2020, https://www.usatoday.com/story/entertainment/celebrities/2020/01/15/lori-loughlins-husband-mossimo-giannulli-emailed-rick-singer-about-usc-plot/4476637002/.

98 United States v. Singer, No. 19-cr-10080-ADB (D. Mass. Mar. 12, 2019), https://www.justice.gov/file/1142876/download.

99 Pinsker, Joe. "The Real Reasons Legacy Preferences Exist," The Atlantic, April 1, 2019, https://www.theatlantic.com/education/archive/2019/04/legacy-admissions-preferences-ivy/586465/.

100 Arcidiacono, Peter, Josh Kinsler, and Tyler Ransom. "Legacy and athlete preferences at Harvard." Journal of Labor Economics 40, no. 1 (2022): 133-156.

101 Kantrowitz, Mark "How Admissions Tests Discriminate Against Low-Income and Minority Student Admissions at Selective Colleges," Forbes, May 21, 2021, https://www.forbes.com/sites/markkantrowitz/2021/05/21/how-admissions-tests-discriminate-against-low-income-and-minority-student-admissions-at-selective-colleges/.

102 Perry, Andre. "Students Need More than an SAT 'Adversity Score'— They Need a Boost in Wealth," Brookings Institution, May 17, 2019, https://www.brookings.edu/blog/the-avenue/2019/05/17/students-need-more-than-an-sat-adversity-score-they-need-a-boost-in-wealth/.

103 Morse, Robert and Eric, Brooks. "How U.S. News Calculated the 2022 Best Colleges Rankings." U.S. News & World Report, September 13, 2021. https://www.usnews.com/education/best-colleges/articles/how-us-news-calculated-the-rankings.

104 "Harvard University." College Scorecard. U.S. Department of Education. Accessed February 27, 2023. https://collegescorecard.ed.gov/school/?166027-Harvard-University.

105 Alvero, A. J., Sonia Giebel, Ben Gebre-Medhin, Anthony Lising Antonio, Mitchell L. Stevens, and Benjamin W. Domingue. "Essay content and style are strongly related to household income and SAT scores: Evidence from 60,000 undergraduate applications." Science advances 7, no. 42 (2021): eabi9031.

106 Gallagher, Sean. "The Write Stuff: 4 College Admissions Essay Editing Services Reviewed." Wired, November 22, 2017. https://www.wired.com/story/college-admissions-essay-editing-services-scribendi-elite-editing-wordvice-scribbr/.

107 "Commentary: What's Less Fair Than the SAT? You Might Be Surprised." Los Angeles Times, February 21, 2022. https://www.latimes.com/opinion/story/2022-02-21/editorial-whats-less-fair-than-the-sat-you-might-be-surprised.

108 Fallows, James. "The Early Decision Racket." The Atlantic, September 2001. https://www.theatlantic.com/magazine/archive/2001/09/the-early-decision-racket/302280/.

109 Henry, Adam L. "An antitrust analysis of college early admission programs." U. Pitt. L. Rev. 66 (2004): 871.

110 Tilitei, Leanna. "Penn accepts 15.6% of early decision applicants to the Class of 2026." The Daily Pennsylvanian, December 16, 2021. https://www.thedp.com/article/2021/12/ed-decisions-penn-class-of-2026.

111 Arcidiacono, Peter, Josh Kinsler, and Tyler Ransom. "Legacy and athlete preferences at Harvard." Journal of Labor Economics 40, no. 1 (2022): 133-156.

THE MOAT

112 "Leland Stanford." Encyclopedia Britannica. Encyclopedia Britannica, Inc. Accessed February 27, 2023. https://www.britannica.com/biography/Leland-Stanford.

113 De Wolk, Roland. American Disruptor: The Scandalous Life of Leland Stanford. University of California Press, 2019.

114 Stanford University. "A History of Stanford." Stanford University. Accessed February 28, 2023. https://www.stanford.edu/about/history/.

115 Siegler, MG. "Peter Thiel Has New Initiative to Pay Kids to 'Stop Out of School'." TechCrunch. September 27, 2010. Accessed February 28, 2023. https://techcrunch.com/2010/09/27/peter-thiel-drop-out-of-school/?_ga=2.128815690.795568111.1660351557-1760881862.1660351556&guc-counter=1.

116 Ferenstein, Gregory. "Thiel Fellows Program Is 'Most Misdirected Piece of Philanthropy,' Says Larry Summers." TechCrunch. October 10, 2013. Accessed February 28, 2023. https://techcrunch.com/2013/10/10/thiel-fellows-program-is-most-misdirected-piece-of-philanthropy-says-larry-summers/.

117 Nasdaq. "Peter Thiel to Step Down from Facebook Parent Meta's Board." Nasdaq. November 12, 2021. Accessed February 28, 2023. https://www.nasdaq.com/articles/peter-thiel-to-step-down-from-facebook-parent-metas-board.

118 Rizzo, Pete. "$100K Peter Thiel Fellowship Awarded to Ethereum's Vitalik Buterin." CoinDesk. June 5, 2014. Accessed February 28, 2023. https://www.coindesk.com/markets/2014/06/05/100k-peter-thiel-fellowship-awarded-to-ethereums-vitalik-buterin/.

119 Waldrop, M. Mitchell. The dream machine: JCR Licklider and the revolution that made computing personal. Viking Penguin, 2001.

120 The New York Times. "Tuition-Free College Could Cost Less Than You Think." July 19, 2019. https://www.nytimes.com/2019/07/19/business/tuition-free-college.html?

121 The Pew Charitable Trusts. "Two Decades of Change in Federal and State Higher Education Funding." October 22, 2019. https://www.pewtrusts.org/en/research-and-analysis/issue-briefs/2019/10/two-decades-of-change-in-federal-and-state-higher-education-funding

122 Waldrop, M. Mitchell. The dream machine: JCR Licklider and the revolution that made computing personal. Viking Penguin, 2001.

123 Ferriss, Tim. "John Doerr — From Introducing 'OKRs' to Investing with Data (The Tim Ferriss Show Transcript)." November 4, 2021. https://tim.blog/2021/11/04/john-doerr-transcript/

124 CNET. "How John Doerr, the old prospector, finally struck Google." June 19, 2008. https://www.cnet.com/tech/tech-industry/how-john-doerr-the-old-prospector-finally-struck-google/

125 The New York Times. (2022, May 4). John Doerr, a Venture Capitalist, Is Giving $100 Million to Stanford for Climate Research. Retrieved from https://www.nytimes.com/2022/05/04/climate/john-doerr-stanford-climate.html

126 Ballotpedia. (n.d.). Election results, 2020: Incumbent win rates by state. Retrieved from https://ballotpedia.org/Election_results,_2020:_Incumbent_win_rates_by_state

127 Fouirnaies, Alexander, and Andrew B. Hall. "The Financial Incumbency Advantage: Causes and Consequences." The Journal of Politics 76, no. 3 (2014): 711–24. https://doi.org/10.1017/s0022381614000139.

128 National Science Board. (2021). Science and Engineering Indicators 2021. Retrieved from https://ncses.nsf.gov/pubs/nsb20213

129 Harvard University. (2020, March 30). Harvard attracts federal funding, supports economy. The Harvard Gazette. Retrieved from https://news.harvard.edu/gazette/story/2020/03/harvard-attracts-federal-funding-supports-economy/

130 Open The Books. (2021). Ivy League, Inc. Retrieved from https://www.openthebooks.com/assets/1/6/Oversight_IvyLeagueInc_FINAL.pdf

131 Caltech Office of the Treasurer. "2020 Endowment Report." Caltech, 2020, https://treasurer.caltech.edu/documents/19249/Caltech_Endowment_Brochure_2020_pages_4.30.pdf.

132 Research.com. "Caltech Academic Programs, Admissions, Tuition, and Campus Life." Research.com, n.d., https://research.com/universities-colleges/caltech-academic-programs.

ARTIFICIAL SCARCITY

133 Mountain View High School. "School Profile 2021-22." Finalsite, 2021, https://resources.finalsite.net/images/v1631644518/fuhsdorg/g7qf5tejcnc4etpely8f/MVHS21-22SchoolProfileFINAL1.pdf.

134 Bian, Yulong, et al. "Over 4,000 People Sign Petition Calling on Penn to Investigate Student Plagiarism Allegations." The Daily Pennsylvanian, 19 May 2022, https://www.thedp.com/article/2022/05/plagiarism-allegations-petition-penn-students-south-korea-justice-minister.

135 Change.org, "Investigate Your Current and Accepted Students for Plagiarism in College Apps," accessed February 27, 2023, https://www.change.org/p/upenn-investigate-your-current-and-accepted-students-for-plagiarism-in-college-apps.

136 Google Docs, "Petition for Investigation of Penn Applicants," accessed February 27, 2023, https://docs.google.com/document/d/1rVNAhrrkznJ0wJgNo_YBk-0QJgh479wAuqnQILjbk4o/edit.

137 Daily Pennsylvanian, "Penn students call for University to investigate alleged plagiarism in South Korea," May 10, 2022, https://www.thedp.com/article/2022/05/plagiarism-allegations-petition-penn-students-south-korea-justice-minister.

138 Hani, "S. Korean justice minister nominee defends daughter's alleged resume-building improprieties," May 10, 2022, https://english.hani.co.kr/arti/english_edition/e_national/1042275.html.

139 The Daily Pennsylvanian, "Penn students call for University to investigate alleged plagiarism in South Korea," May 10, 2022, https://www.thedp.com/article/2022/05/plagiarism-allegations-petition-penn-students-south-korea-justice-minister.

140 Blair, Peter Q., and Kent Smetters. Why Don't Elite Colleges Expand Supply?. No. w29309. National Bureau of Economic Research, 2021.

141 Paumgarten, Nick. "The Tycoon," The New Yorker, July 23, 2007, https://www.newyorker.com/magazine/2007/07/23/the-tycoon.

142 "Investor Relations," Boston Properties, accessed February 27, 2023, https://investors.bxp.com/.

143 "U.S. News Is Sold to Zuckerman," The New York Times, June 12, 1984, https://www.nytimes.com/1984/06/12/business/us-news-is-sold-to-zuckerman.html.

144 Moody, Josh. "The Bob Morse Milestone: Celebrating 45 Years at U.S. News," U.S. News & World Report, February 8, 2018, https://www.usnews.com/higher-education/articles/the-bob-morse-milestone-celebrating-45-years-at-us-news.

145 Thompson, Nicholas. "Playing with Numbers," Washington Monthly, September 1, 2000, https://washingtonmonthly.com/2000/09/01/playing-with-numbers/.

146 "U.S. News Online Strategy Leads to Record Growth in 2013." U.S. News & World Report, January 22, 2014. https://www.usnews.com/info/blogs/press-room/2014/01/22/us-news-online-strategy-leads-to-record-growth-in-2013.

147 "Celebrating 85 Years." U.S. News & World Report, June 11, 2018. https://www.usnews.com/info/articles/2018/06/11/celebrating-85-years.

148 Heath, Thomas. "Value Added: U.S. News and World Report Returns to the Ranks of Profitability." The Washington Post, April 27, 2013. https://www.washingtonpost.com/business/economy/value-added-us-news-and-world-report-returns-to-the-ranks-of-profitability/2013/04/27/2e16c306-ae05-11e2-a986-eec837b1888b_story.html.

149 Time, "Q&A: The Man Behind the U.S. News College Rankings." August 20, 2009, https://content.time.com/time/nation/article/0,8599,1917590,00.html.

150 Thaddeus, Michael. "An Investigation of the Facts Behind Columbia's U.S. News Ranking." Columbia University, accessed February 27, 2023, https://www.math.columbia.edu/~thaddeus/ranking/investigation.html.

151 The New York Times. "Columbia Professor Takes the University to Task Over Rankings." The New York Times, March 23, 2022, https://www.nytimes.com/2022/03/23/nyregion/columbia-university-rankings-professor.html.

152 Tamar Lewin, "With Website to Research Colleges, Obama Abandons Ranking System," The New York Times, September 12, 2015, https://www.nytimes.com/2015/09/13/us/with-website-to-research-colleges-obama-abandons-ranking-system.html.

153 "Columbia University Gets $200-Million Gift." Los Angeles Times. March 21, 2006. https://www.latimes.com/archives/la-xpm-2006-mar-21-na-briefs21.1-story.html.

154 Morris, Laura. "Magazine Owner Gives $10m for Aid." The Harvard Crimson. May 3, 2004. https://www.thecrimson.com/article/2004/5/3/magazine-owner-gives-10m-for-aid/.

155 "PhD Honoris Causa Recipient Mortimer B. Zuckerman." Weizmann Institute of Science. Accessed February 27, 2023. https://www.weizmann.ac.il/WeizmannCompass/sections/people-behind-the-science/phd-honoris-causa-recipient-mortimer-b-zuckerman.

156 Blair, Peter Q., and Kent Smetters. Why Don't Elite Colleges Expand Supply?. No. w29309. National Bureau of Economic Research, 2021.

157 Diaz, Johnny. "How One Student Chose a College During a Pandemic." The New York Times. July 17, 2020. https://www.nytimes.com/2020/07/17/us/college-decision-coronavirus.html.

158 Wong, Alia. "Why The Ivy League Needs to Admit More Students." The Atlantic. September 12, 2018. https://www.theatlantic.com/education/archive/2018/09/ivy-league-acceptance-rates-so-low/571678/.

159 Carnevale, Anthony P., Peter Schmidt, and Jeff Strohl. The Merit Myth: How Our Colleges Favor the Rich and Divide America. The New Press, 2020.

160 Wermund, Benjamin. "How US news college rankings promote economic inequality on campus." Retrieved January 9 (2017): 2021.

161 Morse, Robert and Brooks, Eric. "How U.S. News Calculated the 2022 Best Colleges Rankings." U.S. News & World Report. September 13, 2021. https://www.usnews.com/education/best-colleges/articles/how-us-news-calculated-the-rankings.

162 Blair, Peter Q., and Kent Smetters. Why Don't Elite Colleges Expand Supply?. No. w29309. National Bureau of Economic Research, 2021.

PRICE-FIXING

163 Stannard, Ed. "Yale Graduation Weekend Returns, Complete with Parades, Picnics and Celebrations." New Haven Register. May 21, 2021. https://www.nhregister.com/news/article/Yale-graduation-weekend-returns-complete-with-17185420.php.

164 Litan, Robert. "Why Does Congress Let the Ivy League Operate as a Monopoly?" The New Republic, January 28, 2021. https://newrepublic.com/article/163001/congress-let-ivy-league-operate-monopoly.

165 Merritt, Deborah Jones, and Andrew Lloyd Merritt. "Agreements to Improve Student Aid: An Antitrust Perspective." Journal of Legal Education 67, no. 1 (2017): 17–50. https://www.jstor.org/stable/26453536.

166 Salop, Steven C., and Lawrence J. White. "Policy watch: Antitrust goes to college." Journal of Economic Perspectives 5, no. 3 (1991): 193-202.

167 Gary Putka, Do Colleges Collude on Financial Aid?, WALL ST. J., May 2, 1989, at B1.

168 Depalma, Anthony. "Ivy Universities Deny Price Fixing but Agree to Avoid It in the Future." The New York Times. May 23, 1991. https://www.nytimes.com/1991/05/23/us/ivy-universities-deny-price-fixing-but-agree-to-avoid-it-in-the-future.html.

169 Depalma, Anthony. "Ivy Universities Deny Price Fixing but Agree to Avoid It in the Future." The New York Times. May 23, 1991. https://www.nytimes.com/1991/05/23/us/ivy-universities-deny-price-fixing-but-agree-to-avoid-it-in-the-future.html.

170 "A brief history of overlap and the antitrust suit." MIT News. September 3, 1992. https://news.mit.edu/1992/history-0903#:~:text=MIT%20President%20Charles%20M.,aid%20based%20only%20on%20need.

171 "MIT to propose largest tuition hike in five years." The Tech. February 12, 1989. http://tech.mit.edu/V109/N4/tuitio.04n.html.

172 Goldberg, Debbie. "U.S. Price-Fixing Case against MIT Is Opened." The Washington Post. June 26, 1992. https://www.washingtonpost.com/archive/politics/1992/06/26/us-price-fixing-case-against-mit-is-opened/c70fed5b-a667-4550-b015-c34d9b863232/.

173 "MIT History." MIT News. September 3, 1992. https://news.mit.edu/1992/history-0903.

174 Morrison, Richard. "Price Fixing among Elite Colleges and Universities." The University of Chicago Law Review 59, no. 2 (1992): 807–35. https://doi.org/10.2307/1599922.

175 Austin, Arthur. "Ivy league price-fixing: conflict from the intersection of education and commerce." . John's J. Legal Comment. 21 (2006): 1.

176 Litan, Robert. "Why Does Congress Let the Ivy League Operate as a Monopoly?" The New Republic, January 28, 2021. https://newrepublic.com/article/163001/congress-let-ivy-league-operate-monopoly.

177 Bamberger, Gustavo E., and Dennis W. Carlton. "Antitrust and higher education: MIT financial aid (1993)." The antitrust revolution: Economics, competition and policy (1999): 264-285.

178 Cartel, 568. "Second Amended and Supplemental Complaint." 568 Cartel, January 3, 2023. https://568cartel.com/wp-content/uploads/2023/02/ECF-266-1-2023-01-03-Second-Amended-and-Supplemental-Complaint17318343.1-2-1.pdf.

179 Coy, Peter. "Opinion | How Much Deference Do Elite U.S. Colleges Deserve?" The New York Times, January 14, 2022. https://www.nytimes.com/2022/01/14/opinion/colleges-antitrust-law.html.

180 Li, Joanna. "Class Action Not Dismissed, Fight to Dissolve 568 Presidents Group Continues." The Georgetown Voice, September 19, 2022. https://georgetownvoice.com/2022/09/19/class-action-not-dismissed-fight-to-dissolve-568-presidents-group-continues/.

181 Reuters. "Judge Refuses to Toss Financial Aid Lawsuit Against Top Colleges." New York Post, August 15, 2022. https://nypost.com/2022/08/15/top-colleges-lose-bid-to-toss-financial-aid-antitrust-claims/.

SUBSIDY CANNIBALS

182 New York Post. "Harvard lobbies Dems for tax break — while endowment swells to $53.2B." August 1, 2022. https://nypost.com/2022/08/01/harvard-lobbies-dems-for-tax-break-endowment-swells-to-53-2b/.

183 The Intercept. "Ivy League Universities Push For Special Tax Cut." July 25, 2022. https://theintercept.com/2022/07/25/harvard-university-endowment-tax-cut/.

184 Economic Club. "A Conversation with Lawrence Bacow, President of Harvard University." May 22, 2019. https://www.economicclub.org/sites/default/files/transcripts/lawrence_bacow_event_transcript_-_edited_0.pdf.

185 Tognini, Giacomo. (2021, September 27). Private Equity Billionaire David Rubenstein Donates $10 Million To New York's Lincoln

Center To Expand Civic Activities. Forbes. https://www.forbes.com/sites/giacomotognini/2021/09/27/private-equity-billionaire-david-rubenstein-donates-10-million-to-new-yorks-lincoln-center-to-expand-civic-activities/?sh=45a0de936c6f

186 Mandery, Evan. (2022, September 27). Trump is right about elite colleges and their tax breaks. Politico Magazine. https://www.politico.com/news/magazine/2022/09/27/trump-elite-colleges-taxes-00058697

187 Eaton, Charlie. "Ivory Tower Tax Haven." (2017).

188 Bennett, William. "Our Greedy Colleges," The New York Times, February 18, 1987, https://www.nytimes.com/1987/02/18/opinion/our-greedy-colleges.html.

189 Turner, Lesley J. "The economic incidence of federal student grant aid." University of Maryland, College Park, MD 1000 (2017).

190 Burke, Michael. "Federal spending bill increases maximum Pell Grant by $500," EdSource, March 11, 2021, https://edsource.org/updates/federal-spending-bill-increases-maximum-pell-grant-by-500#:~:text=With%20President%20Joe%20Biden%20signing,%2D%20and%20middle%2Dincome%20families.

191 Fillmore, Ian. "Price discrimination and public policy in the US college market." The Review of Economic Studies (2022): rdac051.

192 Turner, Lesley J. "The economic incidence of federal student grant aid." University of Maryland, College Park, MD 1000 (2017).

193 Delisle, Jason and Dancy, Kim. "Graduate Students and Tuition Tax Benefits: New Analysis" New America, November 7, 2017, https://www.newamerica.org/education-policy/edcentral/gradtaxbenefit/.

194 Lucca, David O., Taylor Nadauld, and Karen Shen. "Credit supply and the rise in college tuition: Evidence from the expansion in federal student aid programs." The Review of Financial Studies 32, no. 2 (2019): 423-466.

195 Chang, Cara and Cho, Isabella. "Harvard Spent $560,000 on Federal Lobbying in Biden's First Year." The Harvard Crimson, March 3, 2022,

https://www.thecrimson.com/article/2022/3/3/harvard-tops-ivy-lobbying-fifth-year/.

196 OpenSecrets. "Education Lobbyists." OpenSecrets, 2022, https://www.opensecrets.org/federal-lobbying/industries/summary?cycle=2021&id=W04.

CONTAGION

197 Jaquette, Ozan. "State university no more: Out-of-state enrollment and the growing exclusion of high-achieving, low-income students at public flagship universities." (2017).

198 Miller Center. "Life Before the Presidency." Accessed on February 27, 2023. https://millercenter.org/president/lbjohnson/life-before-the-presidency.

199 Rozsa, Matthew. "When a President Taught in a Segregated School—and It Changed History." Salon. November 28, 2021. Accessed on February 27, 2023. https://www.salon.com/2021/11/28/when-a-taught-in-a-segregated-school--and-it-changed-history/.

200 American Rhetoric. "Lyndon Baines Johnson - 'We Shall Overcome'." Accessed on February 27, 2023. https://www.americanrhetoric.com/speeches/lbjweshallovercome.htm.

201 Shapiro, Ari. "Navigating Campus For The Not-Rich: Students Launch A Crowdsourced Guide." NPR. April 26, 2018. Accessed on February 27, 2023. https://www.npr.org/2018/04/26/606077648/navigating-campus-for-the-not-rich-students-launch-a-crowdsourced-guide.

202 Weinstein, Liat. "Students respond to college admissions scandal." The Michigan Daily. March 20, 2019. Accessed on February 27, 2023. https://www.michigandaily.com/news/academics/students-respond-college-admissions-scandal/.

203 The New York Times. "Talks Implode During a Day of Chaos; Fate of Bailout Plan Remains Unresolved." September 25, 2008. Accessed on February 27, 2023. https://www.nytimes.com/2008/09/26/business/26bailout.html?_r=1&em&oref=slogin.

204 Mitchell, Michael, and Michael Leachman. "State Higher Education Funding Cuts Have Pushed Costs to Students." Center on Budget and Policy Priorities. October 11, 2022. Accessed on February 27, 2023. https://www.cbpp.org/research/state-budget-and-tax/state-higher-education-funding-cuts-have-pushed-costs-to-students.

205 The Washington Post. "At U-Va., a watch list flags VIP applicants for special handling." 1 Apr. 2017. https://www.washingtonpost.com/local/education/at-u-va-a-watch-list-flags-vip-applicants-for-special-handling/2017/04/01/9482b256-106e-11e7-9d5a-a83e627dc120_story.html.

206 University of Illinois at Urbana-Champaign. "Fall 2017 International Student Enrollment Statistics." (PDF) https://isss.illinois.edu/download_forms/stats/fa17_stats.pdf.

207 Jaquette, Ozan. "State university no more: Out-of-state enrollment and the growing exclusion of high-achieving, low-income students at public flagship universities." (2017).

208 Tampa Bay Times. "USF student, professor file lawsuit against Florida's 'Stop WOKE Act'." 7 Sep. 2022. https://www.tampabay.com/news/education/2022/09/07/usf-student-professor-file-lawsuit-against-floridas-stop-woke-act/.

209 University of South Florida. "USF Rises to Highest Position Ever in U.S. News Rankings." 13 Sep. 2022. https://www.stpetersburg.usf.edu/news/2022/usf-rises-to-highest-position-ever-in-us-news-rankings.aspx.

210 Florida Department of Education. "ICYMI: Florida Public Universities Ranked Among the Nation's Best." 14 Sep. 2022. https://www.fldoe.org/newsroom/latest-news/icymi-florida-public-universities-ranked-among-the-nations-best.stml.

211 Florida Office of the Governor, "Florida Public Universities Ranked Among the Nation's Best," News Release, September 14, 2022, accessed on February 27, 2023, https://www.flgov.com/2022/09/14/florida-public-universities-ranked-among-the-nations-best/.

212 Blair, Peter Q., and Kent Smetters. Why Don't Elite Colleges Expand Supply?. No. w29309. National Bureau of Economic Research, 2021.

213 New York Post. "Judge refuses to toss financial aid lawsuit against top colleges." 15 Aug. 2022. https://nypost.com/2022/08/15/top-colleges-lose-bid-to-toss-financial-aid-antitrust-claims/.

214 OpenSecrets.org. "Lobbying Spending Database - Education." Accessed on February 27, 2023. https://www.opensecrets.org/federal-lobbying/industries/summary?cycle=2021&id=W04.

215 Fillmore, Ian. "Price discrimination and public policy in the US college market." The Review of Economic Studies (2022): rdac051.

SOLUTIONS

216 Yale Daily News. "Abolish Yale." 10 Dec. 2021. https://yaledailynews.com/blog/2021/12/10/abolish-yale/.

217 Chung, Jane. "Besiege the Ivy League." The American Prospect, 16 June 2015, https://prospect.org/education/besiege-the-ivy-league/.

218 Baker, Sam. "Obamacare Website Has Cost $840 Million." The Atlantic, 1 July 2014, https://www.theatlantic.com/politics/archive/2014/07/obamacare-website-has-cost-840-million/440478/.

219 Fillmore, Ian. "Price discrimination and public policy in the US college market." The Review of Economic Studies (2022): rdac051.

www.ingramcontent.com/pod-product-compliance
Lightning Source LLC
Chambersburg PA
CBHW070526220526
45467CB00003B/870